VOLUME 512

NOVEMBER 1990

THE ANNALS

of The American Academy *of* Political
and Social Science

RICHARD D. LAMBERT, *Editor*
ALAN W. HESTON, *Associate Editor*

THE NORDIC REGION:
CHANGING PERSPECTIVES IN
INTERNATIONAL RELATIONS

Special Editor of this Volume

MARTIN O. HEISLER

University of Maryland
College Park

Ⓢ SAGE PUBLICATIONS   *NEWBURY PARK   LONDON   NEW DELHI*

22738454

THE ANNALS
© 1990 *by* The American Academy *of* Political *and* Social Science

From India and South Asia,
write to:
SAGE PUBLICATIONS INDIA Pvt. Ltd.
P.O. Box 4215
New Delhi 110 048
INDIA

From the UK, Europe, the Middle
East and Africa, write to:
SAGE PUBLICATIONS LTD
6 Bonhill Street
London EC2A 4PU
UNITED KINGDOM

SAGE Production Staff: KITTY BEDNAR, LIANN LECH, and JANELLE LeMASTER
*Please note that members of The Academy receive THE ANNALS with their membership.
Library of Congress Catalog Card Number 90-60175
International Standard Serial Number ISSN 0002-7162
International Standard Book Number ISBN 0-8039-3875-6 (Vol. 512, 1990 paper)
International Standard Book Number ISBN 0-8039-3876-4 (Vol. 512, 1990 cloth)
Manufactured in the United States of America. First printing, November 1990.

The articles appearing in THE ANNALS are indexed in *Book Review Index, Public Affairs Information Service Bulletin, Social Sciences Index, Current Contents, General Periodicals Index, Academic Index, Pro-Views,* and *Combined Retrospective Index Sets.* They are also abstracted and indexed in *ABC Pol Sci, Historical Abstracts, Human Resources Abstracts, Social Sciences Citation Index, United States Political Science Documents, Social Work Research & Abstracts, Sage Urban Studies Abstracts, International Political Science Abstracts, America: History and Life, Sociological Abstracts, Managing Abstracts, Social Planning/Policy & Development Abstracts, Automatic Subject Citation Alert, Book Review Digest, Work Related Abstracts, and/or Family Resources Database.*

Information about membership rates, institutional subscriptions, and back issue prices may be found on the facing page.

Advertising. Current rates and specifications may be obtained by writing to THE ANNALS Advertising and Promotion Manager at the Newbury Park office (address above).

Claims. Claims for undelivered copies must be made no later than three months following month of publication. The publisher will supply missing copies when losses have been sustained in transit and when the reserve stock will permit.

Change of Address. Six weeks' advance notice must be given when notifying of change of address to ensure proper identification. Please specify name of journal. Send address changes to: THE ANNALS, c/o Sage Publications, Inc., 2455 Teller Road, Newbury Park, CA 91320.

The American Academy of Political and Social Science

3937 Chestnut Street   Philadelphia, Pennsylvania 19104

Origin and Purpose. The Academy was organized December 14, 1889, to promote the progress of political and social science, especially through publications and meetings. The Academy does not take sides in controverted questions, but seeks to gather and present reliable information to assist the public in forming an intelligent and accurate judgment.

Meetings. The Academy holds an annual meeting in the spring extending over two days.

Publications. THE ANNALS is the bimonthly publication of The Academy. Each issue contains articles on some prominent social or political problem, written at the invitation of the editors. Also, monographs are published from time to time, numbers of which are distributed to pertinent professional organizations. These volumes constitute important reference works on the topics with which they deal, and they are extensively cited by authorities throughout the United States and abroad. The papers presented at the meetings of The Academy are included in THE ANNALS.

Membership. Each member of The Academy receives THE ANNALS and may attend the meetings of The Academy. Membership is open only to individuals. Annual dues: $36.00 for the regular paperbound edition (clothbound, $48.00). Add $9.00 per year for membership outside the U.S.A. Members may also purchase single issues of THE ANNALS for $9.95 each (clothbound, $14.95).

Subscriptions. THE ANNALS (ISSN 0002-7162) is published six times annually—in January, March, May, July, September, and November. Institutions may subscribe to THE ANNALS at the annual rate: $96.00 (clothbound, $120.00). Add $9.00 per year for subscriptions outside the U.S.A. Institutional rates for single issues: $15.95 each (clothbound, $22.95).

Second class postage paid at Philadelphia, Pennsylvania, and at additional mailing offices.

Single issues of THE ANNALS may be obtained by individuals who are not members of The Academy for $13.95 each (clothbound, $22.95). Single issues of THE ANNALS have proven to be excellent supplementary texts for classroom use. Direct inquiries regarding adoptions to THE ANNALS c/o Sage Publications (address below).

All correspondence concerning membership in The Academy, dues renewals, inquiries about membership status, and/or purchase of single issues of THE ANNALS should be sent to THE ANNALS c/o Sage Publications, Inc., 2455 Teller Road, Newbury Park, CA 91320. *Please note that orders under $25 must be prepaid.* Sage affiliates in London and India will assist institutional subscribers abroad with regard to orders, claims, and inquiries for both subscriptions and single issues.

THE ANNALS

of The American Academy *of* Political *and* Social Science

RICHARD D. LAMBERT, *Editor*
ALAN W. HESTON, *Associate Editor*

---FORTHCOMING---

JAPAN'S EXTERNAL ECONOMIC RELATIONS:
JAPANESE PERSPECTIVES
Special Editors: Solomon B. Levine
Koji Taira

Volume 513   January 1991

ELECTRONIC LINKS FOR LEARNING
Special Editors: Vivian M. Horner
Linda G. Roberts

Volume 514   March 1991

AMERICAN FEMINISM: NEW ISSUES
FOR A MATURE MOVEMENT
Special Editor: Janet K. Boles

Volume 515   May 1991

See page 3 for information on Academy membership and
purchase of single volumes of **The Annals.**

CONTENTS

BOOK DEPARTMENT CONTENTS

ECONOMICS

FOREWORD

NORDIC SECURITY: PAST MIRRORS AND FUTURE FACES

The Nordic area has been characterized as a low-tension area during the cold-war period. The Nordic states chose not to constitute their own security organization. Autarchic solutions would have collided with the realities of geography and great-power interests; they exceeded the capacity and inclination of the Nordic states. They chose different roads to security; however, they also chose to take into account the position and interests of their neighbors when making decisions about security. Over time a system of mutual consideration and restraint emerged, particularly in regard to the engagement of external powers in the management of the security arrangements. The Nordic security system was not the product of deliberate design but rather the aggregated result of incremental decisions and adjustment. The factual situation assumed normative functions over time; maintaining the tradition of mutual consideration and restraint became a shared objective in security policymaking.

THE NORDIC SYSTEM OF MUTUAL
CONSIDERATION AND RESISTANCE

The basic structure of the Nordic security system is well known and has been analyzed, some would claim overanalyzed, through the years. It is characterized by a decreasing degree of integration into the Western system of defense arrangements as we move from the West to the East. Iceland's defenses depend on American forces stationed there—the Iceland Defence Force—as the country maintains no military forces on its own. Norway and Denmark are founding members of the North Atlantic Treaty Organization (NATO), but their participation in the military aspects of the alliance is circumscribed by political decisions not to accept the stationing of foreign troops in peacetime or to allow deployment or stockpiling of nuclear and chemical munitions. Sweden pursues a policy of nonalignment aiming for armed neutrality in the event of war. Finland is also nonaligned, but its policy stance is circumscribed by a treaty of friendship and mutual assistance with the Soviet Union. The Nordic security system has sometimes been referred to as a Nordic balance, a term that seems inappropriate as a label since the Nordic states are not poised against each other nor is there any equivalence between the commitments assumed by Iceland, Denmark, and Norway in NATO and Finland's obligations under its treaty with Moscow.

The Nordic states chose their different roads to security in the postwar era largely on the basis of their experiences during World War II. That traumatic watershed continues to condition responses and reflexes in the realm of security policy. All of the Nordic states are Western in terms of social values, political systems, economic structure, and trade relations. Denmark is a member of the European Community (EC), the other four belong to the European Free Trade Association. Both Sweden and Denmark have played in the great-power game of the modern European system. In the postwar era it was the new states of Northern Europe—Iceland, Norway, and Finland—without any tradition and experience in foreign policy, that found themselves responsible for the strategic flashpoints in the area. They shaped the new configuration of security arrangements, including alignment with outside powers.

From the point of view of the East-West balance of power and deterrence, Norway became the most crucial. In the first years of alignment, the principal importance of Norwegian real estate was related to strategic bombing, with airfields in Norway constituting potential staging bases for long-range bombers, their tankers, and escorts. Oslo adhered to the policy of not permitting allied units to be stationed in Norway during peacetime. Moscow tried to constrain Norwegian choices, but Oslo insisted on drawing its own lines. Norwegian authorities chose not to define their policy on foreign military bases inclusively, by specifying the proscriptions, but, rather, exclusively, by enumerating specific measures not prohibited under the policy. The policy is one of unilateral political restraint rather than a legal commitment. The announced restraint is conditional, in the sense of being explicitly valid only as long as Norway is not attacked or threatened with attack.

The policies prohibiting nuclear and chemical weapons deployments are less conditional, in the sense that no preparations have been made for their abrogation or reversal in an emergency. Neither Denmark nor Norway has entered into a program of cooperation agreements concerning nuclear weapons with the United States. Their troops receive no training in the use of nuclear weapons; their weapons systems are not certified for nuclear munitions; no special munition depots for nuclear weapons are maintained on their territories; and allied troops on maneuvers have not been permitted to bring or simulate the use of nuclear weapons. The approved defense plans for Norway are based on conventional defenses only. Norway and Denmark participate in the Nuclear Planning Group in NATO, and no reservations have been registered with respect to the prevailing strategy of flexible response, which does not exclude the use of nuclear weapons, including first use. Both countries tacitly accept the policy of the Western nuclear weapons states of neither confirming nor denying the presence of nuclear weapons on their warships when visiting foreign ports. Norway bases its policy on the assumption that foreign warships respect its position that they not carry nuclear weapons when visiting Norwegian ports and accepts that naval vessels enjoy immunity that prevents inspection by the port state. Norway has refused to demand declarations from the flag states, but it issues clearances with explicit reference to its policy presumptions. The prevailing ambiguity constitutes a target for political action groups, but the Nordic governments have shied away from following the path of New Zealand. Norway in particular remains dependent on allied maritime reinforcements.

Norway and Denmark entered NATO in order to obtain drawing rights on countervailing military power to the regional preponderance of the Soviet Union. They had to trade off considerations of deterrence and reassurance in their security calculus. Deterrence inhered in the capacity and commitment of powerful allies to render assistance in an emergency, thus enabling the aligned states of the North to confront a would-be aggressor with a high risk that a fight for the control of Nordic territory would not be confined to a fight with Nordic countries. In order to make the proposition credible, preparations were made for a reversal of the policy of banning the stationing of foreign troops in an emergency. Joint exercises, prestocking of heavy equipment, fuel, and ammunition, the construction of airfields, harbor installations and the like to receive allied reinforcements, as well as host-nation support agreements, buttressed the policy of proscribing allied stationed troops in peacetime.

As the pattern evolved and crystallized, the self-denying ordinances, particularly in Norway, were viewed as confidence-building measures designed to provide reassurance to the Soviet Union and the other Nordic states. Norway adhered to the policy of not permitting allied maneuvers in the border county of Finnmark and of proscribing allied military flights in Norwegian airspace and allied naval entry into Norwegian coastal waters east of the North Cape. The Soviet Union gradually moved away from a policy of challenging the character of the policies of reassurance to explicitly acknowledging their contribution to stability and the relative absence of tension in the high North.

Denmark's and Norway's allies accepted the geopolitical rationale for the strictures imposed upon allied military cooperation in the beginning largely because they lacked the means to station troops there, later because they recognized that the strictures constituted an important prerequisite for national consensus on the broad framework for national security policy as well as an increasingly important, integral element of the broader security order in Europe. At times there have been whispers about free riders, particularly during the discussions about NATO's dual-track decision concerning intermediate-range nuclear forces in Europe in the late 1970s. The special strictures have, however, come to be viewed as essential aspects of the status quo in Europe.

Sweden has sought credibility by the maintenance of strong national defenses at a high technological level. It has been tacitly recognized that the Swedish contribution to stability in the high North to a large extent constitutes a function of its indirect contribution to the defense of Denmark and Norway by securing the back-door entry, in addition to establishing a high threshold for the forces required to seize and hold Swedish territory. Such forces would not be available to prosecute the war in other theaters and hence would weaken the ability of a would-be aggressor to prevail in a war with the Western coalition. Hence, by derivation, Swedish security is intertwined with that of the West. Escalating costs of modern technology as well as rising unit costs of modern military equipment make it impossible for Sweden to replace its military equipment in a one-to-one ratio. The quantity-quality calculus constitutes a pressing problem for defense planners in all Nordic countries.

Finland has pursued a skillful policy of enhancing its freedom for foreign policy maneuver with the retention of Soviet confidence. Finlandization is not a description of how a small state succumbs to the dictates of a great-power neighbor, but rather how such a state, which had been defeated in war, manages to secure its independence under adverse conditions—of how Finland did not become part of the Soviet empire. Increasingly, Finnish military forces have been structured and deployed also with a view to contributing to stability in Northern Europe, particularly through increased deployments in the North. The credibility of Finland's defenses, in addition to technical capabilities, derives from the history of Finnish military performance during the Winter War of 1939 and perseverance during the Continuation War.

THE STRATEGIC PREDICAMENT

As the infrastructure of the central balance of nuclear deterrence changed from the manned bomber to the ballistic missile, the strategic significance of northwestern Europe did not diminish. The shortest missile trajectories linking the homelands of the two superpowers passed over or in the vicinity of the Nordic area. In strategic terms, the area was important for early warning and forward defense. With the advent of the submarine-launched ballistic missile (SLBM), the waters off Northern Europe became important transit zones for Soviet strategic submarines and forward defense zones for American antisubmarine warfare units. Later, as the range and accuracy of these ballistic missiles increased, Northern waters became an important deployment zone for Soviet strategic submarines, while their Western counterparts could seek deployment in areas further away from Soviet attack submarines than Northern waters.

During the 1980s the Soviet Union emerged as a major naval power, reaching out from the home waters. Admiral Gorshkov, a latter-day Alfred Mahan and head of the Soviet navy, developed a rationale for a global navy in support of Brezhnev's foreign policy. The global navy's Northern Fleet was home-ported at Severomorsk, its Pacific Fleet at Vladivostok. With the advent of the Reagan administration in Washington, the United States launched a naval building program to produce a 600-ship navy and a new maritime strategy based on forward operations. Maritime competition became the dominant military determinant of the strategic predicament of Northern Europe. Offshore production of oil and gas in the North Sea and the prospects of future production further north, including the Barents Sea, pose the issue of competing uses of ocean space.

TOWARD A NEW SECURITY ORDER IN EUROPE

The dramatic political transformations in Eastern Europe in 1989 and the prospects of major arms reductions and troop withdrawals in Europe affect Northern Europe in different ways. Clearly, the threat of war diminishes as the Soviet Union dismantles its forward military structure in Eastern Europe and as political changes in that area remove the options for reconstituting the threat. Moscow could not count on the development of cooperative relations in Central Europe and restraint with respect to integrating the area of the former German Democratic Republic in NATO if it were to apply military pressure in the North. During the cold war, Central Europe constituted the primary tension area while Northern Europe remained an area of low tension. The roles could be reversed in the post-cold-war era, with the possible effect of weakening the links between the center and the northern periphery in Europe. The critical variable is internal developments in the Soviet Union, the dialectics of reform and dissolution of the inner empire.

The Nordic area borders directly on the Soviet Union. There is no intermediate area formed by a forward glacis as in Eastern Europe. Nor are the outer fringes of the Soviet Union in the European northwest made up of non-Russian union republics. Nordic Europe borders directly on Russia. Great Russian reactions to the centrifugal forces of nationalism in the constituent republics of the Union of Soviet Socialist Republics could include chauvinist assertion.

In the event of secession by one or more of the Baltic republics from the USSR, Moscow may face the need to redeploy and relocate forces and military installations from the Baltic area, including nuclear munitions depots, to the Leningrad Military District, thereby changing the security calculus of the Nordic states. The unilateral troop reductions announced by Gorbachev in 1988 were supposed to extend to military units in the Leningrad Military District, including the Kola Peninsula due east of the Soviet-Norwegian border. Implementation was apparently delayed, nurturing Nordic fears of a differentiation of the Soviet military threat, of selective threats against Northern Europe. All of the Nordic states have displayed concern about de-linkage from the core area of the security order in Europe, in connection with East-West negotiations on conventional force reductions in Europe. Regionalization became the specter to be avoided. In the North, regional forces could easily lead to a weakening of the drawing rights of the Nordic states on the general equilibrium in Europe, to an increase in the salience of Soviet military preponderance and options for claiming a *droit de regard* over the security policies of the Nordic states. Nordic concerns had to be harmonized with the concerns of other countries, to constrain the USSR's scope for concentrating its force holdings against specific areas in Western Europe under a collective ceilings regime. The idea of a system of concentric areas extending from the core area of an expanded Central Europe could square the circle in the first round, but the problem could reemerge in subsequent rounds.

In the 1960s defense planning in the Nordic countries tended to focus on the contingency of a limited war confined to a limited area. Surprise attack and fait accompli defined the outbreak scenarios. Perspectives changed during the 1980s in the direction of more holistic visions; the security of Nordic Europe was considered in the context of general wars for mastery in Europe. In the 1990s the pendulum could swing back. Much will depend on the evolution of political culture in the Soviet Union. Available military capabilities will not, by themselves, translate into clear and present dangers. They are circumscribed by the nature of international relations and the nature of the political culture in the states possessing the capability to attack.

Security policy therefore appears to be in the process of shifting from military to political instruments. Relations with the EC occupy center stage in the foreign policy deliberations in Nordic capitals. The basic issues are political rather than economic, although the constitution of the EC internal market by the end of 1992 and the reconstruction of relations between the EC and Eastern Europe, particularly against the background of German unification, create challenges to vital economic interests of the Nordic states. The principal concern is avoiding marginalization and isolation in a context of Soviet internal dissolution and potential turmoil and unpredictability. For Sweden, the issue has been neutrality; but with the waning of the cold war the reference points for nonalignment have been removed. For Norway the issue has been sovereignty, but the nation-state is being drained of sovereignty by the dual impact of transnational processes—environmental destruction, internationalization of business and finance, the universalization of human rights, and the scale of technological development—and the devolution of power from central to local governmental authorities.

Europe's political order is in the process of reformation. It seems likely to most observers in Nordic Europe that the EC will be the principal architect of the new order and that it will constitute a community order. The security order is likely to be shaped by the cooperative structures developed by the Community, by a reconstituted NATO and an essential equilibrium between NATO and the Soviet Union. The interaction will probably be structured and framed by the Conference on Security and Cooperation in Europe. All of the Nordic states have played an active part in its early negotiating phase, and they are likely to play activist roles in a new security order extending across the Northern Hemisphere from San Francisco to Vladivostok.

Four of the Nordic states—Denmark, Finland, Norway, and Sweden—have been the major contributors to the peacekeeping operations of the United Nations. In spite of their different roads to national security, they have joined forces in organizing, training, and planning for U.N. peacekeeping. They have followed the same road in an important, and growing, area of international security. In the future, with the thawing of the cold war, old ethnic and minority conflicts seem to be reemerging from a deep freeze and could constitute one source of instability and uncertainty in Europe's future security order. The Conference on Security and Cooperation in Europe could decide to launch peacekeeping operations within Europe in order to prevent communal strife or local cross-border conflicts from igniting larger conflagrations or in order to protect the human rights of minorities. The Nordic states would be able to contribute not only contingents but also experience. Peacekeeping could become another means to preserve the links between Nordic Europe and Europe as a whole in a future security order.

The new security order will lack the stability that derived from clearly drawn lines of division and confrontation on the one hand and clearly defined commitments on the other. Fluidity, separation, and intervening space will pose military requirements for mobility, defensively accentuated structures, and expeditionary forces. The future military posture of NATO is likely to be designed to preserve a capacity for reconstitution to counter Soviet rearmament and to provide a framework for continued American engagement. It could come to resemble more the current defense arrangements in Norway than in the Federal Republic. It could come to rely more upon reinforcement, prepositioning, and joint exercises than on stationed forces in forward areas.

Norway could provide another model for the European reconstruction. A united neutral Germany could be a source of instability and uncertainty; however, a united Germany in NATO could prove unacceptable to a weakened Soviet Union, particularly if NATO's forces were to move up to the western border of Poland. Hence it is possible that the area of the former German Democratic Republic could be accorded a status similar to that of Finnmark, where allied troops are neither stationed nor permitted to exercise. Such an arrangement could be anchored in a broader European construction of a security zone, extending from Poland through the eastern *Länder* of Germany, Czechoslovakia, and Hungary, in which foreign troops and nuclear and chemical weapons would be prohibited. For Norway, such constructions would reduce the singularity of the Finnmark position and hence tend to integrate the high North into the broader European pattern.

The security of Northern Europe will be dominated by naval competition in the near and intermediate future. Naval competition could evolve according to a different logic from that which is driving the reconstruction of the security order with its Central European epicenter, thereby severing the links between Nordic Europe and Central Europe. Norway will remain dependent on naval reinforcements to forward areas in the North, in order to ensure capabilities that could block the option of a major seaborne assault and in order to obtain air support for a ground defense effort. The Americans will retain an interest in containing a Soviet navy capable of threatening the sea lines of communication that would be essential to a reconstitution strategy. The time urgency of transatlantic reinforcements would probably diminish, however, as Soviet forces are withdrawn from forward positions and drawn down from previous levels.

Norway will pay particular attention to orchestrating arrangements for future naval reinforcement with the reconfiguration of defense structures in Europe. It will strive to maintain a dual claim for drawing rights on both the stability in Europe and transatlantic reinforcements. In this connection, all of the Nordic states have expressed strong interests in naval arms control, starting with confidence-building measures and developing into a regime for preferential reduction of the most offensive components in the force posture, patterned on the original approach to reductions of conventional forces in Europe. Candidates for preferential reduction would be ocean-going attack submarines, which threaten the sea lines of communication, and nuclear-tipped cruise missiles, which threaten the homelands, particularly of littoral states with extended coastlines. The Nordic states share an interest in freedom of navigation, but they also maintain an interest in protecting coastal states from the shadows of military competition at sea. The concern is not that the new maritime strategy amounts to a strategy of horizontal escalation. The risks of escalation to central war are too high and the Kola Peninsula too heavily defended for direct attacks against military installations there to constitute a realistic option with respect to breaking stalemates or compensating for setbacks elsewhere. The concern is, rather, that naval competition could separate Northern Europe from the rest of Europe if it is not subjected to negotiated limitations at a time when arms control negotiations are transforming the military geometry of the cold war.

JOHAN JØRGEN HOLST

Johan Jørgen Holst is director of the Norwegian Institute of International Affairs (NIIA). He was educated at Columbia University and the University of Oslo and has held research positions at Harvard University, the Hudson Institute, the Norwegian Defence Research Establishment, and NIIA. He has held several positions in the Norwegian government, including minister of state for defense (1976-79), minister of state for foreign affairs (1979-81), and minister of defense (1986-89). He is author and editor of numerous books and articles. He is deputy head of the Norwegian Defence Commission of 1990.

Introduction

By MARTIN O. HEISLER

ABSTRACT: The Nordic region is commonly seen to consist of five stable, affluent welfare states, with small and homogeneous populations. Free of war for fifty years, with some of its states neutral, it may seem outside the mainstream of world politics. Yet Finland, by its own efforts and with the tacit collaboration of its Scandinavian neighbors, has maximized its freedom from the influence of its Soviet neighbor, and the three states that are members of the North Atlantic Treaty Organization have similarly managed to "do it their way." Norway adjoins the Soviet Union's heavily armed Kola Peninsula; it is managing several difficult relationships with that country; and, like Finland and Sweden, it pays considerable attention to military security. The region's seas are vital for Soviet and American interests. The area is also a nexus for major environmental and resource regimes, and it has offshore oil and gas resources. The uncertainties confronting the region and its states in foreign policy and security, international economic relations, and the workings of ongoing and potential ventures in international cooperation hold many challenges and opportunities.

Martin O. Heisler, a member of the faculty of government and politics at the University of Maryland, earned his Ph.D. at the University of California at Los Angeles. He was visiting Fulbright professor at Aarhus University's Institute of Political Science in Denmark in 1978-79 and returned to its faculty between 1981 and 1983. He has published widely on comparative and European politics, ethnic relations, and security policy. Currently completing a book on the political theory of the external relations of democracies, he is also engaged in a comparative study of ethnicity and ethnic relations.

PSYCHOLOGISTS tell us that we cope with complex realities not of direct concern to us by simplifying, generalizing, and using stereotypes. That is how most people approach the Nordic region most of the time, since those outside it commonly lack a consistent, broad interest in it. The general literature on it in major languages is sparse, and most of what there is tends to reinforce stereotypical views. Denmark, Finland, Iceland, Norway, and Sweden, the five small states at its core, are usually depicted as boring, albeit in the best sense: free of domestic and international conflict, homogeneous, politically stable, seemingly without crises, altruistic, progressive, productive, and affluent. In this century, the area has attracted attention chiefly for the development and subsequent difficulties of the comprehensive welfare state—particularly in Sweden—and when larger powers introduced, or threatened to introduce, conflict into it. The Nordic nexus and the development of a complex, multidimensional region have been almost entirely ignored.

Specialists see the region very differently. Descending from a global or even European vantage point brings a remarkable variety between—and within—the countries; grounds for military insecurity stemming from great-power interests persist, even at the cold war's end; stability masks aspects of political and social *immobilisme*—an absence of room for maneuver; although they are usually adequately managed, domestic crises abound; altruism is tinged with self-interest and occasional moral arrogance; elements of profound conservatism exist; public sectors are mortgaged and private households stretched thin by high taxes; decreasing competitiveness and growing vulnerability in international economic relations are apparent. In short, the Nordic states are less a world apart than the casual observer might believe.

If, on closer scrutiny, the five countries seem more normal, the region is nonetheless distinctive and important in ways and for reasons that extend beyond the states composing it. The Nordic region is greater than the sum of its parts, even if it is defined to include the seas around it, the Baltic states, and the far northern portions of the Soviet Union. It is a nexus for unique security arrangements that may be apposite models for other parts of the world. Its states have evolved a distinctive style in international relations in the decades since World War II, anchoring actions toward each other and the world outside in deeply rooted and well-structured societal norms. A general disposition toward cooperation is a hallmark of that style. It is evident in—and has had impact out of proportion to the size of these states on —the operations of such international organizations as the United Nations and its functional agencies, levels and forms of assistance to less developed areas, and the Western Alliance and myriad other fora, and it is displayed in the prominent roles the Nordic states have taken in several significant international regimes in the domains of the environment and natural resources. These qualities recommend a closer scrutiny by all with an interest in international relations practice and theory, not just those concerned with Northern Europe's politics, economic relationships, or security *probléma-tiques*. The exploration of the Nordic region as a series of nexi and of the Nordic style in international relations is a major aim of this volume.

SEEDS OF GENERAL INTEREST IN THE NORDIC REGION

One of the region's distinctive qualities is evident in the adeptness with which its small, relatively weak states contributed to the construction of a comparatively benign international security environment in a region of vital importance to the Soviet Union and the Western Alliance. Not only did they crystallize an effective security community among themselves,[1] but, by frequently and in a variety of ways reassuring the Soviet Union of their nonthreatening stance, they defused any aggressive motives their powerful neighbor might have had in the post-World War II period. Their joint security postures—reflecting, in Johan Jørgen Holst's words, "the aggregated result of incremental decisions and adjustment [that] assumed normative functions over time"[2]—effectively neutralized and then eroded Soviet pressures on them in general and on Finland in particular. They managed, simultaneously, to keep America's political

1. Karl W. Deutsch characterized such communities as zones or regions within which states had created the conditions necessary for avoiding the use of force for resolving their disputes. See his *Political Community at the International Level* (Garden City, NY: Doubleday, 1954), esp. p. 33.
2. In the opening paragraph of his foreword to this issue.

levies for its protection tolerable and, on the whole, consistent with their internal norms. The foreword, the articles in part 1, and portions of parts 3 and 4 of this volume depict this quality and explore some of its ramifications for the United States, the Soviet Union, and Europe, as well as for the Nordic region itself.

Both because the region's states are integrally tied to delicate Arctic and sub-Arctic ecosystems and because environmental issues have become salient in their domestic politics, the Nordic states have been active in the creation and operation of several significant international regimes in these domains. In his article in part 2, Olav Schram Stokke shows the routes to success through and the limitations on such cooperation. Jerome Davis considers the potential of regimes for oil and natural gas in the North Sea and provides a carefully reasoned explanation for their failure. Raphael Vartanov and Alexei Roginko, two Soviet specialists on Northern environmental and resource regimes, show convincingly that the Soviet Union is now moving toward broad international cooperation in these domains, but their balanced and realistic assessment also notes embedded political and structural impediments to progress to date. The articles in part 2, then, (1) provide evidence of successful regime formation in the region, (2) show that such readily divisible commodities as oil and gas—and the economic and industrial progress for which they are catalysts—circumscribe international cooperation with politically seminal national interests, and (3) indicate that political and ideological differences are not necessarily barriers to international cooperation.

Consistency between foreign and security policies on the one hand and the normative templates of the five states' societies and polities on the other is a second notable quality. It follows less from coincidence or the pursuit of political expedients by the decision makers of the day than from the political structures and norms that define the domestic regimes—structures and norms that reflect thoroughgoing democratic practice and the accretion of values that permeate many aspects of life. With the passage of time, the norms that define the policy process in each of the five countries became clear and close parameters for external relations in essentially the same fashion and degree that they constrain governments in domestic issue-areas. Put somewhat differently, the *modus vivendi* the Nordic states have developed for coping with the contradictions between democratic governance and the effective conduct of foreign and security policy to which Tocqueville called attention nearly 160 years ago differs from the approaches of other democracies. They have substantially yielded to the exigencies of democratic regime norms.[3] The country-by-country treatments in part 3 suggest the bases for that accommodation and provide less aggre-

gated views of the operation of the Nordic style in external relations. They also delve into the particular problems of each state and adumbrate the limits of joint approaches.

The region has had considerable military significance for both the Soviet Union and Western powers since World War II. While the prospect of a war of aggression against the West or military conflict between the superpowers has receded with the Soviet Union's policy changes and internal travails and the unraveling of the Warsaw Pact, as several of the contributions to this volume show, proximate sources of potential threat remain for the Nordic states. In the far North, the Kola Peninsula, adjoining Norway on the latter's Finnmark border, is arguably the most heavily armed area in the world, with great and lasting strategic value for the Soviet Union. As several contributors to this issue note, Soviet insecurity in the region has been heightened by the autonomy movements of the Baltic republics. Sausage theories aside,[4] sunk costs, clear long-term or open-ended strategic interests, and local, internal insecurities point to the continued maintenance of mas-

---

3. Thus, for instance, a major set of decisions such as those entailed in the ongoing reunification of Germany could not have been made in any of the Nordic states through the policymaking-as-usual procedures used by the coalition of the Christian Democratic Union and the Free Democratic Party.

4. The sausage theory suggests that, with the thinning out of Western and Soviet forces on the Central Front, some of the latter removed from Central and Eastern Europe will be shifted to the northern and southern flanks. While it is not now clear that Soviet forces will be withdrawn faster from East Germany and Eastern Europe than they can be demobilized and reabsorbed—or restationed in Central Asia or elsewhere—it is hard to envision a substantial, simultaneous thinning out of land and air forces on Kola and implausible to argue that the massive Soviet fleets in the far North will shrink in the near future.

sive Soviet military capabilities adjacent to the Nordic states for some time.

Thus a third set of claims the Nordic region has on our attention stems from potential new conflict scenarios that fit neither the military nor, especially, the political templates of the existing Western Alliance. How and to what extent might regionally isolated threats, especially if they stem from domestic disturbances within the Soviet Union, engage the existing structure of international security? Will the North Atlantic Treaty Organization retain its capability and credibility for assurance, reinforcement, and ultimately, nuclear deterrence for its small Northern allies under such circumstances—if general war is not in prospect? If the European Community—Denmark is its only Nordic member—evolves a security dimension, how—politically—and with what —militarily—might it address such sources of potential insecurity? What part will the new Germany play in the defense of Europe? It will be, after the Soviet Union, the largest country adjoining the region. In addition to providing the most important barriers and links to Eastern Europe—a region with greater potential for international conflict than at any time since World War I and soon to be without the pacifying role of the Red Army—the Federal Republic has assumed an increasingly important role of late in the defense of the Baltic. With unification, Germany will have a much more substantial Baltic presence.

These questions assume greater importance in view of the possible implosion of the Soviet Union, the internal preoccupations of Germany and Western Europe, and the largely politically, partly financially driven conservatism of the United States. Most of the articles in parts 1, 3, and 4 probe these questions, but answers cannot be offered with confidence in the flux of the late spring of 1990.

Concerns about a possible marginalization of the Nordic region in the realm of security are partly blurred and partly hypothetical. Concerns with marginalization in the domain of international economic relationships are much sharper and more immediate, and they constitute a fourth reason to focus on the region in the early 1990s. As the European Community moves toward its common internal market—1992 and all that—and seems likely to be occupied for some time with absorbing a unified Germany and with its new relationships with Eastern Europe, it is far from clear what face it will present to the four Nordic states—Finland, Iceland, Norway, and Sweden —that are looking in with varying degrees of anxiety. The articles in part 3 broach each country's perspective, and Donald Hancock's elegant and parsimonious essay in part 4 provides a systemic view. But here, as in the realm of security, we can only sketch the characters and set the stage. There is, in all five Nordic countries, a clearly discernible bent toward standoffishness. Both the historic reluctance of the outside four among the Nordic states to join the European Community[5] and the inward-looking agenda of the latter's

5. Denmark's membership has never enjoyed domestic consensus. While its electorate provided a majority for adherence in a referen-

Delors Plan compel us to wait at least two or three years before being able to provide lines for the actors.

THE AIMS OF THIS VOLUME

This volume has three goals. First, it aims to inform a broad readership about the current and prospective circumstances of the Nordic region and the five small states at its core. Second, as many of the articles show, cooperation—often without formal organization—between Nordic states has, over time, generated regionwide security and foreign policy postures that have served, notably since World War II, as multipliers of the states' individual capabilities. An appreciable, if unmeasurable, increase in security and freedom of action in the proximity of an initially aggressive superpower was one of the significant products of such cooperation. In the midst of the sea change that rose in 1989 and that is continuing, we can do little more than speculate about the region's future security arrangements, and, given changes in Germany, Eastern Europe, and the European Community, our forecasts regarding the positions of the five states in the international economy must remain very tentative. If locating the Nordic region in a rapidly and drastically changing world arena seems slightly less difficult than orienting other affected countries and

areas with respect to those changes, it may be because its states' external behavior is so firmly anchored in their domestic regimes, which provide quite reliable, relatively fixed points of reference.

The domestic regimes from which those states' policies flow have led to myriad cooperative ventures, not only in international politics and security. Over time and through fairly consistent application, the Nordic states may have developed a potential for changing the perspectives of other actors in international relations. At least for some of us, drawing attention to and thus enhancing this normative thrust of the Nordic style in international relations was a third goal. We provide only fragmentary illustrations of this potential, but the years of flux ahead may well contribute some more telling tests.

The table of contents at the front of this volume indicates the large number of scholars—from nine countries, with diverse specialities and intellectual orientations—who created it. It does not show the intellectual stimulation of Oran Young for putting the realist and international-cooperation schools into the same bed, albeit with a bundling board between them most of the time; or the delivery of a superb manuscript by a scholar and friend who, when one of the invited authors indicated long after the deadline that he would not be able to deliver, rescued a crucial part of the volume. To them, and, of course, to all the contributors, my heartfelt thanks.

---

dum in the early 1970s—Norway's voted to stay out—opposition to membership in general, not only to specific obligations and burdens such membership entails, is not trivial in 1990.

The North as a
Multidimensional Strategic Arena

By CLIVE ARCHER

ABSTRACT: Since 1945, the Nordic governments, aware of the increasing strategic importance of their area, have tempered military response with policies favoring restraint and détente and over the years have created their own pattern of security policies. Mr. Gorbachev's New Thinking in foreign policy has affected the Nordic region: some of the states feel less of a threat than before, though new elements of uncertainty have entered the strategic equation. The Nordic states are economically important and have also developed their maritime resources, leading to some jurisdictional disputes. The five countries have had some problems with the institutional framework for their relationships with other West European states. Rapidly changing events on the continent of Europe provide a good opportunity for a reconsideration of relations in the economic as well as military sphere.

Clive Archer is deputy director of and senior lecturer in the Centre for Defence Studies, University of Aberdeen, Scotland. A graduate of the London School of Economics, he earned his doctorate at the University of Aberdeen. He specializes in Nordic and Arctic studies, teaches international organizations, and is the editor of The Soviet Union and Northern Waters *(1988) and author of* Organizing Western Europe *(1990).*

THE Nordic area has often seemed to be the quiet corner of Europe. This perception harks back to the era between the Napoleonic War and World War II, when Europe was the cockpit of the world and Central Europe and the Balkans provided the military and diplomatic battle-grounds for the great powers—with the Nordic states only rarely being involved, let alone being of importance. Since the 1930s the geostrategic position of this northern area of Europe has changed, as military technology has placed it within a much shorter sailing and flying distance of the great powers and, after World War II, as it has become sandwiched between the superpowers.

The importance of the Nordic region is not just limited to its military significance. It is an area of economic strength and a source of trade and resources out of proportion to its small population. The way the Nordic states are developing their resources —human as well as natural—provides another dimension to their special character.

The Nordic countries belong to a penetrated subsystem insofar as they are susceptible to outside influences on their economic and strategic situation. In response, they have established a network of relations between themselves and have also developed their own links with the other European trade and military groupings. In the new strategic situation in Europe, will these strands be rewoven?

THE HISTORICAL EXPERIENCE

Until the 1930s the Nordic region was one of comparative calm in Europe. Sweden remained a neutral bastion. Denmark had been shorn of territories during the Schleswig-Holstein War and kept an uncertain watch on Germany. Norway and Finland had emerged as independent states in 1905 and 1917, respectively. Norway felt it was under the protective watch of Britain, and Finland feared its Soviet neighbor to the east. Even for the Nordic countries the 1930s were testing times. They emerged stronger economically and politically, however; their brand of social welfare and Keynesian policies and their government coalitions of farmers' parties and social democrats formed an effective "middle way" between communism and nazism.[1]

The area was not able to stay out of the military conflict of 1939, despite a joint declaration of neutrality. Finland was attacked by the Soviet Union in 1939, and in April 1940 Germany invaded Denmark and Norway. The strategic situation had changed since World War I. For example, the increased role in warfare of aircraft and submarines had altered Norway's military significance in the interwar period. Germany wanted to protect its vital iron ore imports from Sweden via Narvik and to make sure that Norwegian ports and airports could also be used by Germany against Allied shipping and, eventually, against the United Kingdom.

Only Sweden, with its armed neutrality, managed to survive World War II without being invaded or occupied, though its politicians had often to adapt to the reality of being

1. See Marquis Childs, *Sweden: The Middle Way on Trial* (New Haven, CT: Yale University Press, 1980), esp. chap. 1.

surrounded by a dominant great power, Germany.[2] By 1945 both Denmark and Sweden had found that the Baltic, the approaches to which they guarded, was dominated by the Soviet Union. Up to the early twentieth century, Russia had been painted as a potential adversary of Norway, yet by the end of World War II the Soviet Union was an ally, one that had paid a price to liberate Norwegian territory. As a result of its wars with Finland, however, the USSR also had a common border with northern Norway. Finland itself found that it could not rely on other states to help it in times of crisis or war but had to maintain its independence from the Soviet Union by its own sacrifice.

From the end of 1945 to the end of 1985, the Nordic countries saw their international relations very much affected by the superpowers, and their own relations with the United States and the Soviet Union became of supreme importance in their foreign affairs. At the end of the war, three of the Nordic states had a superpower military presence in their territory. Denmark—Greenland—and Iceland had U.S. Air Force bases, and both Norway and Denmark still had Soviet troops in the areas liberated by the Red Army—Finnmark and Bornholm, respectively. From 1945 to 1948 both Denmark and Norway followed a conscious policy of bridge building between the communist countries to the east and Western capitalist states.

The events of Easter 1948—the signing of the Brussels Pact (19 February), the Communist coup in Prague (25 February), and the Soviet proposal of a treaty with Finland (27 February)—sharpened Danish and Norwegian fears of a Soviet attack. A consideration of a Scandinavian defense union by Sweden, Norway, and Denmark demonstrated that the three Scandinavian states could not agree on a concept, or on the details, of such a defense agreement, and in April 1949 Norway and Denmark—together with Iceland, which had remained on the sidelines during all the discussions—became signatories of the North Atlantic Treaty.

The Atlantic Treaty provided a framework for help from a wider range of Western countries but still, in the beginning, did not have the infrastructure for effective military aid in the case of an attack on Scandinavia. Indeed, membership in the North Atlantic Treaty Organization (NATO) could be seen as a provocation that might have led to an attack by the Soviets before the defenses of Denmark and Norway had been expanded. From the start, Norway and Denmark ruled out the basing of foreign troops on their European territory in peacetime. This was followed in 1957 by the decision of both countries not to accept nuclear weapons —specifically, American ones at that time—on their territory "under present conditions."[3] These base and ban policies were meant to reassure the Soviet Union—and domestic opinion —that Norwegian and Danish mem-

2. Hans Mouritzen, *Finlandization: Towards a General Theory of Adaptive Politics* (Aldershot: Avebury, 1988), pp. 161-218.

3. Denmark, Udenrigsministeriet [Ministry for Foreign Affairs], *Dansk sikkerhedspolitik 1948-1966* [Danish security policy 1948-1966] (Copenhagen: Ministry for Foreign Affairs, 1968), p. 117.

bership in NATO was defensive, but the policies were also conditional and could be changed if "present conditions"—normally interpreted as peace —were disturbed, for example, by a Soviet démarche in the Nordic area.

Since becoming members of NATO, Norway, Denmark, and Iceland have developed security policies that reflect a dual approach similar to that seen in the Harmel Report.[4] On the one hand, the countries' defense capacities have been built up as part of NATO's wider deterrent force. On the other hand, the three states have wished to develop peaceful relations with the Soviet Union wherever possible. From 1949 onward, the three Nordic members of NATO have veered between these two strategies, with alliance and adversary considerations playing varied roles. On some issues, domestic political factors have also been of importance.[5]

During the postwar period, Sweden has developed its own policy of armed nonalignment in peacetime, leading to neutrality in case of war. This is based on support for the United Nations and international peacekeeping, an attempt to ameliorate superpower rivalry, adherence to no alliance or bloc, and a defense posture that made Sweden an unattractive target for any potential aggressor.[6]

After World War II, Finland needed to make sure that there was no repeat of the misunderstandings and aggressive feelings between it and the Soviet Union, as there had been after World War I. The 1948 treaty with the Soviet Union was negotiated to Finnish satisfaction.[7] During the following decades, Finnish foreign policy aimed at establishing Finland as a neutral country that was not beholden to any alliance and whose position was accepted internationally; placed its relations with the Soviet Union on a normal basis; and established itself as a Western country in economic, social, and political terms.

It is clear that the security policies of the countries developed along different lines. Because of their varied geostrategic positions, the opportunities available to each state diverged. The historical experience of governments and peoples, together with other factors bearing on domestic opinion, affected the willingness of ministers in each of the states to choose one option rather than another.[8] External factors—the East-West division from 1948 being the most important—impinged on the Nordic region in such a way as to produce three basic sorts of security policy among its states: the NATO membership, but with certain restrictions, of Denmark, Iceland, and Norway; Swedish nonalignment; and Finland's neutrality and special rela-

4. *North Atlantic Treaty Organization: Facts and Figures* (Brussels: NATO Information Service, 1984), pp. 289-91.

5. Nikolaj Petersen, *Denmark and NATO 1949-1987* (Oslo: Forsvarshistorisk Forskningssenter, 1987), p. 10.

6. Krister Wahlbäck, *The Roots of Swedish Neutrality* (Stockholm: Swedish Institute, 1986).

7. Max Jacobsen, *Finland—Myth and Reality* (Helsinki: Otava, 1987), pp. 68-69.

8. For treatment of the ideas of willingness and opportunity in international relations, see Bruce Russett and Harvey Starr, *World Politics: Menu for Choice* (San Francisco: Freeman, 1981), pp. 22-23.

tionship with the Soviet Union. The Nordic dimension in security policy remained more oblique—it was a recognition by each state that in arranging its own security needs nothing should be done to endanger the requirements of the other Nordic states. Sometimes this link was more explicit and even became known as the Nordic balance, though this term perhaps gives a false impression of the nature of the relationship of the five states in security matters.[9]

THE COLLAPSE OF THE CERTAINTIES

Since Mr. Gorbachev came to power in the Soviet Union in March 1985, the Nordic area has changed in strategic importance. Throughout the 1950s and 1960s the region had been peripheral to superpower conflict—it was considered a flank of the real center of confrontation in continental Europe. Though Northern Europe had importance for NATO as a listening post and was also on the shortest ballistic missile route between the United States and the USSR, its strategic standing was secondary.

Its value increased during the 1970s and 1980s, with the rise of the Kola Peninsula as an important base for the Soviet navy.[10] The growth in the USSR's Northern Fleet led to the fear of Norway's being outflanked, as Soviet naval exercises reached well out into the North Atlantic. This concern was alleviated only when the U.S. Navy, following a more forward strategy during the Reagan presidency, showed greater activity in Northern waters and expounded the idea that the Northern Fleet would, in times of crisis or war, be challenged much closer to home than before.

Technological change also had its effect. From the late 1970s, the longer reach of submarine-based ballistic missiles meant that Soviet strategic submarines could deploy nearer to their base ports and still target the American heartland. Thus, from the mid-1980s, two factors pointed to the Soviet Union's drawing in its naval horns in the North: it was no longer necessary to deploy—and protect— Soviet strategic submarines in the exposed parts of the North Atlantic, and the U.S. Navy's threat to go forward in a crisis underlined the need for the protective resources in the Soviet fleet being on call in the North Norwegian, Barents, and Kara seas. Furthermore, the Baltic was already becoming of less use to the USSR as NATO's ability to close and defend its approaches would mean a bottling-up of Soviet forces there.

The advent of Mr. Gorbachev and the introduction of New Thinking in Soviet foreign and defense policy has had its effect on the Nordic area. The ending of the Cold War, the adoption of concepts of "reasonable sufficiency" and "defensive defence"[11] in security policy, and the eventual sweeping away of Soviet power and

9. Eric Noreen, "The Nordic Balance: A Security in Theory and Practice," *Cooperation and Conflict,* 18(1):43-56 (1983).

10. Robert van Tol, "A Naval Force Comparison in Northern and Atlantic Waters," in *The Soviet Union and Northern Waters,* ed. Clive Archer (New York: Routledge, 1988), pp. 134-63.

11. Edward L. Warner III, "New Thinking and Old Realities in Soviet Defence Policy," *Survival,* 31(1):13-33 (Jan.-Feb. 1989).

communist governments in Eastern Europe could scarcely fail to affect even Europe's quiet corner. But the overall result is variegated. For Denmark, Sweden, and, to a lesser extent, Finland, potentially hostile forces —Polish and East German amphibious troops—have been neutralized on the southern shores of the Baltic and there is the promise of a large-scale withdrawal of the Soviet forces from there.

Previous to 1990, Denmark was a NATO front-line state. Its islands were within hailing distance of the inner-German border, which also formed the NATO-Warsaw Pact land frontier. The Danish island of Bornholm, in the east of the Baltic, is off the coast of Poland. With a Solidarity government in Poland, the coming together of East and West Germany, and the promise of Soviet troop withdrawals from East Germany and Poland, the Warsaw Pact's frontier has shifted to the Soviet Baltic states of Estonia, Latvia, and Lithuania. Indeed, if these continue to assert their rights and perhaps make the stationing of Russian troops there more difficult, then it would seem that the effective military might of NATO's potential enemy has been drawn back to the outskirts of Leningrad, with perhaps a redoubt in the Russian Kaliningrad enclave between Poland and Lithuania.

The events behind this retraction hold some dangers for the Nordic Baltic states of Denmark, Sweden, and Finland, however. Soviet control of Eastern Europe offered certainty; the

loosening of the grip has created an unease. There is the possibility that Poland may descend to civil unrest, that Estonia, Latvia, or Lithuania may come into conflict with Moscow, or that there may be serious interethnic violence in these three lands. This could transform the Baltic into an area of tension with, perhaps, refugees streaming north by sea. This would not be a happy situation for Denmark, Finland, or Sweden, even though the level of conflict would be at the lower end of the scale.

Norway is in a different situation from its Nordic neighbors on the Baltic. Though it has a Baltic shore, its strategic significance lies north. A de-Russification of the Baltic and the reduction of Soviet armed strength in Central Europe—especially in a short timeframe—could mean increased importance for the Kola Peninsula. This is partly because naval arms control and disarmament has not yet been undertaken and partly because troops and equipment may be sent north as the striptease on the Central Front leaves the Soviets few places to store what they have discarded. Furthermore, there are signs that the Northern Fleet, while no longer so active in the North Atlantic, is far from redundant. Indeed, there are Norwegian commentators who believe its exercise patterns closer to home make it more effective.[12] This is significant if, as U.S. troops start to

12. Ellmann Ellingsen and Jan Olsen, eds., *Militærbalansen 1988-1989* (Oslo: DNAK, 1988), pp. 162-67.

return home, NATO becomes much more a maritime alliance, relying on American resupply and reinforcement should crisis occur in Europe.

THE RESOURCE DIMENSION

Traditionally, the Nordic region was a source of primary resources —fish, wood, and agricultural products—but since the interwar period these have been supplemented by commerce and increasingly more sophisticated industry. The population of the Nordic states may be small —no more than 24 million in total— but it is well trained and educated, and, as a result, the area has managed to find its niche in the economic world.

A notable development in the Nordic economies has been the emergence of a strong service sector, quite often associated with the establishment of an extensive social welfare infrastructure in these countries. For example, the share of Sweden's economically active population in the services jumped from 20 percent in 1960 to 37 percent in 1985. Together with 20 percent in commerce, finance, and other similar areas—up from 15 percent in 1960—this accounts for over half of the working population.[13] To sustain a social security expenditure that is, for most of the Nordic states, between a quarter and a third of their gross national product, these countries have to make the best use of whatever resources they have.

13. Nordic Statistical Secretariat, *Yearbook of Nordic Statistics 1988* (Copenhagen: Nordic Council of Ministers and the Nordic Statistical Secretariat, 1989), 27:49.

Indeed, the Nordic region stands up well in international comparisons of its economic activity. The population of the region is 7.7 percent that of the European Communities (EC), 5.8 percent of that of Comecon, 9.4 percent of the United States', and 18.8 percent of Japan's. Yet its trade per capita is far ahead any of these giants—partly, perhaps, because they are giants and need to trade less with the rest of the world—and even the amount of its trade—including that with each other—stands comparison with the major trade blocs. The Nordic export figure is 11.8 percent of the size of the EC total—with Denmark being a member of each group—44.0 percent of the U.S. figure, and 49.0 percent of that of Japan.

The Nordic states also perform well in particular economic areas. Their fish catch in 1986 was greater than that of the EC without Denmark, more than that of the United States, 46 percent of the Comecon figure, and 48 percent of that of Japan. Their crude petroleum production in 1987 was 8.5 percent of the Comecon figure, which included the output of the world's largest petroleum producer, the Soviet Union. Nordic iron ore production in that year was about half that produced by the EC and the United States together, and their output of sawnwood and pulp outstripped that of the EC and of Japan. The tonnage of Nordic merchant vessels launched in 1987 was 40 percent that of the EC total, and the tonnage of the Nordic merchant fleet—14,639—stood up well to that of the EC (66,613), Comecon (35,011), the United States (20,086), and Japan (35,932). The Nordic people were second only to the U.S. population in the number of private cars per 1000 inhabitants in 1986—359 compared to 561 in the United States —and they were only just outstripped by the United States in the number of telephones per 1000 inhabitants: 742 to the U.S. figure of 760.[14]

The economic picture, then, shows a resource-rich area with a small but productive—and therefore wealthy— population. It is also, by tradition and geography, a maritime area that depends heavily on the seas not just for trade and transport but also for resources, especially fish and petroleum. Iceland, heavily dependent on fishing, was the first Nordic state to feel the international consequences of such reliance on the oceans. The extension of its fisheries limits from 3 to 4 miles in 1952 and to 12 miles in 1958 brought retaliation from British trawler owners and government. The Icelanders extended their limits to 50 miles in 1972 and to 200 miles in 1975, and on both occasions the United Kingdom disputed Iceland's exclusive right to fish in the newly created zones. During the last two so-called cod wars, Iceland placed pressure on Britain through the United States, by threatening to reconsider the latter's presence at the Keflavík base. The British were persuaded that the continuation of a base serving NATO interests should be placed before the needs of their deep-water fishermen. The Icelanders had successfully used a security lever to pry open access to a resource supply.

14. Ibid., pp. 26-27.

The division of seabed rights in the North Sea in the 1960s allowed Norway to develop the considerable petroleum reserves there and thereby sustain economic growth in the 1970s and 1980s. A declaration of an economic zone around its coast from January 1977 gave it exclusive or favored access to the resources of these seas. A number of delineation disputes have arisen, however. The disagreement between Norway and Denmark over the fisheries zone and continental shelf between the Norwegian island of Jan Mayen, which is well out into the North Atlantic, and the Danish home-rule territory of Greenland was referred to the International Court of Justice in 1988; a similar dispute between Norway—on behalf of Jan Mayen—and Iceland was settled in 1980 and 1981; but the line between the coast of northeast Greenland and the Svalbard archipelago to the north of Norway remains undrawn.

All these differences are between Nordic states and cover areas of relatively limited economic value. In contrast, the dispute between Norway and the Soviet Union over the boundary in the waters off northern Norway involves a vast area of resource potential and with strategic significance. The Barents Sea—bounded by Svalbard and Franz Josef Land to the north and the Soviet and Norwegian mainlands to the south—provides the approaches to the USSR's maritime bases on the Kola Peninsula, acts as a submarine sanctuary for the Soviet navy, and is a highway to the North Polar areas. It is also fished for cod and capelin and seems to have exploitable hydrocarbon deposits. The Soviet Union and Norway dispute the division of both the maritime zones and the continental shelf in this sea.

In 1977 the two states agreed on a fisheries Grey Zone mainly in the southern part of the 58,000 square miles in dispute, but which also included an area west of the Soviet sector claim in undisputed Norwegian waters and a much smaller zone in Soviet waters, east of the Norwegian median line. A total allowable catch for fish in the zone was divided between Norway and the Soviet Union, with each state policing the vessels it had licensed to fish in the Grey Zone. The arrangement has been renewed annually, but no agreement has been reached on a more permanent delineation. In 1988— just at the time when it had settled a maritime border with Sweden in the Baltic—the USSR suggested joint Norwegian-Soviet exploitation of the disputed area, but the Norwegians feared that without a definitive delineation they would be overshadowed by the Soviet Union in a bilateral arrangement.

Another Nordic territory where the strategic and resource imperatives overlap is Svalbard. This group of islands to the north of Norway came under Norwegian sovereignty in 1920 by the Treaty of Paris, which also allowed the signatories freely to conduct mining on Svalbard with only minimal taxation. The islands were not to be fortified or used for warlike purposes. In 1944 the Soviets tried to persuade Norway to make Svalbard a Soviet-Norwegian condominium, and from then until the end of the 1980s the Soviet Union—with 2000 so-called miners on the island—was slow to obey Norwegian law in Svalbard. The Soviets, however, have challenged Norway's right to introduce a fishery protection zone around Svalbard under the 1920 treaty but have largely complied with fishing regulations.

Thus jurisdictional problems have been created by the Nordic states' having open maritime frontiers giving them access to offshore resources —plus the development in technology that has provided the chance to exploit them.

EVOLVING RELATIONSHIPS

When the West European economic framework was being devised in the 1950s, none of the Nordic states was prepared to join the customs union of the European Economic Community, with its almost supranational institutions, though Denmark gave some consideration to this course.[15] The major Nordic states —Denmark, Norway, and Sweden— supported, albeit with some reservations, the British call for a West European-wide industrial free-trade area with loose institutions, and, when this was turned down by the European Economic Community, they became charter members of the European Free Trade Association (EFTA) in 1960, together with the United Kingdom, Portugal, Austria, and Switzerland. Finland became an EFTA associate, joining fully in 1986, and Iceland signed up in 1970.

15. Gunnar Nielsson, *Denmark and European Integration* (Ann Arbor, MI: University Microfilms, 1967).

When the United Kingdom finally became a member of the EC in 1973, so did Denmark. The Norwegian government had negotiated an accession treaty, but in September 1972 the electorate rejected it and, instead, Norway signed a free-trade treaty with the expanded EC, as did the other EFTA Nordic states.

The current arrangement—four Nordic states in EFTA but with individual free-trade treaties with the EC; Denmark in the EC—is not an easy one. Indeed, even the Danes have had some reservations about being part of the European Communities: they have consistently returned a handful of anti-EC members of the European Parliament, and a referendum accepted the Single European Act, which extended the remit of the EC, by only a 56 percent positive vote. Successive Danish governments have seen their role as a sort of intermediary between the EC and the Nordic area. As Denmark has had to protect its own interests within the Communities and as countries such as Norway and Sweden are anxious to open up a direct dialogue with the EC's institutions, the bridge-building potential of Denmark is now somewhat limited.

Norway has an ambiguous relationship with the EC. On the one hand, Norwegian governments wish to improve the current EFTA-EC links by developing a wider West European market—what has been called the European Economic Space —encompassing the states of the two organizations. Since Norway is a loyal NATO member, they wish to have as close an involvement as possible with European Political Cooper-ation, by which the EC members coordinate, among other policies, their foreign and security stances. On the other hand, Norway is a suitable candidate for full EC membership. Unlike the neutral states, it would not be a brake on European Political Cooperation, and the country has a thriving economy, with almost 70 percent of its current exports going to the EC. The main roadblock to another membership application is political opposition within Norway: sectional interests such as farmers and fishermen and some political groups, mainly on the left, oppose full membership. Furthermore, the Norwegian Labour Party, the country's largest party, seems unwilling to trigger anew the internal conflict involved in the 1972 referendum. Nevertheless, by early 1990, opinion polls were showing a majority of those questioned in Norway to be in favor of EC membership.[16] After all, if East Germany can become part of the Communities, then so can Norway.

Sweden is particularly concerned by the creation of a single European market within the EC by the end of 1992, whereby the barriers to trade, commerce, capital, and labor between the Communities' members are supposed to come down. Sweden sends 51 percent of its exports to the EC and is concerned about its markets there. It is prepared to be involved in all aspects of EC activity except those that might undermine the country's alliance-free policy. It therefore feels that it cannot participate in any binding foreign policy cooperation and is not likely to apply for

16. *Norinform,* 27 Feb. 1990, p. 3.

EC membership. Neutral Finland is in a similar position, and both countries have supported plans to have a closer EC-EFTA relationship. The question remains as to how relevant this wary approach will be in the 1990s, after the Cold War division of Europe has ended, when East Germany has been included in the EC, and with neutral Austria applying for EC membership, possibly being followed by Hungary, Poland, and Czechoslovakia. It may be that the EC will have to consider new forms of membership that could accommodate both neutral and former Communist states.

Major changes in the elements of international relations that have impinged so much on the Nordic region since World War II—in the Cold War and the trade division of Western Europe—have meant that the governments of the area have had to reconsider some of their traditional beliefs. The Nordic states depend for their resilience on their inventiveness, and New Thinking is needed about their institutional links with the rest of Europe, especially with the EC.

ANNALS, *AAPSS*, 512, November 1990

Finlandization as a Problem or an Opportunity?

By GEORGE H. QUESTER

ABSTRACT: While the concept of Finlandization was often used in the past by NATO spokesmen to refer to a problem, the possible intimidation of Western democracies by Soviet military power, it may also suggest a number of positive possibilities for the Baltic republics. An examination of recent history offers a number of analytical insights for comparing the fate of Finland with countries like Poland, subjected to Communist rule, and with Estonia, Latvia, and Lithuania, actually incorporated into the Soviet Union. Models are offered of military and other resistance to foreign pressure, of concessions and withdrawals, and of delicate balances, involving all the Scandinavian countries.

George H. Quester has been serving as chairman of the Department of Government and Politics at the University of Maryland, where he teaches courses on defense policy and international relations. He is the author of books and articles in these areas, and his most recent work is The International Politics of Television *(1990).*

T HE world was quite astounded at the end of 1989 by the pace of events in Eastern Europe. What would have looked wildly unrealistic even at the end of 1988 was accomplished fact by the end of 1989: the tearing down of the Berlin Wall, the establishment of non-Communist government in Poland, the termination of Communist rule in Hungary, Czechoslovakia, and Bulgaria, the fall of Ceausescu in Romania, the assertion of claims to independence in Estonia, Latvia, and Lithuania, and on, and on.

The basic questions, for the balancing of military security and economic progress and of political freedom and general quality of life, may remain the same, but the answers to these questions look far more optimistic, yet also far more unpredictable, than in the past.

The speed and the surprise of these developments were thus frightening in at least two different ways. First, we must always fear that things will fall off the track, that the pace of change may frighten the Soviets into a violent reaction or may lead to some other forms of violence or nonliberal development. Second, the very unpredictability of these events makes us wonder whether we understood any of what was happening over all these years.

Yet the fact that we have been embarrassed by our inability to anticipate the behavior of Gorbachev or the tearing down of the Berlin Wall or the behavior of the Baltic peoples and the Armenians and the Azerbaijanis cannot let us wash our hands of theoretical inferences or analytical judgments here, for a great many problems and questions remain concerning the continuation and completion of these processes.

What kinds of new national arrangements and international arrangements can we envisage around the Baltic Sea? How can we balance considerations of the military security of the Soviet Union against the military security of others and against the national aspirations of the peoples who front on the Baltic? Are there new arrangements that can span alternative economic and social systems, so that one side of the line does not always have to stare jealously at the much higher living standards of the other?

FINLANDIZATION

There was a time when the phrase "Finlandization" produced a great deal of irritation for any Finn, as it was used by the typical spokesperson of the North Atlantic Treaty Organization (NATO) to depict an odious fate for the nations of Western Europe, as they might be compromised in their sovereignty, as they might be rendered less than totally independent in the votes they could cast at the United Nations, in the books they could publish, or in the rulers they elected.[1] The argument was that the latent threat of a Soviet military invasion had hung over Finland since 1945, a threat that never needed to be implemented but that nonetheless somewhat intimidated the Finnish government and people, at times openly, at other times perhaps so

1. For some valuable discussion of the concept of Finlandization, see Max Jakkobson, "Substance and Appearance: Finland," *Foreign Affairs*, 58(5):1034-47 (Summer 1980).

subtly that one hardly noticed it. The fear was that a similar threat of a Soviet invasion, if not countered by the prospect of NATO conventional military or nuclear responses, could also constrict the freedom of choice in nations like Denmark or West Germany or Belgium.

Any Westerner in the 1960s would have been quick to admit, of course, that the situation of Finland was far superior to that of Poland or Czechoslovakia. But, from this same Western point of view, the situation of Finland and the Finns was not as good or free as that of Belgium and the Belgians.

Yet, in the wake of all that has happened since the middle of the 1980s, we might have far less reason to flinch at the phrase "Finlandization," and we might rather see a model here for what we should aspire to for Poland or Hungary, or for Estonia and Latvia and Lithuania.[2] Much of what I will be doing in this article amounts to trying out the model of Finland and asking what would stop it from being adopted for the other countries. Besides treating Finland as a model, therefore, there may be a need now to reanalyze the complicated relationships that have been in effect across all of the Baltic for the past four decades—relationships embodied in the situation, good or bad, of Finland, but relationships drawing in Norway, Sweden, and Denmark and perhaps all of NATO as well.

It has been noted above that Finlandization may never have been such a bad situation, as any visitor to Helsinki in the 1950s or 1960s or 1970s would readily have noticed. Yet the situation of Finland has itself also moved somewhat, in the wake of the turmoil in the Soviet Union, and moved in a good direction rather than bad. If Soviet threats would once have induced the Finnish government to pressure its publishers not to put out a Finnish-language edition of Solzhenitsyn—which led immediately, of course, to the delivery to Helsinki of a large press run of a Finnish translation printed in Sweden[3]—one can hardly imagine any such pressure now, as the Soviets themselves are allowing such literature to be published. Given all the distractions that Gorbachev feels at home, one wonders how he or his colleagues would ever find the time to have any opinions on what should be happening inside Finland.

The model of Finland thus had many positive aspects as we closed the 1980s. On friendly terms with both the West and the East, it was not somehow a vacuum into which contending forces could be drawn, like Afghanistan, but rather a nation that was prospering economically, having surpassed Sweden in per capita income, and quite self-governing politically. Air travelers speculating nervously about which international carrier was the least likely target for terrorists would often hit upon Finnair, as leftist insurgents would not

2. An earlier version of the present author's views can be found in George H. Quester, "America's Interest in Eastern Europe: Toward a Finlandization of the Warsaw Pact," *Conflict*, 5(3):211-32 (Fall 1984).

3. On determining the baseline for measuring relative intimidation and power, see William Pfaff, "Finlandization," *New Yorker*, 1 Sept. 1980, pp. 30-34.

want to offend Moscow by attacking a state with which the USSR professed to be on such good terms and would not be able to depict Finland as some rotten example of bourgeois capitalism like Switzerland or the United States or West Germany and as rightist terrorists would have no bones to pick with the Finnish government either.

The Soviet Union has sometimes described Soviet-Finnish relations as the model for how any two states should be getting along. Such a description, of course, could be seized upon by worriers about Finlandization as evidence that Helsinki was being forced too much to capitulate to Soviet demands. In the absence of such demands for anyone to see, however, it actually indicated that the Finnish model had a lot of positive mileage to it, in terms of getting the Soviet Union to adjust its relations with its other neighbors.

DIFFERING FATES POST-1945

Why did Finland escape the imposition of Communist rule? Why indeed did it escape the fate of Estonia, Latvia, and Lithuania, an outright incorporation into the Soviet Union? Despite the Soviet posture, dating back to Lenin, of a renunciation of the domains of the czar, Stalin seemed intent on reincorporating all that the czar had governed, with the Finns noticing this directly enough in 1939. In the end, Stalin allowed Poland west of the Curzon line to escape this restoration of the old empire, and he allowed Finland to escape; he was also to demand, but not press, claims on the territories that Turkey had

gained after 1918; but he took back everything else.[4]

When anyone speculates today about Gorbachev's likely actions in response to the demands of Estonia, Latvia, and Lithuania, he or she might thus be encouraged by the liberal stance the Soviet leader has taken with regard to Bulgaria, East Germany, and Czechoslovakia but would be discouraged in turn by the vehemence that has been expressed with regard to the Baltic republics.

The difference presumably stems from the nominal relationship by which these are internal parts of the Soviet Union, rather than merely partners of the USSR in the Warsaw Pact. Yet France once described Algeria as part of "Metropolitan France" and was nonetheless, under Charles de Gaulle, brought to renounce this formulation. Is it only because of the embarrassment of having to renounce sovereignty, of having to admit that something that was an internal part of one's country is no longer so, that the Soviets are destined to be much less tolerant of the real wishes of the Estonians? Does a Brezhnev doctrine still make sense for this portion of the Baltic littoral, where a Frank Sinatra doctrine is allowed to apply for the rest?

Some of the problem here, for the Soviets as for any other people or government in the world, will thus hinge on how one backs away from previous declarations without in the process looking too craven, that is, on how to make a concession in a way

4. A useful discussion of Stalin's options and choices in 1945 can be found in Adam Ulam, *Expansion and Coexistence* (New York: Holt, Rinehart & Winston, 1974).

that looks like it is not a mere giving-in to pressure or to naked power. The right time to make a concession is when it can still be viewed as a gesture of magnanimity or statesmanship, rather than as a resignation to force or pressure.

One can indeed find a very interesting model of how this is to be done in the very region we are discussing, in Khrushchev's 1955 decision to surrender the enclave at Porkkala, a prize taken at the end of World War II and awarded to the Soviets by the Finnish peace treaty in perpetuity as a naval base. This basically replaced Hanko, a similar enclave on the Finnish coast awarded to Stalin's USSR by the 1940 treaty and then speedily seized by the Finns and the Germans when Finland joined Nazi Germany in the 1941 invasion of the Soviet Union.

Khrushchev returned Porkkala in the same move as his return to the Chinese of Port Arthur, a prize of the treaty between China and the Soviet Union when the USSR entered the war against Japan. The return of Port Arthur headed off what would have indeed been a very nasty conflict between the Chinese and the Soviets, as we would have seen analogies drawn to Hong Kong, and one could have imagined crowds of Red Guards protesting at the gates of the Soviet naval base. By making the concession, before it was demanded openly by the Chinese, Khrushchev thus prevented what might later have been perceived as weakness. By coupling a concession to tiny Finland with the concession to a huge China, and by declaring an opposition to overseas naval bases on principle,

the Soviets all the more avoided an image of weakness.

Giving up possession of the Baltic republics would be a much greater task in covering any loss of face than giving up Porkkala or Port Arthur, of course. Moreover, the possibility remains that the Russians—we use this term advisedly here, rather than "Soviets"—will have to balk at surrendering what has so long been a part of their own country, simply for fear of the precedent that would then seem to apply to all the Asian republics or to any other portion of the Soviet Union with latent cravings for nationalist self-assertion and independence. Most of us would have credited seven decades of Communist rule with a greater effectiveness at stamping out chauvinism and national assertiveness in places like Armenia and Azerbaijan, assuming that this at least was a blessing of Communist rule, even if the price in economic stagnation and loss of human freedom was enormous. Yet, as the ultimate disappointment with the systems of Lenin and Stalin and their successors, even this benefit of Communist rule does not seem to have been achieved.

EXPLANATIONS FOR THE POSTWAR BALANCE

We will be asking all along here why Finland met one fate and Estonia met another and whether Estonia and the other Baltic republics cannot move up to the situation of Finland. There are many theories of why Finland escaped the fate of the other neighbors of the USSR after 1945. Perhaps this was the result of the military spirit of the Finns, who had made life difficult for any Soviet military advance in two rounds of warfare and would have fought on if they had not been offered an exemption from Soviet occupation. Related to this, it is widely held that Stalin was too intent on moving toward Berlin and hence did not want to tie up forces in the direction of Finland and the north—but why then did he send his army into Bulgaria, which had never even declared war on the Soviet Union all through World War II and had retained diplomatic relations with Moscow?[5]

A somewhat different theory would assign a very important role here to Sweden, as a Nordic-balance counterweight to Soviet designs on Finland. Sweden did not join NATO, as Norway and Denmark did. Had the Soviets imposed a Communist regime on Finland or made Finland into the Finnish Soviet Socialist Republic, the likelihood is much greater that the Swedes would have opted for this kind of an alliance.[6] To complete the reciprocity here, if Sweden had elected in 1949 to join NATO, the risk remains that the Soviets would have retaliated by exerting much greater pressure on Finland, perhaps even launching the kind of invasion that befell Czechoslovakia or Afghanistan.[7]

IDENTIFICATIONS WITH THE BALTICS

For at least two reasons, Finnish involvement with Estonia has to be greater than with Latvia and Lithuania. The Estonian language is very close to Finnish, and in turn totally different from Latvian and Lithuanian, such that an elementary Finnish cultural identification or irredentism might apply to this republic in particular.[8] Estonians have moreover been capable of tuning in Finnish television for decades now and, of course, have been able to understand what was being said and shown, putting them into the same category as the East Germans: subjects of a Communist government who nonetheless had ready access each evening to free-world television news.[9]

Finnish television surely was not designed to destabilize Communist rule in Estonia but rather—like television in most places—was designed to serve some balance of entertainment and cultural interests for the Finns themselves. Unlike other Scandinavian television systems, moreover, Finnish television has for more than a decade relied on commercial advertising to defray its expenses. This might have been irritating to the Finnish viewer, who would have preferred to have television programming unbroken by such advertising

5. On Stalin's choices with regard to Finland, see George Maude, *The Finnish Dilemma* (New York: Oxford University Press, 1976).

6. Some analysts, who have not looked at the continuing size of Swedish defense budgets, might guess that Sweden would have instead deferred to Soviet wishes in some form of Swedenization, but this would be a very misleading inference.

7. Theories of the Nordic balance are discussed in Arne Olav Brundtland, "The Nordic

Balance and Its Possible Relevance for Europe," in *Sicherheit durch Gleichgewicht*, ed. Daniel Frei (Zurich: Schultheiss, 1982).

8. On Estonian national character, see Toivo Raun, *Estonia and the Estonians* (Stanford, CA: Hoover Institution Press, 1987).

9. Estonian watching of Finnish television is described in Philip Taubman, "Estonians' Pensive Refrain: We Are Not Russians," *New York Times*, 18 Mar. 1986.

interruptions. But these commercial advertising messages would have worked to offer Estonians one more input of interest besides the news of the world, namely, a view of what consumers could buy just across the water. Soviet newspapers have at times run commentaries on such Finnish programming, claiming that it was all some sort of Potemkin village, as these goods were not really available in Helsinki. Yet virtually every Estonian viewer—and the data suggest that Estonians have overwhelmingly chosen Finnish television over the Soviet offerings, as they vote with their channel selectors each evening—knows better than this. If there have been any subtle or not so subtle Soviet suggestions that Finnish television should rein in the news commentary or entertainment programs or commercial advertising it has been spilling into Estonia, we have no evidence that any such pressures have worked.

How much would Finns in particular, or Swedes and other Scandinavians, identify with the Latvians or the Lithuanians, as compared with the Estonians? The link of language is not there in the case of these two other republics, but the Latvians at least are predominantly Lutheran in religion, like the Estonians and all the Scandinavians. In an earlier time, a portion of the Balt nobility in both Estonia and Latvia was Swedish, while the bulk was of Germanic origin—Olaf Palme's family had estates in Latvia, for example—but this kind of nostalgic tie is more bitter than sweet, as the Balts were never popular with the peasant majorities that they had exploited and dominated so much. The Lithuanians, by contrast, tended to be governed and exploited more by a Polish nobility and are today predominantly Roman Catholic in religion, which may mobilize the identification of other peoples in the world ahead of the Scandinavians.

One of the bigger questions for the entire future of Eastern Europe indeed pertains to whether these mobilizations of sympathy and interest will stem mainly from such ethnic identifications or rather from a more abstract support for self-determination regardless of the group. By the latter liberal standard of government by consent of the governed, that is, government by majority rule in free elections, Lithuania should draw just as much sympathy around the Baltic littoral as Estonia for its national aspirations. The evidence is that the majority of people living in Estonia would immediately grab an independence like that of Denmark or Sweden—or Finland—if they were given the choice and that probably an even larger percentage of the residents of Lithuania would make this choice.

Latvia becomes a little more difficult by this measure, however, and here we get into the crux of some more complicated issues of self-determination, for less than a majority of the Latvian Soviet Socialist Republic is now Latvian speaking.[10] The great bulk of the Russian speakers in all three of these republics have been brought in since the end of

10. For basic data, see Ronald Wixman, *The Peoples of the USSR: An Ethnographic Handbook* (Eugene: University of Oregon Press, 1983). See also Zbigniew Brzezinski, "Post-Communist Nationalism," *Foreign Affairs*, 68(1):1-25 (Winter 1989-90).

World War II, in some part as a vehicle for Stalin's concern to hold these territories forever as a part of his domain, in part also simply as the personnel for various schemes for massive industrialization.

The variation in the fractions of Russian speakers in the three republics thus reflects the degrees of Soviet-style industrialization—this not always being the kind of modernization that increases prosperity or the quality of life—which to some extent reflected the varying national loyalties and farsightedness of local leaders in the 1940s and 1950s in stalling such schemes. The Lithuanian Communist leadership was thus the most astute or most successful at postponing the kinds of development schemes that would deliberately or inadvertently change the ethnic character of the republic, with the result that the Lithuanian republic has only about 20 percent of its population speaking Russian as its first language—compared with 3 percent for Armenia. Estonia managed to hold its Russian minority to about one-third, while Latvia is now seeing its Slavic group of Russian, Belorussian, or Ukrainian speakers indeed becoming a majority.

One thus has to consider the bizarre possibility here that a Wilsonian free election or plebiscite in Latvia might see Latvian supplanted by Russian as the language of choice and might see a vote for remaining part of the Soviet Union. It may only be the structures by which the Communist leadership has been selected in this republic—as elsewhere in the Soviet Union, selected rather than

truly elected—and the constitutional provisions of the USSR and of its Latvian republic guaranteeing the status of the Latvian language that have kept this from emerging as the natural flow of things.

One of the first demands of all of these republics, as their current legislatures and party leaderships have made unheard-of proposals for special arrangements, has been that the immigration of additional outsiders into their domains be stopped and that some of the migration that has already occurred perhaps be turned around—or that some of the Russian speakers now in these republics be denied the full rights of voters and citizens. In the latter case, they would be treated like *Gastarbeiters* in West Germany, expected to return to their true homes over the longer term, without being allowed to make decisions for the political or cultural future of their temporary home and workplace.

The Russians in Latvia, and in the other Baltic republics, are there, of course, behind the shield of force of arms, of the unwelcome entry of the Soviet army in 1940, followed by a German invasion and then a Soviet counteroffensive in 1944. Fifty years is a long time, by some of the standards of self-determination. Yet people around the Baltic Sea may still have long enough memories to feel that real self-determination should not treat Latvia as a part of Russia but rather as what would have been wanted by the people who lived there before armed aggression.

One could, of course, discuss partitions of Latvia, and of Estonia and

Lithuania as well, whereby the rights of all the ethnic groups were protected, whereby Russian-speaking communities would be free to continue as portions of the Soviet Union. Yet, as they have in most places, such partitions and the plebiscites in favor of them can lead to unmanageable situations and chaos, where the patterns of recent migration have intermingled the communities too much.

Where the issue is ethnic, of course, a Russian-speaking town in any of these republics might like to have borders redrawn so that it was part of the Russian Soviet Federated Socialist Republic, much as the Armenians in the Nagorno-Karabakh Region of Azerbaijan have been demanding a merger with the Armenian Soviet Socialist Republic. Where the issues are rather those of economic liberalization or political liberalization, however, it is not beyond belief that some of these Russian-speaking communities might vote, if their neighbors would only accept them, to remain a part of a newly freed Estonia or Latvia, much as certain so-called ethnic Germans have continued to claim the right to move to (West) Germany, even when they can barely speak any German anymore.

How much is anyone going to tolerate a series of plebiscites that substantially redraw boundaries here, boundaries that are going to have to be very complicated? How much is the outside world going to be mobilizable, and on which side, if the revision of such boundaries is now to be the issue? And would the burden of legitimacy be to assign significance to the language someone speaks or to the preference he or she expresses?

There also continues to be a large Finnish-speaking minority inside the Soviet Union, in what once had the status of a separate Karelo-Finnish Soviet Socialist Republic and even to the south and east of Leningrad, in territory that has always been declared to be part of the Russian Soviet Federated Socialist Republic. If the lid comes off ethnic grievances and demands all across the Soviet Union, will this lid come off, too, with a new issue emerging for the residents of Helsinki to become exercised about again and with new complications for the model of Finlandization?

THE CONTINUING ROLE OF MILITARY PREPARATIONS

In the wake of the collapse of the Communist parties of Eastern Europe, many analysts would now more generally downgrade the significance of military forces for the preservation of peace in Europe, or elsewhere around the world. Close counting of the totals of tanks and infantry and fighter-bombers will seem less relevant; while we very tentatively used to venture some doubts about whether the Soviets could really launch any offensives against NATO with the full-fledged participation of Hungarian and Polish and Czech divisions, this entire possibility now seems more ludicrous than doubtful, as even the East German military forces no longer look like they would ever have been so reliable, as the much more likely military scenarios

—somewhat worrisome nonetheless—might pit such East European forces against the Soviet army.[11]

Yet the distribution of military capabilities has hardly been irrelevant up to the present, and it is not irrelevant for the immediate future either. More hawkish commentators in the United States were fond of noting that the Soviets still had large tank forces in East Germany and across Eastern Europe even as 1990 began, despite the new commitment under Gorbachev to "defensive defense," for there still was much to be done in translating the new pronouncements into changes of force structure and tactical battle doctrine. While real progress was within reach on an agreement on conventional force reductions, such reductions would inevitably have to be larger on the Soviet side than on the NATO side, since the Soviet total of tanks and armored personnel carriers and mobile artillery was so much higher at the outset; and if agreements were close at hand, but had not yet been implemented, a certain degree of inherent threat to Western security would remain.

The past might have been very different for the Baltic region if Norway and Denmark had not been members of NATO, if Sweden had not maintained universal military training and a large military establishment of standing and reserve forces —including perhaps the largest air

11. The momentous changes in the overall East-West military confrontation in Europe are outlined in Rochelle Stanfield, "After the Wall: Where Do We Put the Blocs?" *National Journal*, 25 Nov. 1989, pp. 2872, 2877-79.

force per capita in the world—and if Finland had not similarly maintained a system of universal military training and reserve structures.

Outside military analysts at times deprecated the degree of Finnish military preparedness because of the absence of the most modern of military weaponry, suggesting that a Soviet advance would slice unopposed across Finland toward Sweden and Norway in any future conventional war, just as it might slice across Austria toward Bavaria. While the manning of the Austrian military structure looked less impressive, however —with the Austrian government then belatedly shifting from a small standing-army structure to a larger territorial-reserve army based on the Swiss, Swedish, and Finnish models—the style of Finnish military training and organization looks very impressive indeed to foreign military attachés and other analysts. The brave and effective performance of the Finnish army against the Soviets in World War II probably supported Finnish independence thereafter much more than it threatened it. One would have difficulty in showing that the absence of Estonian military threats to Stalin's domains somehow produced a better deal for Estonia than what the Finns extracted.

In the wake of any mutually agreed-upon, or more spontaneous, conventional disarmament—matched by a further de-emphasis of nuclear escalation and nuclear deployments —it is quite possible that Switzerland and Austria and Sweden and Finland will elect to trim back some of their military preparations as well.[12] It goes without saying that all of this is done best when it is done so as to keep the sides to the confrontation close in comparative military strength and when defensive weapons are favored over offensive, that is, when the weapons that favor the attacker are the first to be eliminated and when those that favor the side sitting still in any future crises are retained in place.

The Finnish models—like the Swedish—are indeed again very relevant here. As part of a new burst of *glasnost* and honest analysis of the real military problems of Central Europe, Soviet commentators have now become very open about admitting that certain kinds of conventional weapons, kinds of which the USSR has had a great number, are particularly menacing and destabilizing. These weapons are also admitted to being offensive, in that they favor the side that takes the initiative to move forward into the other side's territory. The number of tanks and armored personnel carriers, mobile artillery, bridge-building equipment, and certain logistical accoutrements to a forward-moving armored attack are in particular to be reduced, while antitank weapons and fixed fortifications are much less in need of being restricted.[13]

The Finnish army is a valuable model because it is not configured for armored offensive warfare. It has some tanks, provided, ironically enough, by the Soviet Union, even if it remains obvious that the only possible enemy the Finnish army has ever taken seriously is the Soviet Union; the Soviets periodically press Finland to acquire Eastern-bloc military hardware, because the USSR is always hard-pressed to find commodities to sell to the Finns in order to defray the costs of all the things it wishes to buy from Finland. Rather than grouping Soviet-built tanks for armored offensive attacks, the Finns have rather been using this equipment in maneuvers for training—in antitank warfare.

All things considered, it might be beneficial for the military stability and general political future of the Baltic region if Finland and Sweden did not quickly reduce their military preparations; the taxpayers of these countries will be looking for relief at every point, of course, and their most straightforward theory of military and political affairs might thus conclude that reductions in Soviet and NATO military potential should be viewed as a good example for the nonaligned countries in the region. Yet, as noted, these nonaligned countries have already been setting their own good example, in the qualitative thrust of their own forces away from offensive inclinations, and this might well be kept in place until more of what we are discussing here is settled.

12. For an overview of the military preparations of the major neutral states in Europe, see Adam Roberts, *Nations in Arms: The Theory and Practice of Territorial Defence* (New York: St. Martin's Press, 1986).

13. A useful outline of the thinking behind defensive defense can be found in Dieter Senghaas, "Conventional Weapons in Europe: Dismantle Offense, Strengthen Defenses,"

Bulletin of the Atomic Scientists, 43(10):9-11 (Dec. 1987).

THE NUCLEAR-FREE-ZONE ISSUE

The Soviets have often enough proposed a nuclear-free-zone arrangement for the Baltic Sea,[14] with this producing some major irritation and embarrassment when a Soviet submarine ran aground on the Swedish coast in 1981 amid evidence that nuclear warheads were very probably on board. The debate about nuclear disarmament versus conventional disarmament used to be a major source of tension between the Warsaw Pact and NATO more broadly, with Moscow being seen as favoring nuclear disarmament because it had such a large advantage in conventional forces and/or because it was the anti-status-quo force, the power that might one day want to use military action to liberate Belgium or Denmark or France—or at least might want to intimidate the publics of such Western countries by the mere prospect that such an invasion might occur. NATO, content to stand on the defensive and substantially outnumbered in totals of tanks and other conventional forces, would, conversely, have wanted to maintain the threat of nuclear escalation if there were any major war in Europe, thereby deterring Soviet aggressions —and warding off the intimidation of even the prospect of such aggressions —by the likelihood that a war that had gone nuclear would be a disaster for all concerned.[15]

Much of the polarization in this kind of question, of who should favor and who should oppose the maintenance of threats of nuclear escalation, is now undone by the collapse of the Warsaw Pact as a military alliance. Suddenly it is the West that is much more anti-status-quo, and it is the Soviet side that has to worry about military penetrations from the West, or at least about the mere prospect of such interventions by the military forces of NATO.

Given the chaos that can now erupt in Poland or Romania or Czechoslovakia, or even in Estonia and Lithuania, it may soon enough be seen as in the interest of all the parties to get nuclear weapons out of the way, eliminating once and for all the risks of nuclear escalation that are generated by the mere deployment of such weapons in the path of any future combat operations and thus forgoing whatever reinforcements for deterrence this provided, relying for peace and deterrence instead on the very mix of political and military factors that we are discussing throughout this article.

Especially if there is now a breakthrough in conventional disarmament, the likelihood is good of some more extensive and serious nuclear disarmament in Europe. This may resemble the old Rapacki Plan, but with a very different kind of Polish government now endorsing it. It may also include some renewals of the older proposals for a nuclear-free Baltic.

14. On these proposals, see Milton Leitenberg, "The Stranded USSR Submarine in Sweden and the Question of a Nordic Nuclear-Free Zone," *Cooperation and Conflict*, 17(1):17-28 (Mar. 1982).

15. The traditional dialogue between the Warsaw Pact and NATO on nuclear versus conventional armament issues is outlined in Karl Kaiser et al., "Nuclear Weapons and the Preservation of Peace: A German Response to No First Use," *Foreign Affairs*, 60(5):1157-70 (Summer 1982).

Sweden and Finland are already committed by the Nuclear Non-Proliferation Treaty to forgo acquiring nuclear weapons for themselves, Finland already being so committed by the peace treaty terminating World War II. Denmark, Norway, and West Germany are committed likewise. The nonaligned countries also have a declared policy of not permitting the stationing of any other country's nuclear weapons on their territories, and this, at least in peacetime, has also been the policy of NATO members Denmark and Norway. This has decidedly not been the policy, however, of the most important European NATO member, West Germany, which has indeed been relying for decades on the implicit and explicit threat of nuclear escalation posed by the deployment of U.S. nuclear weapons on West German soil.

As a means of exploiting past Soviet positions and exploiting the world's general endorsement of nonnuclear approaches now to arms control, it should not be so difficult to turn the Soviets back to this Baltic option but with a now relevant add-on question on what zone along their side of the Baltic they might be willing to free of nuclear weapons as well. The region immediately to the east of the Norwegian border might strike some Western strategic analysts as an attractive quid to be asked for in a quid pro quo, but this would be to knife much too deeply into the Soviet strategic force potential. With respect to the Baltic region, some Scandinavians may now again support a lessening of the Soviet military presence in the Baltic republics by asking for Latvia, Lithuania, and Estonia as their counterpoint for the formal and final denuclearization of the non-Communist side of the Baltic. Would Poland and East Germany come along in the wake of other events?

Nordic Security in a Europe Without the United States

By STEVEN E. MILLER

ABSTRACT: The five Nordic countries have quite different security problems and geostrategic settings and have made very different choices about their security policy. They will thus react differently to the new balance of forces in Europe that results from the revolutions in Eastern Europe, the disintegration of the Soviet empire, and the unification of Germany. Should these sweeping changes also be accompanied by a U.S. withdrawal from Europe, the Nordic countries would again react in unique ways. An optimistic view of the 1990s would see great benefits to the Nordic region from the end of the Cold War and the confrontation between the North Atlantic Treaty Organization and the Warsaw Pact, and the establishment of a more cooperative pan-European security arrangement. Defense planners in the Nordic countries should also plan, however, for the possibility of greater instability on the Continent, which might generate the need for new security arrangements, different alliance relationships, and a rethinking of the meaning of neutrality in a multipolar world.

Steven E. Miller is currently a senior researcher at the Stockholm International Peace Research Institute and coeditor of International Security. *Formerly he taught defense studies and international relations at Harvard University and the Massachusetts Institute of Technology. He has published widely on arms control and defense studies, especially on Nordic security and naval issues.*

T HE dramatic events of the last year or two have shaken the basic structures of Cold War Europe. Soviet power is in retreat from the center of the Continent and the Soviet state itself is in jeopardy. The Warsaw Pact is moribund and the Soviet empire in Eastern Europe finished. The division of Germany is coming to an end. These developments in turn raise difficult questions about West European institutions and relationships. In particular, it seems clear that the North Atlantic Treaty Organization (NATO), if it is to survive at all, must become something different from what it has been, but many voices doubt whether it can or should be preserved for long in the new Europe. Uncertainties about the future of NATO lead directly to questions about the future role of the United States. Will its nuclear guarantee be preserved? Will its troops remain? Will they be wanted? Will the United States be willing and able to preserve its long-term commitment to the security of Europe, and will Europeans find this necessary or desireable? Whatever political leaders are now saying, the definitive answers to such questions are not yet evident, may not be apparent for some time, may emerge from developments and processes not substantially controllable by political elites, and may not be the answers preferred by present authorities. The possibility cannot be excluded that all the old structures of security in Europe, including NATO and the U.S. role in Europe, will eventually be swept away by the new political currents, the new mass passions, the new national perceptions that could exist in a transformed Europe.

What would this mean for the states of Nordic Europe? Whatever results from the current, uncertain state of affairs, they are likely to feel the need to reexamine their security policies. But the demise of NATO and the retreat of American power from Europe would compel the most fundamental reconsideration in nearly half a century, since the immediate postwar years, when they made the formative choices that governed their security policies in bipolar, divided Europe. Under these circumstances, what sort of considerations and choices would confront them? The aim of this article is to identify the implications and options for Nordic Europe in the event of such a development.

NORDIC DIVERSITY

A first point to be made is that implications would vary widely from country to country. The commonly held impression of Nordic harmony and homogeneity should not obscure the reality that these five countries occupy very different geostrategic settings, have different security problems, and have made quite different choices in providing for their security.[1] This is not simply a matter of alignment, with Iceland, Norway, and Denmark members of NATO while Sweden and Finland are neutral. The differences are more substantial.

Iceland, for example, is physically remote from the rest, occupies a central position—both geographically and intellectually—in naval strategy for the North Atlantic, possesses no

1. As implied, for example, by the title of Johan Jørgen Holst, ed., *Five Roads to Nordic Security* (Oslo: Universitetsforlaget, 1972).

military forces of its own, and is completely dependent on the United States for its defense. Norway is strategically important because its long coastline lies adjacent to waters that represent the only access of the powerful Soviet Northern Fleet to the North Atlantic and the main attack corridor for American naval assets to threaten Soviet bases and forces on the Kola Peninsula. It shares a border with the Soviet Union in the far north, and it fears the Soviet incentive to control the strategically vital northern counties of Norway in the event of crisis or war. While it does not allow foreign bases on its territory in peacetime, its defense strategy relies heavily on reinforcements from its allies, including substantial increments of air and naval capability from the United States. While Norway is not as dependent on the United States as is Iceland, its security policy revolves to a large extent around its relationship with the United States. Denmark, on the other hand, is primarily a Baltic rather than a North Atlantic state, and in security terms, if not culturally, is really more a Central European than a Scandinavian power. Its critical security relationship within NATO is with the Federal Republic of Germany, whose forces have the primary responsibility, along with Denmark's own modest forces, for the defense of Denmark and the western Baltic. Even in terms of reinforcements, American forces barely figure at all in plans for the defense of Denmark. Thus each of the Nordic NATO members has a distinct security

problem and its own unique security policy.[2]

The same is true of the two Nordic neutrals. Finland shares both a long border and a difficult history with the Soviet Union, and its critical security relationship is with its enormous neighbor to the East. That relationship not only plays a pivotal role in Finnish foreign policy but is governed by a formal treaty, the Treaty of Friendship, Cooperation, and Mutual Assistance, which obliges Finland to resist attacks through its territory against the Soviet Union and which gives the Soviet Union a legal pretext, through the treaty's consultative provisions, for involving itself in Finland's security policy—although it has rarely done so.[3] Finland's main security concern is that, in the event of war, the Soviet Union would be tempted to use Finnish territory or Finnish airspace as a shortcut to strategically important areas in western Scandinavia; this Finland seeks to discourage by a policy of armed neutrality that aims to deter by threatening to make transit costly. Sweden follows a similar policy, but from a

2. I have examined in great detail the military implications for the Nordic NATO countries of a U.S. withdrawal in Steven E. Miller, "U.S. Withdrawal and NATO's Northern Flank: Impact and Implications," in *Europe after American Withdrawal*, ed. Jane M. O. Sharp (New York: Oxford University Press, 1990), pp. 303-48.

3. An informative discussion of the Soviet problem in Finnish diplomacy is found in Kari Möttölä, "The Politics of Neutrality and Defence: Finnish Security Policy since the Early 1970s," *Cooperation and Conflict*, 17(4):287-313 (Dec. 1982).

more autonomous position. Buffered by its Scandinavian neighbors from direct contact with the maritime arena to the west and the Soviet Union to the east, Sweden has been able to pursue the most insular security policy of the Nordic states. Because its large territory was wedged between NATO and the Soviet Union in Northern Europe, however, it could not avoid some strategic significance in the East-West competition, and it was sometimes argued that the country benefited from the fact that neither bloc could permit the other to dominate Sweden, thereby allowing Sweden to enjoy the benefits of what amounted to de facto deterrent protection by the superpowers.[4] Nevertheless, like Finland, it has followed its own deterrent policy of armed neutrality that aimed at making it militarily painful for anyone who violated Swedish territory.

It is clear even from this very brief sketch of the security positions and policies of the five Nordic states that this region cannot be treated as a unified whole and that the impact of sweeping changes in Europe that included the departure of the United States would vary considerably from state to state and would pose some distinctive problems for each.

WHAT NEW EUROPE?

A second basic consideration is the character of the new security environment in which the Nordic states

4. See, for example, the very interesting discussion in Ola Tunander, *Cold Water Politics: The Maritime Strategy and Geopolitics of the Northern Front* (Newbury Park, CA: Sage, 1989), esp. pp. 13-15.

would find themselves. The optimistic imagery envisions a Europe democratic, prosperous, and peaceful, integrating economically while managing its security system through pan-European institutions, whether the Conference on Security and Cooperation in Europe or some new European security framework. In this Europe, threat perceptions and levels of forces would presumably both be low, the role of arms control presumably high, and some notion of cooperative security would play a major role in every state's security concept. This Europe, if it were to emerge, would be a very unchallenging security environment to which the Nordic states —and all others in Europe—would have to adapt. While it would clearly require adjustment away from exclusively national policies and toward reliance on what would amount to a collective security system, the hard problems and serious dangers are almost by definition eliminated. This happy outcome, however, cannot be counted upon and for some time to come will remain, if anything, much more a foreign policy objective than a security policy solution; for foreign policymakers, the question is whether and how this harmonious Europe can be created.

Security policy, on the other hand, is a state's insurance policy against worst-case outcomes and is more likely to be preoccupied with problems and risks than with expectations that European comity and institutions will reliably neutralize these problems and risks. In a situation in which the United States—and with it, NATO—had disappeared from the European scene, pessimistic speculations could lead to some quite disturbing scenarios. Most broadly, those factors thought to have provided stability to Cold War Europe —the bipolar structure, including the division of Germany; the inhibition of nuclear weapons; the presence of the superpowers in the center of Europe —would have dramatically changed if not disappeared.[5] The new Europe could be less stable rather than more harmonious. More concretely, removing the stabilizing weight of the superpowers could expose and unleash historical, ethnic, and nationalist antagonisms previously repressed. This is already visible in eastern Central Europe, in frictions between Germany and Poland, in tensions between Hungary and Romania, and in the hostility between Turkey and both Bulgaria and Greece, and it is evident, in more muted fashion, in the widespread concern in Western Europe about containing the power of a unified Germany. Further, in the new Europe, it is distinctly possible that one or more states will disintegrate, including, most significantly, the Soviet Union, but also Yugoslavia and perhaps even Czechoslovakia. Obviously, this could produce both internal violence and severe international repercussions. In short, if the optimistic end of the spectrum of possible outcomes offers a very attractive picture, the pessimistic end offers a bleak view of Europe unstable and ridden with antagonisms and potential conflicts. For the Nordic states, obviously, this would pose much more difficult problems of adaptation.

Let us turn from the broader European security environment to focus more narrowly on the Nordic region. Here several considerations will be especially important in determining the character of the new Nordic security environment. First, there is the question of the character of the U.S. relationship with Europe after a withdrawal. If the United States fully jettisons its European commitment, whether of its own volition or because Europe no longer wishes it, then much of the strategic importance of the Nordic area will disappear; its significance, to both Europe and the United States, has largely derived from the NATO imperative to control the waters of the North Atlantic in order to ensure the safe arrival of seaborne reinforcements and supplies from the United States in the event of war. If this connection is severed, then the geostrategic position of Nordic Europe, particularly Iceland and Norway, is greatly altered. If Europe does not care any longer about the sea lines to America, then in a military sense it would have much less need to worry about what role the Nordic countries are playing, just as the United States would have much less need to rely on its Nordic allies or to concern itself with the wider configuration of the Nordic security environment. In this circumstance, the Nordic area could become strategically marginalized and more isolated from the main security dy-

5. On factors of stability in the old Europe, see John Lewis Gaddis, "The Long Peace: Elements of Stability in the Postwar International System," *International Security,* 10(4):99-142 (Spring 1986). For the argument that the disappearance of these factors will lead to a less stable Europe, see John Mearsheimer, "The Future of Europe," *International Security* (Summer 1990).

namics in the center of Europe. At least some in the Nordic area are likely to welcome this as an attractive alternative to the present, highly militarized and heavily nuclearized nature of their security position. But it could also make it harder for the Nordic states to have their interests and perspectives taken into account in the European framework.

On the other hand, if the United States preserves a commitment to return its forces to Europe if necessary, or if the expectation exists that the United States would do so, then the sea lanes to America would be even more important than at present, since if there are no U.S. forces stationed in Europe, the reinforcements would be everything.[6] Obviously, this would enhance the strategic significance of the Nordic area, would make it a critical factor in new arrangements for European security, and would cause it to remain prominent in U.S. military strategy. In short, whether the Nordic region is strategically more or less important depends directly on the nature of the U.S. security relationship with Europe after a withdrawal.

Second, the security environment for the Nordic states, as for all of Europe, will be heavily influenced by the ultimate disposition of the Soviet

Union. If the USSR emerges from its current travails as benign and democratic, then the security problems for these states are much less acute. But if, after an American withdrawal, events in the USSR develop in worrisome directions and result in alarming external policies,[7] there could be severe difficulties for Nordic security policymakers. However weakened the USSR may seem relative to the combined power of NATO, it will always remain a giant relative to its small Nordic neighbors. All the Nordic states have been exposed to Soviet military pressure to one degree or another.[8] But this has always occurred in a context in which it was understood that most Soviet military power in Europe was oriented toward and preoccupied with NATO, especially in Central Europe. In fact, for Finland, Sweden, and even to some extent Norway, defense planning has been based on the assumption that

7. Sadly, this seems more likely than not. See in particular the thoughtful essay, Barrington Moore, *Liberal Prospects under Soviet Socialism: A Comparative Historical Perspective* (New York: Columbia University, Harriman Institute, Nov. 1989), which argues that the USSR fully meets none of the conditions conducive to liberal democracy. See esp. pp. 20-24.

8. This is true even of Iceland, despite its remote location. See, for example, Albert Jonsson's excellent *Iceland, NATO, and the Keflavík Base* (Reykjavík: Icelandic Commission on Security and International Affairs, 1989), which reports that the U.S. Air Force intercepts more Soviet aircraft around Iceland than anywhere else in the world. See p. 46. It is true also of Sweden, despite its neutral position and lack of a common border with the USSR. On the phenomenon of frequent Soviet submarine incursions in Swedish waters, see Gordon McCormick, *Stranger than Fiction: Soviet Submarine Operations in Swedish Waters* (Santa Monica, CA: RAND, Jan. 1990).

6. This point has been made even about reductions of U.S. forces in Europe. See, for example, Joseph Fitchett, "Norway, Bucking Trend, Shores Up Defenses and NATO Ties," *International Herald Tribune*, 26 Sept. 1989. Fitchett writes, "The importance of controlling . . . Norwegian bases is likely to grow . . . if arms control accords thin the allied force in central Europe. That would increase Western Europe's dependence on U.S. reinforcements crossing the Atlantic."

war in the Nordic area would be a sideshow in a broader European war and that therefore neither superpower could allocate more than a relatively small fraction of its overall capability to Northern European contingencies.[9] It is this assumption that has made credible defense strategies plausible for small states living in the neighborhood of a military superpower. Coping with a Soviet threat in a Europe in which the NATO counterweight does not exist and in which small states are not shielded, directly or indirectly, by American power would be a far more difficult task. Indeed, the near impossibility of devising credible defense postures for small states under these conditions would create strong incentives to find allies, preferably powerful ones.[10] In a Europe without America, a newly threatening Soviet Union could make at least some states yearn again for America.

This leads to a third major consideration, which is whether, in a Europe without the blocs and without the heavy stabilizing weight of the superpowers, there would be room once again for small wars and piece-meal aggression. In Cold War Europe, the confrontation of NATO and the Warsaw Pact strongly inhibited this in several ways. First, it imposed a rigid order on the European continent, and the superpowers had a strong interest in seeing that this order was not disrupted, that stability was preserved. Second, and perhaps most important, because the NATO-Pact framework was so ubiquitous in Europe, because it touched the interests of so many European states, it raised the risk always that a small war might grow into a European war. Third, the bloc-bloc framework contained the power of the larger states and directed their military capability largely at one another.

It is not at all clear what the new structures of security would be in a Europe without the United States, but it is impossible in any case to know in advance whether they will be as effective and as durable as the Cold War framework has been in preventing conflict. In the new Europe, wars of small against small and large against small may seem more feasible and more limitable. What Samuel Huntington has written about Eastern Europe today may be true in the future of a Europe without America: "The sources of initiative have multiplied; the sources of control have vanished."[11] Small states may feel very uncomfortable if they find themselves exposed and isolated in such

9. Tunander, borrowing from Wilhelm Agrell, calls this the "marginal theory." See Tunander, *Cold Water Politics*, p. 14. See also Richard Bitzinger, "Finnish Defense Today," *International Defense Review*, Nov. 1989, p. 1477, which identifies the main problem for Finnish security policy as the need to maintain its territorial integrity in a general European war.

10. The success of Finland in surviving its wars with the USSR during World War II might seem to undermine this point, but it should not be forgotten that Finland paid a high price, suffering one of the highest casualty rates of any state in Europe, that it lost several significant pieces of its territory, and that it ended up allied with Nazi Germany.

11. Samuel Huntington, "Democratization and Security in Eastern Europe," in *Uncertain Futures: Eastern Europe and Democracy*, Occasional Paper no. 16, ed. Peter Volten (New York: Institute for East-West Security Studies, 1990), p. 44.

an environment. For the Nordic states, the prospect of a Europe made safe for piecemeal aggression cannot be separated from their proximity to the Soviet Union or from their relevance to a number of Soviet strategic interests. The conjunction of a conflict-prone Europe with a troublesome Soviet Union would be among the most difficult outcomes for the security policies of the Nordic states.

A fourth major factor that will strongly influence the Nordic security environment in the new Europe is the question of Germany. Again, there is an optimistic image, which envisions an unambitious Germany, preoccupied with internal prosperity and committed to—and restrained by—European institutions, both economic and security. On the other hand, even today, with American power still firmly lodged in Europe, the unification of Germany and the concomitant new assertiveness of German diplomacy are causing visible unease. The concern is often obscured by the niceties and politesse of intra-alliance diplomacy, but it is real nevertheless. It is expressed in refreshingly blunt and undiplomatic terms, for example, by columnist William Safire: "European and American diplomats know a gut judgment cannot be avoided: Is the greater danger to peace in the next generation likelier to come from a domineering Germany or a resurgent Russia?"[12] At issue, of course, is the extent to which the instinct to balance German power is one of the central organizing principles of a new European order.

12. William Safire, "A Question of Trusting in Germany," *International Herald Tribune*, 23-24 June 1990.

A Europe without the United States implies a Germany unanchored to U.S. power and raises the question of whether any effective counterweight to German power would exist in Europe, particularly if the Soviet Union's troubles persist. Such worries could provoke an outbreak of traditional European diplomacy, which a more fluid diplomatic environment would permit. It could result, for example, in the emergence of anti-German coalitions, of which there are a large number of potential combinations, including states of both East and West; this possibility is the curse of Germany's geostrategic position. But Germany, too, would have diplomatic options, some of which could be disturbing to nearby states; in particular, a Berlin-Moscow combination would be an alarming development, especially for the Nordic area and Eastern Europe but also for the rest of Europe.[13] Thus, in a Europe without the United States, Germany's relationship with Europe and the Nordic states' relationship with Germany would be crucial elements in determining the new security environment.

In sum, the problem of Nordic security in a new Europe will depend very much on the character of that new Europe. As former Norwegian

13. See Huntington's very interesting discussion, in which he notes the existence of a "condominium pattern," involving Berlin-Moscow collaboration, with a "sandwiching pattern," involving the efforts of others to contain Germany. Huntington, "Democratization and Security in Eastern Europe," p. 45. See also Thomas Christensen and Jack Synder, "Chain Gangs and Passed Bucks: Predicting Alliance Patterns in Multipolarity," *International Organization*, 44(2) (Spring 1990).

Defense Minister Johan Jørgen Holst puts it, " 'Even if we are located in Northern Europe, we cannot confine our outlook to our region, because we are very much dependent on what happens in the rest of Europe.' "[14] If the optimistic visions come to pass, then the problems are few and unpressing, and pan-European institutions may assume some or much of the responsibility for ensuring the security of their members. It is the more negative scenarios, which in my view are more realistic, that raise more challenging issues for Nordic security policymakers.

WHAT NORDIC OPTIONS?

In the face of such challenges, what options could Nordic policymakers consider? In the confines of this article, it is impossible to examine the separate debates that would exist in each of the Nordic countries. But it is possible to sketch more generally the range of options that are likely to be evident in these debates, understanding that some will be more salient in some Nordic states than in others. Clearly, the debate in each country will be heavily colored by the security policy traditions that currently exist. There are four policy paths that are likely to figure prominently in any fundamental reexamination of security in the Nordic states. They are not all mutually exclusive, and some of the debate could well focus on what mix of these policies is desirable.

14. Quoted in Brigitte Sauerwein, "The Russians Won't Come by Train," *International Defense Review*, Nov. 1989, p. 1160.

First, neutrality will remain an option, but perhaps a more complex one. Since World War II, it has been defined largely by way of reference to the blocs. It may be necessary to reconsider the meaning of neutrality if the Europe of blocs is replaced by a Europe of states or a Europe of pan-European structures.[15] Of course, neutrality does not depend on the Cold War—some of Europe's neutrals have traditions of following this policy that long antedate the postwar era. But the Cold War has given neutrality a clear and distinctive meaning. As the *Economist* recently put it, "The Cold War provided . . . neutrality with an abnormally clear context. Europe was set in a state of not-quite-war. By eschewing both alliances they showed themselves to be noncombatants in the non-war."[16] Neutrality in a new Europe would have to find a new meaning.

The attractiveness of neutrality would be determined by perceptions of advantages versus disadvantages in the new conditions. These perceptions could well be very different from those that exist today. In general, neutrality provides two substantial advantages: autonomy and the ability to stay out of the problems and troubles of others; for countries like Sweden and Switzerland, this latter in practice has meant the ability to stay out of a war even when all of Europe is in flames. Understand-

15. See, for example, the call for discussion by Sweden's General Bengt Gustafsson, reported in Roger Magnerård, "Neutraliteten måste djiskuteras," *Svenska dagbladet*, 5 Feb. 1990.

16. "Neutrality's Identity Crisis," *Economist*, 3 Feb. 1990, p. 20.

ably, this is regarded by these societies to be a considerable benefit. But there are real costs to this policy as well: it isolates and marginalizes states and deprives them of the protection that alliances can provide. Thus Sweden and Finland have, by their own choice, been excluded from direct participation in many of the most important decision-making and negotiating fora in Europe, including NATO institutions, various East-West arms negotiations, and even the European Community (EC). Naturally, such exclusion limits their voice and circumscribes their influence. Neutrality can have more tangible costs, as well, for it can be expensive in monetary terms to acquire the military capability necessary to buttress a policy of armed neutrality.[17]

A second option would be to attempt some sort of Nordic security arrangement. This was one of the alternatives under discussion in the immediate postwar period, but it was not the first preference of the Nordic states and therefore failed. But such a notion is compatible with the tradition of high levels of Nordic cooperation and could well seem more feasible in a harmonious Europe. Further, it could seem attractive to those in Scandinavia who would like to remain apart from the security concerns of the United States and the rest of Europe but nevertheless see the value of being part of a group. This idea has several handicaps, how-

ever. One is that all the Nordic states together still represent a fairly weak military grouping compared to the larger states in Europe or combinations thereof. In an alarming security environment, a Nordic arrangement might seem insufficient. Second, it would have to transcend the different political orientations of the Nordic states. To create a regional alliance would require the abandonment of neutrality, unless the Nordic security group were to profess a kind of collective neutrality. Third, it would have to encompass the diverse security positions and requirements of the Nordic states. But for all the problems, this is still an idea that could resurface on the agenda of debate in a Europe of sweeping changes.

Third, the Nordic states could consider some sort of Eurocentric solution. As noted, pan-Europeanism has considerable appeal, in the Nordic area as elsewhere. There are many advocates of the idea of employing some existing institution, such as the Conference on Security and Cooperation in Europe or the Council of Europe, or of creating a new pan-European institution to serve as the basis of a future European security system.[18] Most likely, something along these lines is likely to happen and the Nordic states are likely to participate. The real issue is whether and how such an institution solves the security problems of individual states. There has yet to be a durably effec-

---

17. Erling Bjöl, *Nordic Security*, Adelphi Paper no. 181 (London: IISS, 1983), emphasizes this point with respect to Sweden, for example, and raises the question of whether it will be able in the future to afford a credible armed neutrality posture. See pp. 16-21.

18. For one illustrative discussion among many, see Eva Nowotny, "The Role of the CSCE and the Council of Europe in Facilitating a Stable Transition toward New Political Structures in Europe," in *Uncertain Futures*, ed. Volten, pp. 51-61.

tive collective security system, and there is no particular reason to believe that we know how to construct one now. Hence this will probably be at best a partial solution to the security problems of European states; in the ultimate recourse, their security is likely to continue to depend on their own resources and arrangements.

A related but distinct Eurocentric path is the integrationist approach. This would involve linking the future of the Nordic states more directly to the European Community. Initially, this would be primarily an economic relationship, but the integrationist aspiration explicitly includes a political and a security component. It represents a kind of gradual and more functional route to the pan-European solution. There is no doubt that the EC will be important to the future of the Nordic area. Economically, it is already very important. Furthermore, there is no doubt that the Nordic states will have to address explicitly their future relationship with the European Community, whether singly or jointly through their collective membership in the European Free Trade Association.[19] Indeed, many in the Nordic area believe that all of these states will be members of the EC by the middle of the 1990s.[20] The

issue, again, is whether this represents a genuine solution to the security problems of individual states. Except in the case of quite optimistic outcomes in Europe, it probably does not. So while the integrationist approach will surely figure prominently in Nordic foreign policy debates, it is again at best a partial answer.

There is another European approach, one that might be relevant if a difficult security environment should emerge: this is the traditional coalitionist approach of finding allies and seeking great-power protectors. This might seem a remote or backward-looking possibility, but it is the traditional behavior of small states with serious security problems.[21] Almost by definition, small states alone are incapable of defending themselves against large powers, and alliance politics is therefore a critical element of their security policy. In Cold War Europe, the choices were clear and the problem of alignment fairly simple. In a future, more fluid Europe, the possible patterns are less clear, as the identity of potential threats and potential protectors depends on the resolution of a number of uncertainties. But in the future some Nordic states could be worrying about whether to align with Moscow against Germany or Germany against Moscow, or even choosing between a London-Paris combination and a Moscow-Berlin coalition. If Europe really is, as many believe or hope, moving beyond power politics, then such considerations and choices

19. Discussions between the European Free Trade Association and the EC are already under way. See, for example, John Palmer, "Sinking EFTA Raises Stakes for EC Deal," *Guardian*, 15 June 1990.

20. For an overview of this issue, see "Europe and the Nordic Countries," *European Affairs*, 3(4):93-116 (Winter 1989). Illustrative of the mood is Catherine Ryan, "Majority of Norwegians Now Favor EC Membership," *Norway Times*, 15 Mar. 1990.

21. See, in particular, the discussion in Stephen Walt, *The Origins of Alliances* (Ithaca, NY: Cornell University Press, 1987).

will never arise. But if international politics continues in its long, historical pattern, then such issues and choices could very well confront Nordic decision makers.

A fourth possible path, which is a non-European variant of the coalitionist approach, is to try to preserve or re-create a security relationship with the United States. For countries like Norway and Iceland, which have had close relations with and a heavy dependency on the United States, there would undoubtedly be a temptation to try to preserve a bilateral relationship even if the broader NATO framework collapsed. This would have the advantage of hooking their security to that of the world's greatest power.

CONCLUSION

Indulging in speculation about a hypothetical scenario is inherently a murky exercise. Here I have tried to outline briefly some of the factors and choices that would affect the Nordic security environment in a radically changed Europe. Inevitably, uncertainties predominate, but identifying key issues and critical conditions can at least help to give a sense of the range of possible outcomes. I have here tried to keep in mind the possibility of optimistic as well as more problematic outcomes. Unfortunately, if history is any guide, the problematic outcomes are more likely and the states of Nordic Europe are likely to face some difficult choices in their future security policies.

ANNALS, *AAPSS,* 512, November 1990

The Northern Environment: Is Cooperation Coming?

By OLAV SCHRAM STOKKE

ABSTRACT: Current Arctic regimes are narrow and shallow, but the potential for increased cooperation seems high. In the areas of science, petroleum development, fisheries management, and marine protection, the predominance of strategic considerations is increasingly being challenged in key Arctic states. Groups such as scientists, industrial firms, and environmental organizations portray these problems in terms of cost efficiency rather than competition, and the assessment of national interests is less straightforward than before. In this situation, processes of regime formation will be less structured, and senior policymakers in the Arctic will be more influenced by situational factors. Today these are very favorable for cooperation, due to the sense of urgency present in certain areas, the entrepreneurial activity of some actors, and the presence in each issue area of cooperative salient solutions.

Olav Schram Stokke received his master's degree in political science at the University of Oslo, Norway, where he has also lectured. He held a position at the University of Tromsö before joining the Polar program of the Fridtjof Nansen Institute in Oslo. His publications are in the field of international political economy, with a focus on resource management issues in the North.

THE industrialization of the North implies common opportunities as well as shared problems among the Arctic states. Today the idea of cooperation is much in vogue in political rhetoric, as shown by Gorbachev's Murmansk speech and the recent Finnish initiative to set up an Arctic conference on environmental issues of the North. The purpose of this article is to describe, explain, and project the pace and form of Arctic cooperation. The focus is on science, resource extraction, and environmental management, and toward the end I will comment on the interplay of the Nordic and Arctic levels.

In general, the Arctic environment is vulnerable to industrialization for a cluster of reasons. A harsh climate means greater strain on the equipment employed. Accidents are more likely, and efforts to rectify damage will be hampered by long distances and poor infrastructure. Low temperatures inhibit the natural assimilation and breakdown of pollutants, and a disruption of one link in the simple ecosystems may have serious implications for the rest. Improved catching and localization technology have boosted efficiency in the extraction of living resources to the point of eradication, and some of the most important Arctic fish stocks are threatened by overexploitation. The degree of marine pollution in the Arctic is still very low and for the most part originates outside the region itself. The current spread of offshore petroleum activities may threaten this situation. Moreover, while most of it originates further south, the winter and spring concentration of air pollutants such as sulphur dioxide in the Arctic is as high as in the northeastern United States.[1] Some alarming reports indicate a thinning of the ozone layer above the Arctic. The so-called greenhouse effect will entail regional temperature rises above the global average, effecting a melting of the ice cap, with serious if yet unclear consequences for global climatic conditions.[2]

THE WHATS AND WHYS OF ARCTIC COOPERATION

By "cooperation" I mean coordination of policy in order to realize mutual gains or avoid mutual losses. Cooperation may be ad hoc or tacit, but more often it requires a mechanism I term regimes and define as "practices consisting of recognized roles linked together by clusters of rules or conventions governing relations among the occupants of these roles," in "well-defined activities, resources, or geographical areas."[3] Regimes may facilitate cooperation by changing the structure of actor incentives in a number of ways. Clearly, there may be instrumental reasons for complying with a regime, such as fear of being punished by other states or in domestic elections. Usually, however, the compliance decision will be the result of standard operating

1. John McCormick, *Acid Earth: The Global Threat of Acid Pollution* (Washington, DC: International Institute for Environment and Development, 1985), p. 176.

2. J. B. Maxwell and L. A. Barrie, "Atmospheric and Climatic Change in the Arctic and Antarctic," *Ambio*, 18(1):46 (1989).

3. Oran R. Young, *International Cooperation: Building Regimes for Natural Resources and the Environment* (Ithaca, NY: Cornell University Press, 1989), pp. 12-13.

procedures rather than a calculus of costs and benefits.[4] In this article I shall focus on the formation of cooperative regimes in the Arctic. While the concept is often given broader meaning, I will concentrate on regimes that are formalized by international agreements.

A regime involves a set of rights and rules and usually a more or less formalized procedure for handling social or collective choice.[5] Two dimensions of this concept are especially salient for our discussion. One is the breadth of the regime, or the number of members. Judging from the many bilateral agreements concluded in the Arctic in the past decade, narrow regimes seem easier to establish than broad ones. In many situations, however, the actors will have no incentive to join a regime unless it involves a critical minimum of others. A second dimension is the depth of the regime, or the extent to which it limits the autonomy of states in a given issue area. At a moderate level, a regime may imply no more than an obligation to exchange information. It is less shallow if it involves mechanisms for joint planning or regulation, as do the fisheries and environmental commissions in the Barents Sea. At an exalted level, regimes may provide instruments for joint enforcement of regulations, but usually this is left to the participant states. Clearly, shallow regimes are generally easier to negotiate than deep ones because they infringe less on the sovereign rights of states. Yet they may for the same reason be less effective in realizing cooperative gains.

EXPLAINING THE FORMATION OF REGIMES

Some authors are concerned with spontaneous processes of regime formation, beyond the intention or even the comprehension of purposive actors.[6] I will conceive of regimes here as emerging from the interplay of intentional actors who pursue more or less distinctive goals. As cooperative regimes imply a certain loss of national sovereignty, states will not participate in them unless they are likely to derive some benefit. Underdal identifies two types of interdependence that may render uncoordinated behavior suboptimal and thus create an integrative potential.[7] One is cost efficiency, implying the presence of synergy or contingency relationships between actors. The second type is incongruity, where the costs and benefits produced by actor behavior are represented by a nonproportional subset in their calculi. This will be the case if the problem involves externalities or competition.[8] In general, integrative potentials stemming from cost-efficiency interdependence are tapped more easily than those from incongruity interdependence.[9] Though it is not always done, power can be introduced in such

4. Ibid., p. 78.
5. Ibid., p. 18.

6. Robert Axelrod, "An Evolutionary Approach to Norms," *American Political Science Review*, 80(4) (Dec. 1986).
7. Arild Underdal, "International Cooperation: Transforming 'Needs' into 'Deeds,'" *Journal of Peace Research*, 24(2) (1987).
8. The term "externalities" denotes effects on others of an actor's behavior that is not included in his or her cost-benefit calculus. If competition is present, these effects are included in the actor's calculus, but in an inverted form. Underdal, "International Cooperation," p. 171.
9. Ibid., p. 137.

a scheme by delimiting the set of integrative solutions, either directly through coercion or benevolence as in hegemonic stability theory or indirectly as unequal ability to manage without cooperation.

Young, however, offers several reasons for reducing the focus on power and acceptance zones in the analysis of regime formation.[10] When negotiating a new regime, power is usually employable only at prohibitive costs. Moreover, national interests are often unclear, because a proposed regime will apply across a wide range of situations and over an extended period. In this setting, three kinds of situational factors will influence the negotiations: first, the presence of solutions with certain properties that make them attractive to all parties, such as simplicity, previous application, apparent equity, or ready implementability; second, the presence of entrepreneurs or active participants who are able to discover these solutions and rally support for their realization; and, finally, exogenous shocks that put pressure on policymakers to provide an agreement.

We can combine these approaches by assuming that the process of regime formation will vary fundamentally with the clarity of the national interests involved. Clarity is the degree of domestic consensus about what the national interest is on a particular issue. If the interests are very clear, the process will be structured and predictable, and the poten-

tial for cooperation can be analyzed by a straightforward assessment of cost efficiency, externalities, and competition. If, on the other hand, the state decision makers perceive themselves as weakly or ambiguously affected by the possible regime, the negotiations are likely to be more anarchical and more prone to the situational factors highlighted by Young. States are the main actors in the model and they are clearly satisficers. Yet, by contending or confirming the established definition of national interest, nongovernmental organizations can significantly influence political processes. The main thesis of this article is that many of the traditional Arctic policy issues are being invaded by various domestic or even transnational interest groups that stress the benefits and not the dangers of cooperation. The public is more aware of environmental issues and less afraid of military ones than in the early 1980s. This increases the leeway of state policymakers engaged in international negotiations, and we can expect Young's situational factors to grow in importance. It is not easy to establish adequate objective criteria for clarity of interests. The empirical assessment of this variable obviously requires hermeneutical practice by the analyst. This involves a risk that the key variable will be selectively specified and the model immune to falsification. That risk is basically inevitable in social science, however, as the objects to be studied are themselves subjects, and in most cases it will be possible to reach reasonably well-founded assessments.

10. Oran R. Young, "The Politics of Regime Formation: Managing Natural Resources and the Environment," *International Organization*, 43(3) (Summer 1989).

REGIME OPPORTUNITIES
IN THE ARCTIC

With the exception of the Svalbard Treaty and the 1973 Polar Bear Convention, there are no circumpolar environmental or resource regimes in the Arctic today. Generally, bilateral agreements are the most common, and the regimes are fairly shallow.

Scientific cooperation

Ever since the Phipps expedition in 1775 or the better-known first Polar Year in 1882-83, there have been many efforts to organize multilateral cooperation in Arctic science. Many analysts have commented on their lack of success.[11] Today, however, there are two processes under way that challenge pessimism. A network of recent and fairly comprehensive bilateral agreements is emerging in the science area, often crossing the East-West divide.[12] I will look more closely at a second process, the movement toward setting up an International Arctic Science Committee.

How clear-cut are the national interests involved? The policy arena varies from country to country, but in general there seem to be two types of concerns that compete for the definition of national interest. One is a knowledge-motivated interest in pooling resources, in order to avoid duplication and secure access to data from the full circumpolar area. Not sur-

prisingly, the major domestic proponents are members of the scientific community, in all the Arctic states. At this level, the problem is the benign one of realizing cost efficiency. However, when moving from basic to applied science, concerns of another kind appear. Certain fields of Arctic research have military or direct industrial applications and are thus highly competitive: oceanography, physics of the upper atmosphere, and Arctic engineering. Still, as the proposed agreement will clearly enable the avoidance of sensitive areas in the cooperative programs, the intensity of these other concerns must be deemed low. It is not surprising that in both the United States and the Soviet Union, the Ministry of Foreign Affairs has played a secondary role in the process.[13]

The lack of clear national interests of a competitive kind leads us to expect a fairly anarchical process, with ample room for action for entrepreneurial groups eager to reap cooperative gains. This would go a long way toward explaining developments in the early phase of the preparations for the International Arctic Science Committee. An informal international network of scientists developed an organizational model that was apparently much influenced by two salient solutions, namely, the Antarctic Treaty System and later the Scientific Committee on Antarctic Research, confined to the nongovernmental level. The more concrete the plans, however, the more they touched upon

11. Willy Ostreng, "Polar Science and Politics: Close Twins or Opposite Poles in International Cooperation," in *International Resource Management*, ed. S. Andersen and W. Ostreng (London: Belhaven Press, 1989).

12. Olav Schram Stokke, "The Arctic: Towards a Cooperate Region?" *International Challenges*, 8(4):18-26 (1988).

13. Oran R. Young, *The Arctic in World Affairs* (Seattle: Washington Sea Grant Program, 1989), p. 29.

symbolic, competitive issues, such as the breadth of the regime. This issue was brought to a head when West Germany, France, and Great Britain declared to the United States their interest in joining the decision-making machinery of the new organization. The process was rendered less anarchical by the introduction of dormant competitive concerns such as U.S. loyalty to allies and a long-standing Soviet position that Arctic affairs should be dealt with by Arctic states alone.[14] But, as the negotiations are now at an advanced stage, it seems unlikely that this element will kill the regime. A probable outcome is a privileged position for the so-called Arctic Eight in the central decision-making bodies but a larger role for the more broadly based scientific working groups.

Groundfish: Exploitation and management

With the introduction of 200-mile economic zones, the cross-boundary interdependence in the fishery area was sharply reduced, and the existent regimes are predominantly bilateral. The 1982 Law of the Sea Convention sets up a global regime to be specified differently in each region depending on the biological distribution of the fish stocks. I shall focus on two regions, the Bering Sea and the Barents Sea.

In the Bering Sea, off Alaska, industry-level cooperation in the exploitation of groundfish has been very intense since the United States set up its 200-mile zone. The main actors were foreign fishing companies and U.S. trawler owners, who lobbied for continued foreign quotas in the zone in return for at-sea processing and marketing services. The Alaskan infrastructure was unable to assimilate all the fish taken in the Bering Sea and Gulf of Alaska. Thus, at an early stage, U.S. interests were reasonably clear and compatible with cooperation, and a number of international fisheries agreements were concluded with long-distance fishing nations. The main actors were Japanese, Soviet, and U.S. industry organizations, with the Soviets as front-runners. As they had previously set up similar arrangements with Norwegian firms in the Barents Sea, this option stood out as a possibly salient solution to the problem posed by the U.S. phasing-out policy. Complementary capabilities and probable synergy effects made the issue very benign, but there was also an element of competition for the raw material between the foreign factory vessels and domestic processors. U.S. legislation settled this issue to the benefit of the processors.[15] Only moderate at first, this competition was intensified as a U.S. fleet of factory trawlers emerged in the late 1980s. As the domestic factory-trawler owners were able to redefine the perceived U.S. interests at the cost of the

14. This was a contended issue in the negotiation of the Polar Bear Agreement as well, and the Soviets had given a concession on this point already by allowing the inclusion of the non-rim states Finland, Iceland, and Sweden. Young, *Arctic in World Affairs.*

15. By the 1979 processor preference amendment to the 1976 Magnuson Fisheries Conservation and Management Act.

small joint-venture trawler owners, industry-level cooperation in the U.S. Arctic zone was terminated in 1988. It is unlikely to reappear. Cooperation might occur in Soviet waters, but only for a limited period. The complementarity[16] on which it will be based is as vulnerable in the Soviet setting as in the American.

Instead, groundfish cooperation is likely to move from exploitation to the management area, where it has been negligible in the past.[17] With the U.S. stakes in the Arctic groundfish industry so much higher than before and the health of the pollack stocks in partial jeopardy, the need for coordinated action by the two coastal states increases. An immediate task is to improve knowledge about the marine ecosystems. U.S.-Soviet coordination in this area will probably increase, both bilaterally and within a broader Pacific framework. There are three multilateral processes under way: the growing activity of the International North Pacific Fisheries Commission groundfish group, the series of international scientific symposia on Bering Sea groundfish,[18] and the efforts to establish the Pacific Council for the Exploration of the Seas. Moreover, if they can take the lead in setting up an international groundfish commission for this area, the United States and the Soviet Union will enhance their ability to

regulate troublesome third-country fishing in the Donut Hole, a high-sea area located between their zones.[19] Realizing these gains from bilateral cooperation involves no significant problems of externality or competition. Cross-boundary stock interdependences are probably moderate, and the two coastal states serve different markets.

In the Barents Sea the policy arena has been very different, for three reasons. Because of the link in international law between exercised authority and claims to sovereignty, the issue of cooperative management by Norway and the Soviet Union is deeply embedded in the territorial disputes in these waters. Second, Norway's domestic fisheries sector is regulated by a detailed network of explicit rights and obligations. Any cooperative effort that is perceived to infringe upon the interests of certain subsectors is likely to be effectively resisted. Third, overcapacity has marked the fishing fleets of both coastal states for the last 15 years. Accordingly, there is scant room for anarchical processes in the formation of regimes; and cooperation has proceeded in a cautious manner. The 1978 Grey Zone agreement allows regulation of fishing operations in the disputed section of the Barents Sea by separate systems of enforcement. The Grey Zone is not identical with

16. That is, U.S. technology in this area, which is fairly standardized.

17. The International North Pacific Fisheries Commission has always concentrated on salmon.

18. The first meeting was held in Sitka, Alaska, in 1988, and the Soviet city Khabarovsk hosted a second symposium in April 1990.

19. Edward Miles and William T. Burke, "Pressures on the United Nations Convention on the Law of the Sea of 1982 Arising from New Fisheries Conflicts: The Problem of Straddling Stocks" (Paper delivered at the Joint Soviet Marine Law Association and Law of the Sea Institute Symposium on the Law of the Sea, Moscow, 28 Nov.-2 Dec. 1988).

the disputed area, thus reducing the basis for creeping jurisdiction and, with it, a basic competitive element in the problem of shared management. The second competitive element, distribution of shared stocks, has been removed in a manner that reminds us of Young's concept of a salient and apparently equitable solution. Norway and the Soviet Union have settled on fixed keys based on rough, one-shot assessments of biological abundance.[20] Thus cooperative bilateral management has proceeded far in the Barents Sea. The current resource crisis has also enhanced the potential for cooperation on the exploitation of groundfish. The Soviets need hard currency and lack the ability to process high-quality products for Western markets. In the past years agreements have been set up to allow direct deliveries from Soviet vessels to Norwegian processors short on raw material. This is still a small-scale phenomenon, highly vulnerable to changes in the domestic supply situation; but it might spill over to other sectors such as the shipbuilding and equipment industries.[21]

Bilateral but fairly deep fisheries regimes are already in operation in the Arctic. There is no reason to expect broader membership in these regimes, but conditions are favorable for increased coordination of man-

agement in the Bering Sea and, to a lesser extent, exploitation in the Barents Sea.

Arctic oil and gas

Today there is very little cooperation in the area of mineral exploitation in the Arctic. Apart from a dormant Norwegian-Icelandic accord, no specific regimes exist to regulate such cooperation. When discussing future prospects, we must distinguish between disputed and undisputed waters. The disputed boundaries in the Barents, Bering, Chukchi, and Beaufort seas[22] involve problems of the most malign type, as cooperative arrangements might subvert national claims to shelf resources. The issues under explicit negotiation have not proceeded beyond the specification of property rights. These issues involve hard-core national interests. Accordingly, entrepreneurial actors who may benefit from cooperation will have a hard time persuading governments to give concessions in order to achieve cooperation. Nor is there great urgency to enter the disputed areas, as vast areas of undisputed waters are still unexplored. This may explain why the Soviet proposal for a joint development zone in the Barents Sea, deemed reasonable by outside analysts[23] and clearly modeled on the rather successful Grey Zone agreement, was re-

---

20. Brit Floistad and Olav Schram Stokke, "Common Concerns—National Interests: Norway, the Soviet Union and the Barents Sea Fisheries," *International Challenges*, 9(2) (1989).

21. The Soviet Union has set up a number of barter trades with Denmark and West Germany, trading fish for engineering services and fishing equipment.

22. For a presentation and analysis of these disputes, see Dorien Donders, Arnfinn Jorgensen-Dahl, and Olav Schram Stokke, *Northern and Arctic Boundary Disputes*, R-008 (Oslo: Fridtjof Nansen Institute, 1989).

23. Robert L. Friedheim, "The Regime of the Arctic—Distributional or Integrative Bargaining?" *Ocean Development and International Law*, 19:504 (1988).

buffed by Norwegian authorities demanding a clear boundary line. In undisputed waters the cooperative problem seems more benign, especially between Western oil companies and the Soviet Union. The Soviets have already invited a number of West European companies to participate in the exploitation of their Arctic shelf resources. They have relaxed domestic restrictions on the size and transfer of foreign ownership shares in joint ventures.[24] The employment of more cost-efficient Western technology may enable the Soviets to identify and extract resources earlier and probably at a lower cost than without cooperation.

Two competitive elements may obstruct the realization of this integrative potential, however. An argument against licensing technology is the fear of nourishing the growth of a strong competitor. On the other hand, the Finnish experiences of joint ship construction with Soviet partners suggest that the deterioration of a technological advantage is a slow process, especially in an area so close to the technology frontier. Likewise, the very strict regulations on technology transfers from Western countries to Eastern-bloc states, coordinated through an increasingly formal organization called COCOM,[25] is gradually being phased out. Another competitive element is the issue of marketing. Because of the depressed state of world oil markets, some cooperative efforts have stumbled over disagreement on market channels.[26] Nevertheless, industrial cooperation within undisputed areas of the Soviet Union would not require much political innovation as the restrictions on technology transfers dwindle and the competitive elements become surmountable. The main obstacle to cooperation is beyond the control of Northern governments and oil companies; it is, namely, the state of the international oil markets, which may not encourage large-scale investments in the Arctic frontier areas. Still, as shown by the recent lease sales in the Chukchi Sea, the oil industry is still willing to put money into high-risk, long-term exploration.

The Arctic environment: Marine pollution

In recent years a number of bilateral and fairly shallow environmental agreements have emerged in the Arctic. Due to increased petroleum activity and the related density of shipping operations, a need for deeper international cooperation in the area of marine pollution is probably growing. Today there are no agreed-upon emission standards corresponding to those found in the North Sea or the Baltic.

When assessing the problem structure of marine pollution, we must bear in mind that it is a strongly contested issue in all Arctic states.

24. David Scrivener, *Gorbachev's Murmansk Speech: The Soviet Initiative and Western Response* (Oslo: Norwegian Atlantic Committee, 1989), p. 38.

25. The Coordinating Committee (COCOM), based in Paris and historically dominated by the United States, issues a list of products and technologies banned from export to members of the Warsaw Pact. Besides all the countries of the North Atlantic Treaty Organization, Japan is a member.

26. Scrivener, *Gorbachev's Murmansk Speech*, p. 38.

The traditional predominance of industrial concerns is in decline. Nongovernmental organizations are very active in this area, operating within as well as outside the regular political channels. Decision makers have scant knowledge about the costs of various measures, including that of nonaction. Thus, in general, this is a changing policy arena where the domestic actors are many and national interests unclear. A rather anarchical policy process is likely to evolve, sensitive to situational factors such as sudden crises, salient solutions, and entrepreneurial activity.

This statement needs to be qualified. A shallow regime concerned mainly with the exchange of information and some coordination of scientific operations would clearly be cost-efficient. The present network of bilateral environmental and scientific agreements in the Arctic states may be able to tap parts of this potential. Still, broadening the membership would be more efficient and would not introduce significant externalities or competition. Such a broadening of existent regimes may actually be propelled by entrepreneurial spillover from the cooperative institutions in the scientific area. The problem of negotiating an explicitly regulative regime is more malign. The costs of conforming to given rules will depend on unevenly distributed factors, like the volume and composition of industrial production and the command of reasonably clean technologies. Therefore the specific rules are bound to be strongly contested by the participants to a regime even though

the notion that regulations will be collectively helpful may not. There is a model for a solution to this type of problem, exemplified by the United Nations Environmental Programme's Regional Seas Programme. A broad umbrella agreement is negotiated and later specified through protocols when perceived national interests permit. In the highly topical area of Arctic shipping, the 1973/1978 MARPOL convention could be useful, as all the Arctic states are members. As pointed out by Roginko, it might be possible to achieve a "special area" status for the Arctic Oceans, which would imply especially strict regulations.[27] Due to the density of boundary disputes in Arctic waters, cooperative systems of compliance control and enforcement will be very difficult to achieve.

Thus, as long as the regime proposals are fairly shallow or general at first, they are not likely to infringe upon clearly defined interests in any of the Arctic states. On the contrary, there is considerable domestic goodwill to be won by showing political strength in this area. This implies that external shocks like the recent tanker accident off Alaska and entrepreneurial activity such as the Finnish initiative to organize a broad ministerial convergence on the environment may push marine pollution to the top of the Arctic policy agenda.

27. Alexei Roginko, "Arctic Environmental Cooperation: Prospects and Possibilities" (Paper prepared for the Joint International Studies Association/British International Studies Association Convention, London, Mar. 1989).

*A special role for
    the Nordic countries?*

In this setting, the Nordic countries may prove important to the realization of Arctic cooperation in two ways. First, it may seem farfetched to search for salient Nordic solutions to be emulated by the broader set of Arctic states. Despite strong cultural homogeneity and deep economic interdependence, Nordic cooperation has not been a linear success story. Many ambitious attempts to set up regional regimes in the strategic and economic areas have failed, largely because of centrifugal forces toward broader solutions in the North Atlantic Treaty Organization, the European Free Trade Association, and the European Community. Whenever this has happened, the Nordic countries have settled for less controversial mechanisms of coordination. While there are a number of institutions, the dense network of informal intra-Nordic contacts at almost every level of political activity is equally important. Thus both the incrementalist response to setbacks and the low-key nature of Nordic coordination may provide lessons for the Arctic process.

Second, as demonstrated also by the Finnish Initiative, the Nordic states are particularly well suited to act as entrepreneurs for cooperative processes in the Arctic, for three reasons. It is a matter of routine to coordinate their own positions on issues related to Arctic cooperation, and together they make up five of the eight Arctic states. Also, geography implies that they are ill served by tensions in the region, and this provides a strong incentive to promote cooperative solutions to collective problems. Finally, their very smallness and varying strategic orientations have often led the Nordic states to see themselves as East-West bridge builders.

CONCLUDING REMARKS

Current Arctic regimes are narrow and shallow. In the areas of science, petroleum development, fisheries management, and marine protection, however, the predominance of military considerations is increasingly being challenged in key Arctic states. Scientists, industrial firms, and environmental organizations portray the problems in terms of cost efficiency rather than competition. The assessment of national interests is less straightforward than before; the positions of various Arctic players are being loosened up. Accordingly, the process of Arctic regime formation will be more influenced by accidental situational factors. Today these are very favorable for cooperation, due to the sense of urgency present in certain areas, the entrepreneurial activity of some actors, and the presence in each issue area of cooperative salient solutions.

ANNALS, *AAPSS*, 512, November 1990

New Dimensions of Soviet Arctic Policy: Views from the Soviet Union

By RAPHAEL V. VARTANOV and ALEXEI YU. ROGINKO

ABSTRACT: Radically new approaches to the formation of both foreign and domestic Arctic policy have been established in the USSR. Design of a real Arctic policy founded on these approaches is proceeding at a slow pace, however, and all means of dealing with Arctic issues through departmental approaches have been exhausted. Of all the Arctic problems facing the country, questions related to a radical restructuring of the social outlook of the North and developing its infrastructure are being brought to the forefront. Development of the Soviet North has resulted in a deep conflict between the economic interests of industrial civilization and the Arctic ecosystems now functioning at critical levels. More important, the interests, the identity, and the very existence of small Northern aboriginal peoples are at stake. Yet a certain optimism is inspired by several factors: awareness of the challenge facing the Soviet Union in the Arctic; active involvement of a major scientific effort; institutionalized participation of the native peoples in decision making; and an ever expanding role played by a sphere of international cooperation.

A head of the Section of Environment and Ocean Development in the Institute of World Economy and International Relations (IMEMO), USSR Academy of Sciences, Raphael V. Vartanov graduated from the Moscow Aviation Institute in 1974 and received his Ph.D. in economics in 1979. He is author of numerous articles and monograph chapters on international ocean management and environmental policy.

Alexi Yu. Roginko is a research associate in the same section of IMEMO. A graduate of the Geographical Faculty of Moscow University in 1975, he has published many works on international marine and Arctic environmental-protection problems.

F OR obvious reasons, the Arctic region has always played a special role for the Soviet Union. The USSR is by far the largest Arctic-rim nation. Roughly half the land area of the circumpolar North lies within the Soviet Union, and this land area in turn constitutes half of the territory of the country. Historically, the dominant factors determining Soviet Arctic policy have been military-strategic and economic. The latter has been tied almost exclusively to the development of abundant mineral and fossil-fuel resources in the area.

The priority of the military factor in using Arctic space can be explained in terms of international relations in the region, which long before World War II became a part of the sphere of military confrontation between the two opposing socioeconomic systems. Since the beginning of the Cold War, relations between the United States and the USSR, the closest neighbors in the Arctic and at the same time the major political and military opponents, determined the essence of this confrontation, thereby markedly intensifying it. This situation was aggravated by progress in military technologies, including the advent of long-range bombers and nuclear missiles, which expanded possibilities for the military use of Arctic spaces. "Consequently the Arctic became something of a military flank, or a northern extension of East-West confrontation."[1] As a result, the Arctic has been viewed in the USSR primarily in terms

1. Pertti Joenniemi, "Competing Images of the Arctic: A Policy Perspective," *Current Research on Peace and Violence*, 12(3):113 (1989).

of strategic interests, and cooperation in economic, scientific, and environmental fields has been accorded secondary, if any, priority.

In such a situation, the idea of a sector that allegedly protected and secured the USSR's interests in the Arctic seemed very attractive to Soviet political, military, and even scientific circles. At the same time, this very concept, despite its long—since 1926—existence, turned out to be, in our view, insufficiently elaborated. It did not—and, in fact, could not at the time of its promulgation—take into account the development of economic activities in the Arctic, their expansion in the ice-cover, air, offshore, and even underwater spaces. Today there is an apparent need to define more precisely the correlation of the sectoral principle with the provisions of the contemporary law of the sea and to reconsider radically the approach to the whole international legal regime of the Arctic.

THE MURMANSK INITIATIVE

President Gorbachev's Murmansk initiative in October 1987 marked a turning point in Soviet Arctic policies. In his speech he called for an "Arctic zone of peace," and he set forth a six-point program for international cooperation in the area, including establishment of a Nordic nuclear-free zone in Northern Europe, limiting naval activity in the seas adjacent to that region, peaceful cooperation in exploiting the resources of the North and the Arctic, scientific research in the Arctic, cooperation between Northern countries in environmental protection, and the opening up of the Northern Sea Route to foreign vessels.[2] The most striking feature of the Murmansk initiative was that it represented an authoritative exposition of a unified approach to Arctic policy by the Soviet Union, bringing together security, resource, scientific, and environmental issues. It reflected a broadening of the concept of international security, a close connection between its civil and military elements, and an understanding that economic development and environmental protection are both, in considerable measure, contingent upon controlling the arms race.

Several Western observers dismissed the new Soviet Arctic initiatives as little more than a public relations ploy. Some of them argued that Gorbachev was merely trying to gain one-sided advantages with his speech;[3] arms control provisions in the Murmansk initiative have been widely discounted as self-serving proposals that only "repackage" or "elaborate" on previous Soviet propositions.[4] But the analysis of subsequent Soviet Arctic policy cannot but prove the seriousness of Soviet intentions to pursue the goal of genuine international cooperation in the region. More has been done by the Soviet Union to develop Arctic cooperation since the Murmansk speech than during the previous seventy years. A number of bilateral agreements on Arctic issues have been concluded with the United States, Canada, Norway, and Finland; in December 1988, an international conference of Arctic and Nordic countries on coordination of research in the Arctic took place in Leningrad, with the aim of establishing an International Arctic Science Committee; with active Soviet participation, the process of creating a comprehensive international regime for Arctic environmental protection, proposed by the Finnish government, is developing; cultural links between Northern ethnic groups have begun, with visits between Alaskan and Siberian Inuits.[5] Thus the Arctic region has been accorded one of the highest priorities in Soviet foreign policy in general.

Embodying the principles of a new political thinking, the Murmansk initiative could not but have a profound impact on the domestic dimension of Soviet Arctic policy, radically changing the order of priorities in the use of Arctic resources and space. What is the essence of these changes? First, it is the realization of the need for Arctic policy to serve a variety of interests. If previously it was designed primarily to address strategic, resource, and, to a certain extent, sci-

2. Mikhail S. Gorbachev, "Speech at a Ceremonial Gathering Dedicated to the Presentation of the Order of Lenin and Gold Star Medal to the City of Murmansk," *Pravda*, 2 Oct. 1987, p. 1.

3. See Willy Ostreng, "The Changing Mood of the Kremlin: Security and Cooperation in the Arctic," *International Challenges* (Fridtjof Nansen Institute), 9(2) (1989).

4. Dan Hayward, "Gorbachev's Murmansk Initiatives: New Prospects for Arms Control in the Arctic?" *Northern Perspectives*, July-Aug. 1988, pp. 9-11; Ronald G. Purver "Arctic Security: The Murmansk Initiative and Its Impact," *Current Research on Peace and Violence*, 11:4, 9-25 (1988).

5. See Gail Osherenko and Oran R. Young, *The Age of the Arctic: Hot Conflicts and Cold Realities* (New York: Cambridge University Press, 1989), pp. 292-95.

entific concerns,[6] the contemporary approach is marked by a clear shift of priorities toward the social domain. A whole complex of military, environmental, scientific, economic, and social factors is taken into account in formulating current Soviet Arctic policies.[7] A drastic increase in the importance of a socioenvironmental sphere, accompanied by a relative reduction in the weight of strategic problems, has resulted in a leveling of the significance of various policy issues. But the existing possibilities for dealing with each of them, the experience already acquired, as well as the extent of their neglect vary substantially. Of particular concern today are environmental issues and the entire complex of problems related to the needs and interests of Northern native peoples.

It is evident that Soviet Arctic policy is succeeding in surmounting sizable obstacles. Quite naturally, opti-

6. Scientific research in the Arctic received primary attention in the USSR as far back as the 1930s. Polar researchers were admired as national heroes in the Soviet Union. The successes of Arctic science have been at least partly regarded as political issues. At the same time, the priorities in Arctic science have remained unchanged for decades. These were, first of all, basic research, hydrometeorological studies aimed at the support of navigation, and resource-oriented research in the areas of the far North.

7. One indication of a unified approach to dealing with Arctic issues at a governmental level as well as of the seriousness with which the Soviet government regards the Arctic is the establishment in June 1988 of a new State Commission on Arctic Affairs of the USSR Council of Ministers. Chaired by a first deputy prime minister, Presidential Council member Yu. Maslyukov, this commission includes representatives of all major ministries and state committees in the Soviet government.

mists expecting rapid progress in Arctic activities after Gorbachev's Murmansk speech, which has drastically changed the level of Arctic thinking in the USSR, were somewhat disappointed. This is not accidental, in our opinion, but has occurred mainly for two reasons. First, the advancement of the Arctic from the lowest to one of the highest priorities in Soviet policy has been an objective result of a new political thinking, of fundamental changes in Soviet foreign and domestic policies; however, it has not been precipitated by a real evolution of the Arctic policy itself or by concrete activities in the Arctic. It emerged as a challenge to the entire previous policy. Second, current Soviet Arctic policies are being shaped under conditions of intense conflict between the new constructive processes, born of *perestroika,* and the still-strong administrative, economic, and military structures of the past. The latter have lost the initiative but still display firmness and an ability to resist. These structures, occupying solid positions in economic ministries and agencies, are resisting the ongoing changes primarily by blocking new positive and radical decisions taken at the national level.[8]

8. To cite just one example, back in November 1984 an *ukaz* ("edict") of the Presidium of the Supreme Soviet was passed named "On the Strengthening of Nature Protection in the Regions of Far North and Sea Areas Adjacent to the Northern Coast of the USSR." It envisaged the establishment of a network of natural reserves, placed strict limitations on transport use, tourism, and industrial development in the Arctic, provided for special standards for vessels operating in the Arctic waters, and so forth. But the problem is that the concrete norms and rules upon which the execution and

For decades, Soviet economic policy and practice in the use of Arctic resources and spaces were dominated by the attitude that the more the country takes from the Arctic, the better. At different periods, this approach was typical, in our opinion, of other industrialized countries as well. It was an inherent feature of the period of extensive scientific and technological progress in the economic sphere. When contradictions emerged concerning different uses of the Arctic, or between environmental and social priorities, on the one hand, and resource development, on the other, they were, as a rule, resolved to the detriment of the former. For a long time all economic activities in the North were exclusively resource oriented, and mostly they still are. This can be accounted for, if not justified, by our history, by initial low levels of economic development, by low living standards, and so forth. Still, the Soviet Union relies heavily on the Arctic for the supply of fossil-fuel resources. The Siberian Arctic accounts for almost two-thirds of national oil and more than 60 percent of natural gas production,[9] and these percentages are bound to increase substantially, especially when Arctic offshore oil and gas development starts.

Such an approach to the development of the Soviet North has resulted in a deep conflict between economic interests and the Arctic ecosystems now functioning at critical levels. Even more important, the interests, identity, and the very existence of small Northern aboriginal peoples are now at risk.

INDUSTRIAL DEVELOPMENT

Plans for industrial development of the Arctic and subarctic areas have always been met with great anxiety everywhere. Governmental and public organizations usually require reliable safeguards from private companies for the protection of indigenous peoples' needs and interests. These safeguards are also provided for by International Labor Organization convention 107, concerning the protection and integration of indigenous and tribal populations, to which the Soviet Union is a party. As the experience of other countries suggests, there exists a real possibility of harmonizing the interests of native peoples with industrial development.

What is the situation in the Soviet Union with regard to the protection of Northern natives' interests and their human environment? The answer is unequivocal—until the present it has been extremely alarming. These interests were not taken into account in the 1950s, when large-scale nuclear tests were performed in the Arctic; they are not allowed for today, as geological prospecting in the tundra and taiga, oil and gas production, and the construction of enormous pipelines across pastures and hunting areas, among other activities, are carried out.[10]

enforcement of the edict depend have still not been elaborated. To date, the ministries involved have been blocking the issue. Thus good intentions have not been translated into action and still remain mainly on paper.

9. A. Granberg, "Siberian Economy—Goals of Structural Policy," Kommunist, 1988, no. 2, p. 32.

10. A. Pika and B. Prokhorov, "Large Problems of Small Peoples," Kommunist, 1988, no. 16, p. 78.

The few improvements that industrial civilization and technology have brought to Northern natives are far outweighed by the damage inflicted upon the Arctic environment by the ministries, agencies, and organizations conducting large-scale, practically unregulated and uncontrolled industrial development.

According to official data, during the past twenty years more than 20 million hectares of reindeer pasture have been destroyed in the North, including about 6 million hectares in the Yamal-Nenetz Autonomous District alone. In fact, the situation is even worse, because these figures do not include the so-called recultivated lands, which will become suitable for grazing again in fifty years or so, provided they are not used in the meantime.[11] As a result of all this destruction, the reindeer population decreased from 2.4 million in 1965 to 1.8 million in 1986.[12] According to an assessment made by local scientists from the Yamal Agricultural Station, the damage inflicted on the environment of the district is estimated at approximately R60 billion.[13] In comparison, the total national defense budget for 1988 amounted to about R77 billion.

The Soviet North was being developed with outright violations of environmental legislation. Three gigantic natural gas fields in western Siberia —Medvejye, Urengoi, and Yamburg —were developed without any environmental impact assessment. Most valuable species of fish and fur animals have disappeared here completely; dozens of small rivers have been polluted and destroyed. Moreover, according to the data of the Committee of People's Control, the quantity of pipes, construction materials, machinery, and equipment abandoned in the North would have provided a reliable material basis for the development of an average-sized European state.[14] In fact, today there is more abandoned scrap in the tundra than there are wild animals. Thousands of square kilometers of man-made Arctic desert that, taken together, could have constituted a second Alaska, bear silent witness to a triumph of a mindless technocratic approach.

The environmental situation in the industrially most developed area of the Soviet North, the Kola Peninsula, causes the gravest concern. Emissions of sulfur from the peninsula are twice as great as those in all of Finland. The so-called industrial desert in this region, supporting practically no plant life, covers an area of about 100,000 hectares.[15] The boreal forest line is gradually moving south, and if this trend is not curbed, the peninsula will turn into rocky tundra in a few decades. The same is true of the Norilsk area. Up to 60 percent of the local Kola population suffers from respiratory and other

11. V. Sangi, "For the Crown Top Not to Fall Off . . .," *Literaturnaya gazeta*, 15 Feb. 1989, no. 7, pp. 1, 7.

12. Pika and Prokhorov, "Large Problems of Small Peoples," p. 78.

13. F. Sizyj, "The Price of Yamal," *Ogonyok*, 1988, no. 46, p. 20.

14. Ibid., p. 21.

15. Martti Varmola, "The State of Forests in Finnish Lapland" (Background paper prepared for the Consultative Meeting on the Protection of the Arctic Environment, Rovaniemi, 20-26 Sept. 1989), p. 2.

environment-connected diseases.[16] In other words, the Kola Peninsula has already turned into an environmental disaster area.

Reckless, aggressive exploitation of the Northern environment by Soviet industrial ministries undermines the natural basis of the existence of small indigenous peoples. Their human environment, traditional life-styles, material culture, and social organization are being changed so drastically that it is difficult to guarantee their survival in the coming decades. Forced resettlement of Northern natives, for example, has led to the organization of large soviet farms (soukhozes), usually operating at a loss, replacing formerly quite profitable small farms. Uncontrolled overgrazing in their vicinity has undermined the feed basis for reindeering. Being isolated from traditional trade businesses and the environment to which they had been accustomed, the tundra natives have considerably reduced their settlement and hunting areas and have shortened their migration routes. As a result, they are gradually losing their traditions of reindeering, hunting, and fishing. When living in small towns, as a rule they occupy the lowest rungs of the social status ladder; the results of the destruction of their traditional life-style are unemployment, high criminal and suicide rates, alcoholism, and so forth. The average life expectancy of many small Northern peoples is comparable only to that in the least developed countries: 43-45 years for men, about 55 years for women. Infant mortality has also been exceptionally high.[17]

What are the roots, the principal causes, of the current conflictful situation—even crisis—in the Soviet North? First, there is a property issue. The resources of the Northern rivers, forests, and tundra, as well as the Northern lands and waters themselves, long ago ceased to be collective property of the native population. They passed over to the state, and state property, especially in the North, has long been a fiction. In reality, it is the property of ministries and agencies. As these are guided primarily by selfish, narrow-minded interests, they do not even try to coordinate their activities with the urgent, vital needs of the Northern natives. Having seized lands and waters without the real owners' permission, the ministries just pay compensation to each other in case of environmental damage. The Northern natives have been forgotten. Their living standards are extremely low: in their settlements more often than not there are no schools, hospitals, or electricity, let alone such modern conveniences as water supply and sewerage. Their average wages are 10-15 times lower than those of the oilmen working and living nearby.[18] This is happening in the region that supplies a large part of Europe with its energy resources.

The second factor is insufficient, scanty knowledge about the state of the Arctic environment. One of the

16. V. Kiselev, "What Is Ahead, Monchegorsk?" Sovetskaya kultura, 14 Jan. 1989.

17. Yu. Golubchikov, "Losing Second Alaska," Sovetskaya kultura, 13 July 1989; Pika and Prokhorov, "Large Problems of Small Peoples," p. 80.

18. Ibid., p. 77.

important reasons for this lack of information is that the study of the North has been fragmented into a number of separate branches. Analytical approaches have prevailed and, moreover, a type of scientist has been created who is ready to carry out any order of the financing agency. Environmental research in the Norilsk area is financed by the Ministry for Nonferrous Metals, in western Siberia by the Ministry of Oil and Gas Construction. Needless to say, those environmental protection departments that are functioning within the ministries' structure serve more to cloud and conceal the real situation than to clarify it.[19]

Third, there is a lack of financing, which is really a national rather than a regional problem. About R10 billion is spent on environmental protection annually for the country as a whole, compared with $80 billion in the United States. This problem is particularly acute in the North, where sums allocated for the prevention of environmental damage and the restoration of disturbed parts of the environment are incomparably smaller than the damage already inflicted. For instance, out of R32 billion initially allocated for the development of natural-gas fields in the Yamal Peninsula, only R300 million —less than 1 percent of the total project cost—was to be spent on "compensational measures," including environmental protection. By comparison, environmental outlays during the construction of the Alaska pipeline accounted for about 15 percent of the total project cost. In Yamburg, where natural-gas production is already

under way, the Ministry of Oil and Gas Construction plans to spend some R150 million for the restoration of the environment and for damage compensation, while the real cost of environmental damage is on the order of billions, not millions.[20]

The final cause, really the result of all the factors enumerated previously, is the absence of a comprehensive strategy for the Arctic, a clear concept of sustainable development in the North, which could have balanced economic and environmental concerns.

SOLUTIONS

What has to be done, and done immediately? Undoubtedly, a new economic mechanism for environmental management and resource use needs to be developed as soon as possible. Several experts have suggested, for example, the development of a new system for assessing land value in the Arctic that should take into account possible environmental damage costs. Of course, more effective legal measures not only for compensation of such damage costs but for the prevention of damage should be elaborated. As academician V. Kotlyakov has suggested, until such measures are developed, it might be better to suspend temporarily all industrial development in the Arctic and to concentrate efforts on the development of central regions.[21]

19. Golubchikov, "Losing Second Alaska."

20. See an interview by I. I. Mazur, the deputy minister for oil and gas construction, in *Energiya: Ekonomika, tekhnika, ekologiya,* 1989, no. 3, pp. 20-25.

21. See V. Kotlyakov and G. Agranat, "Tropics of the North," *Pravda,* 9 May 1989.

What is most important to realize is that no comprehensive solution can be reached without the active involvement of the Northern natives themselves. All attempts to implement any, even the most helpful, measures from above—from Moscow or Tyumen, from Magadan or Krasnoyarsk—are doomed to failure. The central authorities should curb the expansion of industrial ministries to the North and make them respect and consider the needs and interests of aboriginal peoples.

A specific national policy is required to assist not just the people living in the North but the native peoples of the Arctic and the North in their striving toward survival and preservation of ethnic identity. That means more than just providing equal rights and equal opportunities to the entire population of the North. Under those equal conditions, the strongest will always win—and the Northern natives are not yet the strongest in their native land. The independence of their development is the only possible means for their survival, because no support from outside can help if the barrier of social passivity and alienation is not broken by the natives themselves. Active participation of the Northern natives in regional and local development programs in all their stages—from design to fulfillment—should be recognized as a major political principle.[22] It should be for the natives themselves to decide what is better for them—traditionalism or industrial development, reindeer or oil,

privileges from the state or economic prospects.

One of the most commonly proposed ways of achieving this aim is to organize a network of reserves in the North, with land, waters, and resources owned only by the native population and at its exclusive disposal.[23] This has already been done in the United States and Canada, where about 25 percent of the Northern territories have been turned into biosphere reserves. It is a hope-inspiring fact that the Communist Party Platform on National Policy, adopted by the Central Committee plenary meeting in September 1989, envisages granting to the soviets of the territories where the Northern natives live "exclusive rights for their economic development, that is, for their hunting areas, pastures, inland and offshore waters, forests, as well as the right to establish natural reserves with the aim of restoring and preserving these peoples' settlement areas."[24] At the end of March 1990, the first Congress of Peoples of the North was held, and the Association of Small Northern Peoples was established. Its aims are the promotion of political, social, and economic rights of the Northern natives, preservation of their cultural identity, control over resource exploitation in the territories of their residence, as well as the representation of these peoples' interests at all governmental levels. In

22. See Pika and Prokhorov, "Large Problems of Small Peoples," p. 82.

23. See, for example, L. Shinkarev, "Tundra: How to Help Northern Natives to Preserve Ethnic Culture," Izvestiya, 15 June 1989; Sangi, "For the Crown Top Not to Fall Off."

24. "National Policy of the Party in the Current Situation (the CPSU Platform)," Pravda, 24 Sept. 1989.

the declaration adopted by the congress, its participants called for a revision of the principles of the Northern territories' industrial development. They demanded, in particular, that any large-scale project concerning utilization of natural resources should undergo the examination of the relevant regional native peoples' associations.[25]

The realization of the measures envisaged will pave the way for the establishment of real Northern natives' self-government structures, enabling them again to feel masters of their own lands and waters, tundra pastures and reindeer herds. Only economic self-government, an opportunity to dispose of cooperative property in Northern communities independently, will return to the natives both personal and social *raison d'être*. That is exactly what they need to assist them in their striving toward self-preservation and cultural identity.

CONCLUSION

We can now attempt a general assessment of the situation related to resolving the Arctic problems in the Soviet Union.

First, fundamentally new approaches to the formation of Arctic policy have been established in the USSR. They are based on positive policy shifts in the economic and so-

25. *Izvestiya*, 1 Apr. 1990, no. 92.

cial life of the nation as well as on a deep realization of the problems that have accumulated in the region. A real Arctic policy founded on these new approaches has not yet been formulated, however. The process of its design is proceeding at a slow pace, due to a number of objective and subjective factors. At the same time, all the means of dealing with the Arctic issues through departmental approaches have been exhausted.

Objectively, of all the Arctic problems, questions related to a radical restructuring of the social outlook of the North and developing its infrastructure are being brought to the forefront today. Their solution requires substantial investments both in the region itself and outside it; the latter could even include the closure of enterprises. The returns on these investments will probably be delayed.

Yet, a certain optimism is inspired by several factors. There is a profound awareness of the challenge the Soviet Union is facing in the Arctic, at least partly reflected in concrete decisions; active involvement of a major scientific effort, a multidisciplinary one, as distinct from the exclusively technocratic one of former times; institutionalized participation of the native peoples of the North in decision making; and, finally, an ever expanding role played by a sphere of international cooperation—at various levels and in different directions.

ANNALS, *AAPSS*, 512, November 1990

International Oil:
The Scandinavian Dimension

By JEROME D. DAVIS

ABSTRACT: The recurrent energy crises of the past 17 years and the not unrelated rapid development of North Sea oil and gas reserves have had an impact on all the Scandinavian countries, both those with offshore interests and those without. Yet despite calls for Nordic cooperation in this field, such cooperation is virtually nonexistent. It is argued here that this failure is due to the nature of the international oil and gas regime. The analysis is based on four arguments: (1) there is an international oil and gas regime; (2) the dynamics of this regime do not necessarily further intergovernmental cooperation; (3) the current moribund status of Scandinavian cooperation can be ascribed to the nature of this regime; and (4) while the future is uncertain, there is little basis for hope that cooperative institutions can be designed to conform to the diverse expectations of the states involved.

Jerome Davis currently occupies the Chair of Public Economics at the Institute of Economics and Planning, Roskilde University, Roskilde, Denmark. He received M.A. and Ph.D. degrees from the School of Advanced International Studies, Johns Hopkins University. He worked at the Economic Research Service of the U.S. Department of Agriculture, the Brookings Institution, and Aarhus University, Denmark. He has been assistant and later associate professor of international political economy at the Institute of Political Science, Aarhus University, and has held his present chair since 1984. He has served as a consultant on oil and gas issues and is the author of numerous books and articles on international political economy and oil and natural-gas resources.

F EW events in the past twenty years have had more impact on the Scandinavian economies than the successive oil crises of 1973-74 and 1979, and the emergence of one major—Norway—and one minor—Denmark—exporter of oil and natural gas. Given the prominence of Nordic cooperation in the political agendas of the Scandinavian nations, as well as the importance of energy-security issues, one would expect a relatively high degree of Scandinavian cooperation in this area.

In fact, the opposite seems to have been the case. The discovery and development of oil and gas resources in the Norwegian and Danish offshore sectors has led to only minimal Scandinavian cooperation, despite the expression of widespread support for such cooperation. This is an apparent paradox. Other industries, such as the electrical power industry and the airline industry, are characterized by significant Nordic cooperation. In the airline industry, moreover, there is a jointly owned and operated company, the Scandinavian Airlines System. The unfulfilled promise of intergovernment Scandinavian cooperation in the oil and gas industry is the focus of my attention here.

What can explain this lack of intergovernmental Scandinavian cooperation in oil and gas? The answer, I argue, is to be found in the nature of the international oil and gas regime. First, I shall outline the main features of the international oil and gas regime. I then investigate why this regime has failed to yield formalized intergovernmental cooperation, both internationally and in Scandinavia. Finally, I consider what forms of Scandinavian cooperation might emerge in this field in the future.

THE INTERNATIONAL OIL AND GAS REGIME

Two of the distinctions made by Kratochwil and Ruggie on the nature of regime theory are of interest. The first concerns the placement of regimes in their proper international context:

In sum, in order to resolve both disciplinary and real world puzzles, the process of international governance has come to be associated with the concept of international regimes, occupying an ontological space somewhere between the level of formal institutions on the one hand and systemic factors on the other.[1]

Regimes, then, can be seen as a link, a leitmotiv, between formal institutional arrangements and the more diffuse international system. This is critical to my argument, for only a portion of the international oil and gas regime is formally institutionalized in organizations such as the Organization of Petroleum Exporting Countries (OPEC) and the International Energy Agency (IEA).

The second distinction lies in the difference between the positivist epistemology surrounding the definition of a regime and a theory that is, by its very nature, intersubjective—that is, ontological—in its approach.[2] International regimes are fundamentally normative in the sense that they presuppose certain shared norms as their

1. Friedrich Kratochwil and John Gerard Ruggie, "International Organization: A State of the Art on an Art of the State," *International Organization*, 40(4):760 (Autumn 1986).
2. Ibid., pp. 764-67.

essential underpinning. Although not disagreeing with Kratochwil and Ruggie's critique of the normative basis of regime theory, I will proceed to define the international oil and gas regime on the basis of shared inter-subjective norms among states as regards industry practices nationally and internationally, a consensus based on principles, norms, and rules, not always explicitly formulated but nonetheless generally present.

The existence of institutionalized forms of interstate cooperation in organizations such as the IEA, OPEC, and the Organization of Arab Petroleum Exporting Countries, is a reflection of the limited ways in which states cooperate institutionally in this regime. Institutional cooperation here has limited ends: security of energy supplies in the event of an international crisis; collective maximization of producer revenues; a coordinated Arab policy on oil and gas issues. A further analysis of the nature of the regime, while beyond the scope of this article, could indicate the strengths and weaknesses of these institutions, as well as provide reasons as to why they function as they do.

While a characteristic of this regime is the strong position of the transnational oil and gas corporations—and these still serve as conveyors of regime practices—the regime is constantly changing and is in many ways vastly different today from what it was ten years ago. Two ways in which it has changed are especially relevant here: first, the ongoing restructuring of the industry, a consequence of the dampened demand for oil and oil products as well as loss of access to key reserves; and, second, the replacement of OPEC's role as price setter and quota enforcer by more flexible contractual relationships in which prices are linked to existing market prices—spot or futures.

It is not possible to cover all aspects of this international regime here. The discussion will be confined to the three sets of characteristics most salient to my arguments. These are the regime characteristics inherent in the exploration for and production of oil and gas; the regime characteristics pertaining to the refining and marketing of oil; and characteristics underlying the transport and marketing of natural gas.

There are five principal types of petroleum hydrocarbon exploration and production systems: a concession system, also termed license or lease system; the joint venture; the production-sharing contract; the service contract; and state ownership. While these types may seem widely disparate, the differences are more apparent than real. The first four cover oil exploration and exploitation terms for 134 different countries.[3] The fifth, state monopoly ownership through a national company, exists in only 10 countries, and even these often utilize one or another form of transnational engagement through service contracts.

More important, when factors of cost, risk, and stringency of exploration and production terms are taken into account, there is a striking in-

3. United Nations Centre on Transnational Corporations, *Alternative Arrangements for Petroleum Development* (New York: United Nations Centre on Transnational Corporations, 1981).

verse correlation. The more oil and gas resources, the lower the risk—and to a lesser degree, the cost—and the more stringent the terms of exploration and exploitation.[4] Finally, a comparison of many of these exploration and production arrangements reveals a remarkable similarity of legal language—boiler plate—and other elements, such as the use of the International Chambers of Commerce in arbitration arrangements. There is little doubt that sufficient international norms exist here for oil and gas exploration and production to qualify as a major part of the international oil and gas regime.

The refining and marketing of oil has been and remains, with some exceptions, a prerogative of oil companies. Oil refineries have been constructed—and, more recently, dismantled—on the basis of their proximity to market, advantages in transport differentials and refinery scale, and match of product mix to evolving market demand. Here again, states may—and often do—directly or indirectly subsidize refineries, as these can confer substantial balance-of-trade advantages, if not gains in consumer product prices. Where the state has itself taken an active interest in the construction of state-owned refineries, the ultimate fate of these refineries has largely been conditioned by the same economic factors determinative of refineries owned and operated by the transnational oil companies. Here, too, regime change is

evident. Refineries, especially if tied to regional markets, have become important assets in the ongoing industrial restructuring currently characteristic of the international oil and gas regime.

Perhaps no other single element in our regime is characterized by more diversity than the transportation and sale of natural gas.[5] In contrast to practices elsewhere—most notably in the United States—continental European transport and sale of natural gas takes place within an oligopsony market. Consortium ownership of major international transmission lines has led to a situation where bulk producer sale of natural gas is a function of an essentially bilateral bargaining relationship in which producer prices are directly linked to oil-product—and more recently coal —prices, the volumes negotiated are large, and load factor and other delivery terms are very stringent and often inflexible. The situation in the United Kingdom is somewhat different: the privatized British Gas still enjoys a monopoly position and serves at all times as an alternative to Northern gas sales to the European continent.

THE INTERNATIONAL OIL AND GAS REGIME AND FORMALLY INSTITUTIONALIZED INTERNATIONAL COOPERATION

A logical feature of my approach is that a regime occupies the ontological space between formalized institu-

4. Jerome Davis, "Is There a Relationship? Risk, Cost, and Concessionary/Licensing Terms in Oil and Gas Exploration and Production" (Manuscript, Institute for Economics and Planning, 1989).

5. Jerome Davis, *Blue Gold: The Political Economy of Natural Gas* (New York: Allen & Unwin, 1984), chaps. 1-5. For a more Norwegian perspective, see Helge O. Bergesen et al., *Natural Gas in Europe* (London: Pinter, 1988).

tional cooperation and the characteristics of the international system. We have previously noted the limited nature of international cooperation in OPEC, the Organization of Arab Petroleum Exporting Countries, and the IEA. It remains to examine why the regime characteristics under discussion in this article have not led to more extensive, formally institutionalized, international cooperation.

The answer is that the tangible benefits arising from international cooperation in oil and gas often do not outweigh those of noncooperation. To develop this argument, I will refer to the three salient aspects of the regime briefly described earlier.

With regard to exploration and production, seldom do reserves of oil and gas lie in domains where there is uncertainty of national ownership. One exception in this regard is access to oil reserves in the Barents Sea, described by Stokke in another contribution to this issue. Where ownership is contested, cooperation may eventually ensue but can be accompanied by considerable conflict. The contentious issues surrounding the exploitation of the Saudi Arabian-Kuwaiti Neutral Zone are a case in point.

Where ownership is certain, there is little incentive for the national owner to share its benefits with other states. The reasons for this are well known. The state, in its role of owner of the resources, is also a rent captor; it can expect to receive up to 70 percent or more of net revenues from any oil or gas find. Given the economic stakes involved, there is justified concern that the find be properly exploited, that its exploitation contribute to national well-being, and that the oil companies be responsive to the state. These concerns have led to the familiar pattern of bureaucratic supervision, the creation and operation of a state oil company that is also responsible for supervision and rent capture. An associated concern is that the national economy benefit from the secondary and tertiary effects of oil exploitation—for example, minimization of adverse environmental effects, procurement of offshore orders, and so forth. Almost by definition, there is little room for intergovernmental cooperation in this field.

The location of refining and marketing assets also poses problems for intergovernmental cooperation. A refinery in one country can work to the disadvantage of the siting of a refinery in another country. What ensues in the politics of refinery siting is a form of intergovernmental overbidding, reminiscent of international competition for major automobile plants and other major investments undertaken by transnational corporations. The reverse is true of refinery closures; arguments are advanced as to why such closures should occur in other countries and not in one's own. Neither case presents logical reasons for increased international cooperation.

Natural-gas transmission and sale on the European continent is a function of extensive cooperation between the various European transmission companies, with a very low degree of accompanying intergovernmental cooperation. In the United Kingdom, the transmission and sale of gas has been conducted on terms that allow for import of Norwegian gas but that have effectively barred export of British gas to the Continent. Thus, in the world of natural gas, as in so many other aspects, Britain remains the "emerald isle," removed from the ongoing cooperation between the European transmission companies as well as from other forms of European Community initiatives having to do with possible liberalization of English offshore practices.

SCANDINAVIA AND NORTH SEA OIL AND GAS: THE LACK OF FORMALLY INSTITUTIONALIZED COOPERATION

If we consider active membership in the formal institutions connected with the oil and gas regime, a major reason why a Nordic Council or another Scandinavian solution was not sought by the Scandinavian states was that other institutional answers were more appealing. For security of energy supplies, the consuming Scandinavian nations could turn to the IEA. Norway's reserved attitude toward this organization contrasted significantly with Danish and Swedish support; Norway became only an associate member.

Furthermore, the exploitation and development of offshore resources have revolutionized the Norwegian economy. Norway has become dependent on oil exports in much the same way that one could superficially say that the Mexican economy has become dependent on Mexican oil or the Egyptian economy has become dependent on Egyptian oil, to name two

other major non-OPEC producers.[6] This has recently led Norwegian policymakers to institute a 7.5 percent production cutback from Norwegian fields—now 5.0 percent—in an effort to aid OPEC in its goals of price maintenance and stabilization. Cooperation with OPEC is in some respects more attractive than any formalized cooperation with the other Scandinavian states.

Exploitation of North Sea oil and gas: The Scandinavian factor

There are only two producers of oil and natural gas in the Nordic region: Norway and Denmark. Norway is by far the more important, currently producing 1.2 million barrels of crude oil and 2.9 billion cubic feet of natural gas per day. Denmark's oil production amounts to 100,000 barrels a day; its gas production, to 515 million cubic feet a day. While there has been much talk of cooperation in the exploitation of Norwegian oil and gas reserves among the non-Norwegians in the Scandinavian community, Norway has been noticeably reticent in this regard.

Such cooperation as there is has taken the form of Swedish and Finnish companies entering into offshore exploration consortia. Volvo has purchased 20 percent of Saga Petroleum, the major private Norwegian participant in offshore Norwegian licenses. Petro-Swede, owned by the Swedish

6. These concerns are reflected in Olav Bjerkholt and Erik Offerdal, eds., *Macroeconomic Prospects for a Small Oil Exporting Country* (Dordrecht: Martinus Nijhoff, 1985).

government, is also a member of several consortia. It owns shares of a number of commercial finds and at least one producing field, Valhall in southern Norwegian waters. Neste OY of Finland has acquired all of Atlantic Richfield's interests in several offshore blocks. These include shares in various prospects in the Haltenbanken region.

No non-Norwegian Scandinavian corporation, it should be emphasized, has an operator status with a major Norwegian North Sea producing field. Furthermore, the presence of other European firms, either state-owned or with significant state ties, far outweighs the Scandinavian presence. These include firms such as OMV, of Austria; Elf, of France; Agip, of Italy; Deminex, of West Germany; and even the non-European Petrobras, of Brazil.[7]

In terms of larger policy issues, if OPEC is disregarded, Norway seems to have more in common with the United Kingdom than with its Scandinavian neighbors. The British are major purchasers of Norwegian gas; the others are not. Norwegian and British policymakers have been involved in delineating and establishing ownership rights to fields straddling their respective offshore areas. Policymakers on both sides of the North Sea are intensely aware of what their counterparts are doing. Actions by

7. Oystein Noreng, The Oil Industry and Government in the North Sea (London: Croom Helm, 1980), and Jerome Davis, High Cost Oil and Gas Resources (London: Croom Helm, 1981), give a good impression as to the nature of licensing and industry-government interrelationships for Norway and Denmark, respectively.

one country can be contingent on what happens in the other.

While no Danish company is involved in the Norwegian sector of the North Sea, both Norsk Hydro and Statoil have shares in Danish licenses, although these have yet to yield tangible results.

Refining and marketing:
Conflicting or
converging interests?

Nor has there appeared any notable degree of Scandinavian intergovernmental cooperation downstream in oil refining and marketing. Between 1976 and 1990, when European refining capacity fell by 35 percent, no refineries were retired in Scandinavia. Norway's Statoil has in fact progressed with an ambitious refitting of its Mongstad refinery.

Refining and marketing in Scandinavia, as elsewhere, are being affected by the restructuring of the industry in general. This has been perhaps most remarkable in Denmark. Of the Seven Sisters, all of whom had markets in Denmark in 1973, only three remained in 1990. In this massive transfer of ownership, Statoil purchased Esso Denmark, thereby acquiring a 22 percent market share in Denmark. Together with the state-owned Norsk Hydro's purchase of Chevron assets, the Norwegian share of the Danish market has increased to 26 percent. Yet there was nothing distinctively Scandinavian in these moves. In the same time period, for example, Kuwait Petroleum acquired Gulf Oil assets—the Stigsnaes refinery—and took over all of British Petroleum's operations, with the exception of British Petroleum's lubricant business, and now has an overall market share of 19 percent.

Elsewhere in Scandinavia, Statoil acquired Esso Sweden, at the same time as its acquisition of Esso Denmark. Finland's Neste OY has purchased a major share of the Swedish OK concern. Here, too, despite the growing prominence of Statoil, there is little to indicate that anything but commercial motivation has been present in these acquisitions.

Natural gas in Scandinavia

Of the various areas of potential cooperation, the establishment of a Scandinavian natural-gas network has attracted the most official government attention, most notably in a recent Nordic Council publication, *Towards a Scandinavian Natural Gas Network.*[8] Ten years ago, except for Finland, none of the Nordic countries had a domestic market for natural gas. Reserves in Norway and Denmark were substantial. Prospects for developing a common natural-gas market seemed, on the surface, attractive.

But were they? The large-volume, high-load-factor oil-product indexing characteristics of inter-European trade were hardly suitable for the relatively small Scandinavian markets then available. Norwegian policymakers were preoccupied with sell-

8. Kjell Roland, ed., *Et integrertgass-marked i Norden* (Copenhagen: Nordisk Ministerraad, 1989), nr. 18. See also B. Berndt Andersson et al., *Naturgasmarknader i Norden* (Gothenberg, Sweden: Gothenberg University, Center for Energy Economics, 1989).

ing some 30 billion cubic meters (1.1 trillion cubic feet) of natural gas per annum to well-established markets on the Continent and in the United Kingdom. The widely dispersed, relatively uneconomic markets in Denmark and Sweden were unattractive or, at best, a second or third preference. The Finnish market was already importing Russian gas. Prospects for major expansion there were dubious. The discovery of the gigantic Troll reserves, or the very expensive, inaccessible reserves in the Norwegian north, have not changed this outlook in essence.

Scandinavian natural-gas cooperation began inauspiciously, with a contract between the Danish Oil and Natural Gas Company and Swedegas in 1978. This and three other Danish-Swedish contracts constitute the only intra-Scandinavian trade in natural gas to date. Three things are notable about this trade. First, far from being based on intra-Scandinavian cooperation, this deal was essential to the national development of the Danish natural-gas market, which could not take the entire 2.5 billion cubic meters per annum that were to be produced from the Danish shelf and had to dispose of the surplus. Second, the geographical distances involved were relatively small compared to the Norwegian alternative. Third, although it was and is relatively small—it will peak at 1.1 billion cubic meters, or approximately 40 billion cubic feet per annum—it has preempted large portions of the Swedish market, making the possibility of future Norwegian exports there even more problematic.

CONCLUSION: THE QUESTION OF
ORGANIZATIONAL DESIGN

In retrospect, it would seem clear that prospects for formal Nordic intergovernmental cooperation in oil and gas were never very auspicious, given the relatively weak authority of the Nordic Council and the greater attractions of other formalized organizations such as the IEA. The noninstitutionalized aspects of the international oil and gas regime do not appear conducive to formal Scandinavian institutional arrangements.

The logic of our international regime, as applied to a possible future establishment of a Scandinavian institutional arrangement—the question of organizational design—remains to be examined.[9] The possibilities for such a design do not appear good. To participate in the development of Norwegian oil and gas, Swedish and Finnish national oil companies have had to submit to Norwegian licensing policies. Downstream acquisitions of refineries and markets by Scandinavian oil companies have been more the result of established oil transnationals' selling their European assets than of any overarching concept of Nordic unity.

Cooperation in natural gas had its origins in developing a national gas market in Denmark, cooperation occurring largely because the Danes could not support the purchase of the minimal amounts of natural gas involved from their own North Sea, and they saw Swedegas as a purchaser of the necessary surplus. Additional quantities traded between the two

9. Kratochwil and Ruggie, "International Organization," p. 772.

countries were as much a function of the problems of Danish natural gas planning as they were of any desire for greater Scandinavian cooperation in the field.

Furthermore, as Norway's attention turns toward the Barents Sea and its unresolved differences there with the Soviet Union, it is not unlikely that its efforts toward organizational design will be focused in this direction, to the detriment of Norway's more traditional ties with its Nordic neighbors. Similarly, Danish energy policy—including its hydrocarbon policy—will be influenced more and more by Danish membership in the European Community. Here much will depend on the other Nordic states' future policies toward the European Community, of which they are not at present members.

Yet the Nordic world is in constant change, and the future is particularly hard to predict in 1990. A Scandinavian natural-gas net may yet evolve, if the Swedes decide to continue the dismantling of their nuclear reactors. Such a scenario will lead to sufficient demand to sustain the economics of natural-gas lines to Sweden from the Haltenbank and Barents Sea provinces and to support a connection to the Soviet lines through Finland. Similarly, events in Poland, East Germany, and the Baltic republics could also lead to forms of Northern cooperation unconceivable at present. Finally, the establishment of a common energy market, a portion of the European plans for the internal market in 1992, could well change the nature of Scandinavian policies. Whether this would be better or worse remains to be seen.

Denmark's Foreign Relations in the 1990s

By NIKOLAJ PETERSEN

ABSTRACT: Denmark faces, in the 1990s, a radically transformed security and political-economic environment, which is likely to have a profound impact on the relative importance of the five traditional arenas in Danish security and foreign economic policy, namely, the Nordic, the Atlantic, the West European, the All-European, and the global arenas. After a detailed analysis of Danish postwar security and foreign economic policies, which focuses on the effects of eroding domestic agreement in the 1980s, it is concluded that consensus has been largely reestablished and is likely to prevail in the 1990s, despite fundamental challenges to established policies and attitudes. Finally, Denmark's likely responses to four main challenges of the 1990s are discussed; these are the changing threat environment, the prospects for a European union, German unification, and possibilities for cooperation in the Baltic region.

Nikolaj Petersen, Professor of International Relations at Aarhus University, is cochairman of the Danish Commission on Security and Disarmament and vice-chairman of the Danish Institute of International Affairs and of the Nordic Cooperation Committee for International Politics and Conflict and Peace Research. His publications include monographs and articles on Danish foreign policy, West European defense cooperation, foreign policy theory, and strategic issues. He is currently engaged in a project on the implications of changes in Eastern Europe and Germany for West European security cooperation.

A S a small, modern country located at a strategic and economic crossroads, Denmark faces serious problems in reconciling its security, economic, and other interests with external constraints and influences. This classical problem of adaptation[1] has variously been solved by policies of withdrawal or isolationism, policies of dependence or appeasement, and policies of balancing off domestic and external demands. Until World War II, Danish security policy fluctuated between withdrawal and appeasement in light of its uncomfortable position in the hegemonic shadow of Germany, while a more independent trade policy was possible by balancing off Britain and Germany, its major markets. Since 1949, security policy has followed a balancing mode by virtue of the North Atlantic Treaty Organization (NATO) guarantee, while balancing has become increasingly difficult in economic affairs due to growing interdependence with the European Community (EC).

ARENAS AND INTERESTS IN DANISH FOREIGN POLICY

An important characteristic of Denmark's postwar foreign relations is their diversification across five broad arenas: the Nordic, the West European, the Atlantic, the all-European, and the global. This diversification is linked with functional specialization,

which sometimes approaches compartmentalization.

All five arenas serve as fora for multilateral policy cooperation, so important for a small country with little independent clout. But each is also a setting for specific interests: the Nordic arena mainly serves the expression of a Nordic identity and the coordination of low politics; Western Europe is the main forum for economic interests, while security interests have been served by participation in NATO. To date, the all-European arena has primarily been used for pursuing value-promotive interests, especially human rights, while Denmark's global policy—that is, toward the Third World—is motivated mainly by goals such as economic development.

This scheme represents the traditional perspective of the foreign policy establishment, a coalition of Social Democrats, Conservatives, and Liberals that has controlled foreign policy making since World War II, with the Social Democrats as the dominant force. But it has not gone unchallenged. The leftist parties, the most important being the Socialist People's Party, oppose both NATO and the EC, and the centrist Radicals—important as supporters of governments during the entire postwar period—also harbor doubts about aspects of official foreign policy.

External developments continually challenge this neat, compartmentalized scheme. Recent upheavals in Eastern Europe will increase the importance of the all-European arena, with respect to economic and security policy and to the changes in NATO and EC cooperation, which are

---

1. Cf. Nikolaj Petersen, "Adaptation as a Framework for the Analysis of Foreign Policy Behaviour," *Cooperation and Conflict*, 12:221-50 (1977); Hans Mouritzen, *Finlandization: Towards a General Theory of Adaptive Politics* (Aldershot: Avebury, 1988).

likely to affect the existing security policy framework.

Not only are boundaries between arenas becoming blurred, but the neat distinction between security and welfare politics is eroding as well, both in Europe and in the transatlantic relationship. Thus a main theme for Danish foreign policy in the 1990s will be the broadening context of its security policy as well as the increasing interconnectedness between security and welfare policies in Europe.

THE GAMES OF DANISH SECURITY POLICY, 1949-89

Since 1949 security policy has emerged from a triangular interplay between the threat (that is, the Soviet Union), the guarantee (NATO and the United States), and domestic politics.[2] Borrowing from Glenn Snyder, we can speak about "the adversary game," "the alliance game," and "the domestic game" of Danish security policy.[3]

2. Analyses in English of Danish security policy are few. The following, however, give good overviews: Martin O. Heisler, "Denmark's Quest for Security: Constraints and Opportunities within the Alliance," in *NATO's Northern Allies. The National Security Policies of Belgium, Denmark, the Netherlands, and Norway,* ed. Gregory Flynn (London: Croom Helm, 1985), pp. 57-112; Carsten Holbraad, "Denmark: Half-Hearted Partner," in *Semialignment and Western Security,* ed. Nils Ørvik (London: Croom Helm, 1986), pp. 15-60; Nikolaj Petersen, *Denmark and NATO 1949-1987* (Oslo: Forsvarshistorisk Forskningssenter, 1987).

3. Glenn H. Snyder, "The Security Dilemma in Alliance Politics," *World Politics,* 36:461-95 (1984).

"The domestic game": Security policy and domestic policy

For over a century security policy has been intimately associated with the vagaries of Danish domestic politics. Historically, the Left has been neutralist, pacifist, and antimilitarist, with the Right being more pro-defense and power oriented. After 1945 this difference was muted as the Social Democrats, abandoning pacifism and neutralism, joined with the Liberal and Conservative parties to bring Denmark into NATO—in 1949—and to steer the complicated process of adapting to alliance membership. Other parties joined subsequently, notably, the Radicals, the embodiment of home-grown neutralism and antimilitarism, and by 1960 a broad consensus had formed, excluding only the Socialist People's Party and minor parties on its left.

Consensus was never perfect, however. The Radicals' support has been consistently lukewarm, but, more important, the Social Democrats and the major bourgeois parties have never been in total agreement. The latter usually follow the so-called NATO mainstream, while the Social Democrats have steered a more independent course, especially on nuclear issues.[4] Until the late 1970s, consensus was upheld by a mixture of genuine compromises—for example, on defense policy—and bourgeois acquiescence in Social Democratic initiatives—for example, concerning base

4. On the history of Danish nuclear politics, see Erik Boel, *Socialdemokratiets atomvåbenpolitik 1945-88* (Copenhagen: Akademisk Forlag, 1989).

and nuclear policy. But in the 1980s that consensus eroded. In 1979 the bourgeois parties[5] protested the Social Democratic government's proposal to postpone NATO's dual-track decision, and from 1982, when a Conservative-led minority coalition under Poul Schlüter came to power, conflict became endemic. The Radicals supported the Schlüter government on most domestic issues. On security policy, however, they joined a so-called alternative majority in the Folketing with the Social Democratic and left-wing parties, which until 1988 voted through a total of 23 parliamentary resolutions against the government, mostly concerning nuclear politics, such as deployment of intermediate-range nuclear forces (INF) and a Nordic nuclear weapons free zone.[6]

Matters came to a head in April 1988 over a resolution requiring the government to inform visiting warships of the long-standing Danish ban against nuclear weapons on its territory in peacetime. The government, fearing confrontation with Britain and the United States, called an election—the first since 1929 to be

fought on a security issue.[7] After the election the alternative majority evaporated, as the Radicals now joined the Conservatives and Liberals in a new three-party government. Since then, consensus between the Social Democrats and the bourgeois parties has been gradually restored, in part due to the changing parliamentary scene but also because external events have made old disagreements less relevant. Thus in January 1990 a broad official Defense Commission could release an agreed-upon majority report, with only the People's Socialists dissenting.[8]

"The adversary game": Threat perceptions

Danish threat perceptions in the postwar period fall into two categories: actor-oriented perception of the Soviet Union and Warsaw Pact as the primary military threat, and perceptions of structural threat emanating from the bifurcated international system and the risk of nuclear war.

Until the late 1980s, the Soviet threat was the main rationale for Danish alliance and defense policy. But in the 1980s perceptions of structural threat, especially of nuclear war, became widespread in the alternative majority, and as the Right stuck to its traditional threat perceptions, disagreement arose about the

5. Since 1973 the bourgeois group has consisted of five parties: the Conservatives, the Liberals, the Center Democrats, the Christian People's Party, and the right-wing Progress Party.

6. On this episode, see Ib Faurby, Hans-Henrik Holm, and Nikolaj Petersen, *Kampen om sikkerheden. Nye tendenser i dansk politik* (Århus: Politica, 1986); Hans-Henrik Holm, "A Democratic Revolt? Stability and Change in Danish Security Policy 1979-1989," *Cooperation and Conflict*, 24:179-97 (1989); Nikolaj Petersen, "The Security Policies of Small NATO Countries: Factors of Change," *Cooperation and Conflict*, 23:145-62 (1988).

7. See Nikolaj Petersen, "Sikkerhedspolitik og indenrigspolitik," in *Dansk udenrigspolitisk årbog 1988*, ed. Nikolaj Petersen and Christian Thune (Copenhagen: DUPI, 1989), pp. 30-54.

8. *Forsvaret i 90'erne. Beretning fra Forsvarskommissionen af 1988*, 3 vols. (Copenhagen: Defense Commission, 1990).

very definition of the national security problem.

Such differences have become less pronounced. There is considerable uncertainty now as to the nature of the threat after the virtual disintegration of the Warsaw Pact. In its report the 1988 Defense Commission sketches two scenarios, a best case and a worst case, defining the parameters of the Danish defense problem in the 1990s. In the former, now probably overtaken by events, the Warsaw Pact would continue, despite internal changes, as a stabilizer of not only East-West but also East-East relations. The scenario also includes an early agreement on conventional forces in Europe (CFE), possibly followed up by a more radical CFE II. The worst-case scenario envisages the breakup of the Eastern bloc, fundamentally changing the context of the present disarmament process as well as giving rise to new conflict patterns in Europe. Thus destabilization in Eastern Europe and the Soviet Union is the dominant Danish risk perception on the threshold of the 1990s rather than premeditated aggression or accidental superpower war.

"The alliance game": Denmark's NATO policies

Until World War II, Denmark's main response to external threats was neutrality, appeasement, or a mixture of both. But after five years of German occupation, neutrality lost its attraction. Faced with the threatening proximity of the Soviet Union and the uncertainties of the early Cold War, Denmark first sought, in 1948-49, security in a Nordic defense union and then, when this proved unattainable, as an original, though late-coming, signatory of the North Atlantic Treaty, in 1949.[9]

Since then NATO has been the main framework of Danish security policy. Denmark's NATO policy has been a blend of association and dissociation, that is, policies aiming at bolstering deterrence and alliance guarantees through a cooperative policy, on the one hand, and policies to reduce tension and provocation through a semi-independent stance, on the other. Observers have generally focused on the dissociative elements and pictured Denmark as a "NATO member on minimum conditions" or as "semi-aligned"; some have even coined the term "Denmarkization" to denote an alleged free-riding policy in the alliance.[10] These stereotypes capture part of the picture, but they are incomplete and hence misleading. In important respects Denmark has followed a cooperative policy in NATO. Denmark has rarely, if ever, joined European lamentations about the U.S. leadership in NATO or the frailty of its nuclear guarantee, and in the 1980s it kept a low profile in discussions over the so-called Europeanization of defense. Specifically, it has recognized the preeminent U.S. defense interests in Greenland. The United States operates two bases on Greenland, the most important being

9. Nikolaj Petersen, "Optionsproblematikken i dansk sikkerhedspolitik 1948-49," in *Studier i dansk udenrigspolitik tilegnet Erling Bjøl,* ed. Niels Amstrup and Ib Faurby (Århus: Politica, 1978), pp. 199-236.

10. On this question, see Holbraad, "Denmark: Half-Hearted Partner."

at Thule, the hub of the recently modernized ballistic missile early warning system.[11]

Since 1950 the defense of Denmark proper has been closely integrated with the defense of NATO-Europe as a whole, since 1962 within the framework of the BALTAP (Baltic Approaches) command, covering Denmark, Schleswig-Holstein, and Hamburg. BALTAP, which is NATO's most integrated multinational command, has worked effectively in the defense of the Western part of the Baltic and the Baltic exits, but its future may now be in the balance due to uncertainties about Germany's future place in NATO. If a united Germany were to leave NATO's integrated military command, Denmark would face very difficult questions about the future structure and framework of its defenses.

Cooperative policies have, however, been modified by more independent postures, reflecting mainly the Social Democratic Party's preferences and values. One is the 1953 ban on the peacetime stationing of foreign troops, which, however, goes along with detailed preparations in the 1970s and 1980s for Allied reinforcements in crisis or war. The corresponding ban on nuclear weapons was formulated in 1957. It has a broader scope by also covering Greenland and the Faroe Islands. Although officially it applies only to peacetime, it is extremely difficult to imagine that the Folketing would accept nuclear weapons in wartime, let alone in a crisis short of war.

After the formation of the alternative majority, the government was forced in December 1983 to footnote the INF deployment decision in the NATO Council. Later the alternative majority also enforced footnotes to NATO endorsements of SDI. As early as 1985, the Folketing also spoke out against the modernization of NATO's short-range nuclear forces, an issue that could have become highly divisive had it not been buried at the NATO summit in May 1989.

By the late 1980s many of the contested nuclear issues had somehow solved themselves, a fate that also threatens the Nordic nuclear-free zone, which became the pet project of the alternative majority after INF. The zone is still officially on the Nordic agenda but shows little movement.

Compared to nuclear issues, defense policy has largely retained a consensus.[12] The tradition dating to the early 1950s of broad defense agreements covering several fiscal years was sustained through the 1980s, albeit with more conflict than before, especially over the defense budget; the bourgeois parties supported NATO's 3 percent decision of 1978, but the Social Democrats managed to enforce zero solutions, in both 1981 and 1984. In the spring of 1989, however, a new zero-plus defense agreement was negotiated, and despite some pressures to cash the peace dividend, it appears that coming defense cuts will not be enacted indepen-

11. See Clive Archer, *Greenland and the Atlantic Alliance* (Aberdeen: Centre for Defence Studies, 1985); Nikolaj Petersen, "Denmark, Greenland, and Arctic Security," in *The Arctic Challenge,* ed. Kari Möttölä (Boulder, CO: Westview Press, 1988), pp. 39-73.

12. Christian Thune and Nikolaj Petersen, "Denmark," in *Nordic Defense: Comparative Decision Making,* ed. William J. Taylor and Paul M. Cole (Lexington, MA: Lexington Books, 1985), pp. 1-36.

dently but as part of a CFE agreement or in concert with NATO.

THE CONSTRAINTS OF EXTERNAL ECONOMIC RELATIONS

Denmark is vitally dependent on external trade. Exports have diversified substantially in the postwar period, away from agricultural products and dependency on the British market. Its most important trading partners, as of 1987, are the Federal Republic (17 percent of exports, 24 percent of imports), Sweden (11 and 12 percent, respectively), Britain (12 and 8 percent), and the United States (7 and 5 percent). About half the foreign trade is in the European Community (48 percent of exports, 52 percent of imports), while the balance is evenly divided between the European Free Trade Association (EFTA) and the rest of the world. Denmark's economic freedom of maneuver is also curtailed by a huge foreign debt, contracted in the 1970s and 1980s, which now amounts to about half of its gross national product.

The domestic aspect of European integration

Denmark's trade pattern reflects both political and market forces. It followed Britain's lead, both as cofounder of EFTA in 1960 and as an EC applicant in the 1960s. Eventually, in 1973, Denmark joined the EC, following a heated public debate and a national referendum in which 57 percent voted for membership and 33 percent against. This division reflected misgivings mainly on the Left, including many Social Demo-

crats—in fact, most of the present leadership of the party opposed the EC in 1972—and Radicals, who feared a loss of sovereignty. These fears were dismissed by the majority of the Social Democrats as well as by the Liberals and Conservatives who concentrated on the expected economic benefits of membership.

These divisions are still perceptible. The public remains divided, and many EC supporters continue to doubt its political aspects, especially the notion of a European union. In 1986, the parties of the alternative majority rejected the Single European Act. The Social Democrats feared for Denmark's right to pursue independent environmental and job-safety policies; the Radicals objected to the formal inclusion of European Political Cooperation (EPC) in the EC, while the Left opposed it as part of its general anti-EC stance. In response, the government unexpectedly called for another referendum to secure the approval of the act, which was obtained, though with a reduced majority compared to 1972: 53 percent for, 47 percent against.

Since this defeat the Social Democrats have gradually edged toward a more pro-European attitude, and recent events in Europe, especially the drive toward German unification, appear to be eroding many remaining reservations. As a consequence, Foreign Minister Uffe Ellemann-Jensen, a Liberal, has felt able to call for an acceleration of the European integration process—an unlikely pronouncement from a country usually accused of foot dragging in the EC. In April 1990 the Folketing almost unanimously adopted a resolution on the strengthening of EC cooperation,[13] and the new-found consensus even survived the proclamation of the goal of a European union—previously anathema to Danish Social Democrats —at the EC summit in Dublin later in the month.

The economic aspects of EC membership

While the political aspects of EC membership have been hotly debated, the economic side is less controversial, despite the fact that, objectively, economic integration has a significant impact on the Danish state's economic-political freedom of maneuver. Thus Denmark has generally supported the plans for Europe 1992, the EC's inner market without physical, technical, or fiscal barriers to trade. As a matter of fact, Denmark had by 1990 translated more 1992 directives into national legislation than any other EC country.

On the other hand, some doubts have been voiced concerning the impact of accelerating integration on the national freedom of action. For instance, Denmark is highly reluctant to harmonize its indirect taxes as part of the inner market. The Danish welfare state is more comprehensive and certainly much more expensive than those of its EC partners, and the level of taxation is the highest in the Community. A genuine harmonization of taxes would therefore have profound effects on Denmark's ability to finance its welfare state.

Since 1978 Denmark also has participated in the European Monetary System, which has served to stabilize the Danish krone after a series of competitive devaluations but has also curtailed the role of currency policy as an economic instrument. For this reason there have been some doubts—especially among Social Democrats— about the Delors Plan for an Economic and Monetary Union. Denmark has accepted its first phase—mainly a perfection of the European Monetary System—but is divided over the later phases, which would establish firm and unalterable exchange rates and—especially problematic—limit the budgetary freedom of the members. But again, recent developments in Europe appear to sweep aside many doubts and reservations, so that Denmark now is more willing to accept further economic integration than just one year ago.

The political aspects of the Community

Traditionally, Danish politicians have preferred to view the EC as a framework for trade and economic cooperation, though they have also learned to appreciate its foreign policy forum, the EPC, both for the information it provides and the possibilities for foreign policy consultation. With respect to the inclusion of secu-

13. See *Folketingstidende 1989/90. Folketingets forhandlinger*, 18 Apr. 1990, col. 8455 ff. The relevant passage is: "The Folketing enjoins the government to pursue an active European policy on the basis of . . . support for a strengthening of EC cooperation . . . which makes possible majority decisions to secure environmental protection and employees' rights, larger democratic control and openness, and a strengthened economic and monetary cooperation for securing growth and employment while respecting . . . the independent distributive policies of the member countries." Ibid., col. 8480f.

rity and defense issues, Denmark has been status-quo-oriented and has, until recently, opposed all attempts to give the EPC—or the EC itself—a broader security policy role.[14] As a consequence, the Western European Union (WEU)—of which Denmark is not a member—has become since 1984 a major forum for West European security policy, placing Denmark somewhat on the sidelines. Basically, Denmark sees little need to change the organization of Western defense radically, even though some lip service has been paid to the idea of a European pillar in NATO. Most —especially the Social Democrats— would probably prefer the EPC rather than the WEU as the basis of this pillar, though Foreign Minister Ellemann-Jensen, a Liberal, has declared himself ready for membership in the WEU, provided Denmark were welcome.

COOPERATION AND SECURITY IN THE ALL-EUROPEAN CIRCLE

As early as 1966 Denmark gave its support to the idea, proposed by the Soviets, of a Conference on Security and Cooperation in Europe (CSCE), and it played an active role in the early CSCE negotiations, for example, as the Western coordinator on basket III—that is, humanitarian —questions. Partly as a result of this, Denmark has always stressed the humanitarian aspects of CSCE along with confidence building and politi-

14. Thus Denmark opposed those parts of the Tindemans Report of 1975, the Genscher-Colombo Plan of 1981, and the Dooge Report of 1985 that envisaged the inclusion of security policy issues in the EPC or EC.

cal cooperation. Since the 1960s Denmark has also pursued active political contacts with individual Eastern European countries, a policy that is now being reinforced. In 1989 the Folketing voted to set up a major fund for Eastern Europe.

PERSPECTIVES FOR THE NEXT DECADE

At the beginning of the 1990s, prospects for Danish foreign policy appear unusually blurred. The Cold War system is breaking down, and Europe, East and West, is undergoing dynamic, even revolutionary change. A major systemic transformation is under way, but its direction, intensity, and rate are almost impossible to gauge. In this situation, many of the issues that preoccupied Danish policymakers in the 1980s are fading into relative insignificance, while new opportunities and challenges appear on the political horizon. Most likely the neat functional compartmentalization of Danish foreign policy—already somewhat undermined by the dynamics of European integration—will erode in the 1990s. Issue areas like security, welfare, and human rights and democracy will be increasingly interwoven, and the three hard-core foreign policy arenas—the Atlantic, the West European, and the all-European—will become intertwined in a multitude of ways.

Like most other European countries, Denmark was taken unawares by the revolutionary developments of late 1989, and its responses are only slowly being formulated. A leading consideration in this situation is reducing uncertainty and imposing at least some order on a turbulent environment. Another important Danish interest is to coordinate its responses with those of others within a broad multilateral framework, including not only NATO and the EC, but also —and to an increasing degree—the CSCE. As Denmark faces the 1990s, its position differs significantly from its Nordic neighbors' as a member not only of NATO, like Norway and Iceland, but also of the EC, which is likely to become the hub of European developments in the next decade and beyond. Political, military, and economic interdependence with uniting Germany adds another important aspect. In this situation Denmark's main strategy will be to build upon existing structures as well as to help create new institutions for the management of change and instability. Somewhat ironically, the relaxation of European tensions may give Denmark less scope for independent action than the Cold War did; in the emerging European system, bandwagoning seems to be mandated. I will discuss these strategies in relation to four issues likely to dominate the foreign policy agenda of the 1990s: the changing threat environment; the expanding role of the European Community; the future of Germany; and the politics of the Baltic basin.

The changing
threat environment

Denmark's traditional threat perception is being rapidly replaced by a feeling that a relatively nonthreatening situation is evolving in the Baltic area. On the other hand, possible spillovers from domestic unrest in Eastern Europe, from an upsurge of national rivalries there, and from instabilities connected with the dismantling of the Soviet empire and the restructuring of Soviet society have entered the risk calculations. With this background of uncertainty, there is an emerging consensus in Denmark that existing arrangements should not be wantonly destroyed and that NATO should be maintained as part of a coming European security system to provide a forum for the coordination of Western policies; a framework for a continued American presence in Europe, now important as a counterweight to the new Germany; and a guarantee against the unforeseen and unforeseeable.

But Denmark also favors the strengthening of other institutions, especially the CSCE, in order to contain the insecurities inherent in the German and Eastern European situations. Efforts to give the CSCE more permanence and substance as a forum for all-European security talks— Foreign Minister Ellemann-Jensen has talked about a European Security Council with peacekeeping functions—and to make it the overall framework for cooperation between East and West in Europe are viewed with much sympathy in Copenhagen.

The future of the
European Community

As a member of the EC, Denmark is the only Nordic country directly affected by the growing pace of European integration, which is already challenging many customary Danish views.[15] As mentioned, the acceleration of history has undermined many Danish reservations concerning the expansion of the EC. At present it seems entirely possible that Denmark will come to accept the enlarged security policy role foreseen for the EPC under the recent Franco-German initiative for a political union, provided that the Atlantic nexus is retained and the EPC is not given operational functions.[16]

As far as the future shape of the Community is concerned, two alternative models vie for influence. One is the European Union, propagated by Commission Chairman Jacques Delors and now also by France and West Germany. In this view, the Community can only play its proper role in Europe by perfecting its own union, that is, by completing the inner market, creating an Economic and Monetary Union, and capping the enterprise with a political union. In this way the EC would become the powerful nucleus of the future Europe, surrounded by concentric rings of associates with varying attachment, such as the EFTA countries, the East Europeans, and perhaps also the Soviet Union. Lately, this model has acquired the added attraction of an acceptable integrative framework for a unified Germany and is now—after the EC summit in Dublin on 28 April 1990—the dominant concept.

The competing, now less favored concept is the Europe of variable geometry, in which the EC would still be the core and motor but in a more flexible structure in which institutions like EFTA, the Council of Europe, and the CSCE would also be important. In the 1980s there was a good deal of sympathy in Denmark —especially among Social Democrats —for the less stringent demands of variable geometry, and in the present situation this model could have some appeal by facilitating cooperation with Eastern Europe and EFTA and by possibly providing relief from the pressures toward West European union. With the present dynamism of the European-union concept, however, the leading Danish politicians, including the leadership of the Social Democratic Party, seem convinced— or resigned—that the union is going to come. On the other hand, Denmark will continue to advocate a wide-ranging, outward-looking EC posture, including a broad program for the economic rehabilitation of Eastern Europe and the stabilization of political and social conditions there.

15. This is one reason why Foreign Minister Uffe Ellemann-Jensen has been conducting an energetic and outspoken campaign in 1990 to convince Norway and Sweden about the necessity of early EC membership—so far with little appreciation.

16. On the other hand, there is also an argument for concentrating on the WEU—and perhaps joining it—namely, that burdening the EC with defense and security issues would make it politically less attractive both to the EFTA countries, which Denmark would like to join, and to the East Europeans.

The German problem

One troubling aspect of a multi-tiered, rather than a unionist, approach to Europe could be its ineffectiveness as a restraint on a unified Germany. The looser the future European structure, the more freedom of maneuver for Germany. Therefore France and other European countries, including Denmark, have become more integrationist lately. In any case, the prospect of German reunification is enough to give pause to a nation that in the past has had unpleasant experiences with German unity.[17] On the other hand, Denmark has—like other NATO countries—consistently supported the goal of German reunification, and, more decisively, Denmark has, of course, no chance whatever to block it. After some uncertain initial reactions, reflecting gut feelings among many politicians including Prime Minister Schlüter, Denmark now supports unification unreservedly. But it is also pointed out that unification must be compatible with other nations' security interests and take place within an agreed European context.[18]

The politics of the Baltic basin

In most scenarios for the 1990s, the Nordic area appears as a slightly marginalized zone, as an appendix to the political center of gravity in Central Europe. Apart from Denmark, which through geography and politics is firmly attached to Europe, the other Nordic countries may—for better or worse—come to feel isolated and perhaps even forgotten. Nordic cooperation could therefore come to have an even lower priority in Danish foreign policy than now.

There is, however, a scenario, that yields a different prediction, by focusing on prospects for increasing political and economic cooperation in the Baltic basin between the Nordic countries, the emerging Baltic states, Poland, and possibly also the Soviet Union and Germany. Cooperative ventures were already created around the Baltic in the 1970s and 1980s, mostly in the area of pollution control, where the region constitutes a highly interdependent ecosystem— in which Denmark unfortunately is at the receiving end as far as pollutants are concerned.[19] Denmark is therefore vitally interested in Baltic cooperation in this area, including substantial technical and economic assistance programs.

But Baltic cooperation could come to include other aspects as well. In the new post-Communist Eastern Europe there is, besides huge economic and environmental problems, a gaping lack of expertise in running a modern market-oriented and democratic state. Given the wide appeal of the Nordic model in these states, it would be natural for the Nordic countries to assist in the process of transition, not only with economic support but also with educational support.

Apart from this, Baltic cooperation could be politically important for these countries as a counterweight to dependence on the Soviet Union or a unified Germany. The inclusion of the Soviet Union and Germany might therefore create some difficul-

---

17. Denmark was—in the 1864 Schleswig War—the unlucky, though not totally innocent, victim of the first of Bismarck's three wars on the way toward the German unification of 1871.

18. See remarks by Prime Minister Poul Schlüter in Berlin, quoted in *Politiken*, 18 May 1990.

19. Cf. Arthur Westing, ed., *Comprehensive Security for the Baltic: An Environmental Approach* (Oslo: Universitetsforlaget, 1989).

ties, even though they need not be insurmountable.

Baltic cooperation is still in its infancy, and much depends on events in Lithuania, Latvia, Estonia, and the Soviet Union itself. A new and interesting perspective has opened for Danish foreign policy, however, and, judging from initial responses, it will be explored in the next decade, on both a national and, if possible, a Nordic basis.[20] In this way the increased integration into the emerging European framework, which most signposts predict for the 1990s, could be somehow moderated by the creation of a new Baltic arena for Danish foreign policy.

CONCLUSION

The previous discussion about the future did not treat domestic politics very extensively. In conclusion, it should be pointed out that different perspectives will continue to flavor the responses of the Danish Right and Left. The bourgeois parties, and especially the Liberal Party, are more positive about a European union than are the Social Democrats. They also stress the continued need for NATO, while the Social Democrats are more likely to countenance far-reaching changes in the security sphere. But despite continuing disagreements, there is a tacit agreement between government and opposition not to repeat the luxury of the 1980s of a broken consensus and the resulting loss of external influence. In the confused foreign policy environment of the 1990s, consensus will become an important, even necessary, asset for a small country near the European center of gravity. For, as mentioned earlier, the paradoxical consequence of the breakup of the Cold War system may very well be a reduction, rather than an expansion, of Denmark's freedom of maneuver. Situational pressures may compel Denmark to accept solutions it would otherwise have resisted. On the other hand, within the constraints and limitations of what in the nineteenth century was called Denmark's European necessity, there will be plenty of scope for Danish initiatives, most notably in the Baltic area and vis-à-vis individual East European countries.

20. In April 1990 an effort by Foreign Minister Ellemann-Jensen to commit his Nordic colleagues to a joint declaration in support of Lithuania failed, because of both poor preparation and resistance on the part of Sweden and Finland. The prospects for joint Nordic policies in the Baltic therefore seem limited, as long as Moscow has not accepted the principle of Baltic independence.

ANNALS, *AAPSS*, 512, November 1990

Norway:
Domestically Driven Foreign Policy

By OLAV F. KNUDSEN

ABSTRACT: Norway is a typical small industrial democracy, experiencing a continuous tension between external pressures and internally generated aspirations. In security policy a compromise—the reassurance policy—softens the collision between the two forces. When the Storting or the electorate decides policy directly, foreign policy may become the nonlogical outcome of complex, underlying lines of domestic conflict. A major instance, the 1972 referendum rejecting membership in the European Community (EC), has had a traumatic effect on the subsequent European policy of all parties for two decades. A corporatist participatory system, coupled with external economic dependence, often makes economic foreign policy salient. When ministries are the decisional locus, interest groups often have privileged access. The Labor Party will continue to play a key role in foreign policy making as long as it bridges the main foreign policy cleavages. The Conservatives and European-Atlanticists in the Labor Party have made up an implicit and durable foreign policy coalition fundamental to the nation. The EC-membership issue remains the largest challenge to their future policymaking role.

Olav Fagelund Knudsen earned a Ph.D. from the University of Denver. He is currently director of research at the Norwegian Institute of International Affairs; previously he was professor of political science and dean of social sciences at the University of Oslo. His publications include The Politics of International Shipping *(1973), and he is currently writing a general analysis of the strategies of small neighbors of great powers.*

TRADITIONALLY, small states have had their foreign policies determined largely by the givens of the international politics taking place around them. The level of great-power tension in the small state's environment has always served as a constraint on its aspirations: greater leeway with détente; less with renewed tension.

With the introduction of democratic government these simple relationships were confounded. Today small industrial democracies experience a continuous tension between external pressures and internally generated aspirations. Increasing and intensifying democratization in recent decades has reinforced the pressure from within.

This is true of all the Nordic states and is a trait likely to remain with them for the foreseeable future. To a greater extent than other Nordic states, however, Norway has a complex structure of domestic politics that to an exceptional degree reaches into its foreign relations. This makes it an interesting case for studying the interplay of foreign and domestic politics. Norwegian foreign policy often results from such complexity rather than being based on simple calculations of national interest.

BACKGROUND

Norway has at different times been protected and exposed by its geographic position, topographical features, and climate. Resources have been scarce and have only recently made Norway rich—for as long as it lasts. These factors, many with an enduring influence, will be sketched out in this section.

Physical features and social adaptation

Topography and climate have tended to make for national fragmentation. The long and narrow shape of Norwegian territory makes distances considerable, a trait aggravated by mountains and innumerable deep indentations and fractures of the coastline. Thus land-based transport and communications have always been difficult and developed only slowly before the latter half of this century.

Coastal archipelagos, on the other hand, provide shielded waterways along the coast. The often mountainous coastline gives attractive shelter from raging elements on the North Atlantic and Arctic oceans. In the face of growing depopulation of peripheral areas, political consensus in recent years has supported a policy of subsidies, allowing the scattered settlement pattern to remain for reasons of national cultural heritage as well as defense.

The physical features facilitate sea-based transport and communications along the coast and overseas. Links across the sea were more convenient and thus became more important than land links. Cultural impulses followed the same routes.

Natural resources and related industries

Resources have historically been scarce. Only minimal parts of the land are tillable. Timber and fish were the national staples and are still important. The fish stocks of the North Atlantic have been overtaxed, however, and conservation is a pressing concern. Forest resources currently supply the paper industry but are insufficient for the country's own needs.

Mining has never been rich but has provided some industrial development. Copper, silver, and iron have formed the backbone of a mining industry since the 1600s. A few specialty mines remain, but the output is not of strategic interest.

The plentiful waterfalls played a key role in industrialization, first as power for sawmills, later as a source of cheap hydroelectric power. On this basis a new line of Norwegian industry emerged in this century, exploiting abundant energy to process imported raw materials—for example, bauxite into aluminum—for reexport. The economy became gradually more integrated in the world economy.

Today, submarine deposits of oil and gas, mainly in the North Sea and off the western coast, have yielded energy and unprecedented wealth, paired with technological development. The international oil industry has played an important role in these ventures, in cooperation with state-owned Norwegian companies.

Exports of oil and gas via pipelines to Scotland and the Continent during the 1980s amounted to about 50 percent of Norway's total exports by value. Oil exports will start to decline during the 1990s, while gas exports are expected to increase and last several decades into the next century. Development of submarine resources in the north has been deferred for security reasons and is awaiting an agreement with the USSR on separation of the two countries' maritime economic zones.

Economic system

The economy is a typical mixed type. Banking and insurance are primarily private; the social security system is, of course, a major exception. State ownership is concentrated in infrastructure such as utilities and communications. In industry and finance, state activity is limited primarily to areas of special national importance—such as oil—or need, such as regional development. Agriculture and, to some extent, fisheries are heavily subsidized.

Industries competing in export markets employ about 20 percent of the labor force. Import-competing industries are significantly larger employers. Germany, Sweden, and the United Kingdom are Norway's major trading partners. Wages are ordinarily set in broad, centrally negotiated agreements on the national level with locally negotiated supplements.

Social system

Norway's fragmentation and modest wealth are reflected in the social system. The current population of about 4 million is highly homogeneous. Small numbers of ethnic Samis in the north, and recent urban immigrants from Western Europe and Islamic countries break the monotony.

Average nominal income is high by international standards, though disposable personal income relative to cost of living is not. Income distribution is concentrated around the median; outright wealth and poverty are rare. Class differences in material terms are not noticeable. Social welfare is provided for as in the other Nordic countries.

Social values are strongly egalitarian and leveling. There are consequent tendencies to exclude those who seem different and toward group introversion. Many reject immigrant groups and strangers generally. Racist attitudes are more frequent than the predominant ethos of the nation would lead one to expect.

Democracy is seen as legitimated more by opportunities for popular participation than by decision-making efficiency. Socialism as a humanistic, egalitarian ideal has long had a strong position. Capitalism has few positive connotations in Norwegian culture.

There is great interest in international affairs and in learning about other cultures, yet a strong belief in Norwegian sociocultural superiority. Distinctive, oppositional cultural patterns add to this. Especially in southwestern rural areas, a strong abstentionist movement goes together with fundamentalist religious movements and rejection of the High Norwegian language.

Political system

Since 1814 Norway has been a constitutional monarchy and a representative democracy. A conflict between the Storting (parliament) and the Swedish king in 1884 led to the introduction of the parliamentary principle. A multiparty system gradually developed, with the social-democratic Labor Party in a leading position —35-45 percent—since about 1935. The Conservative Party is the second largest party—20-35 percent. Notable current features of the party system include

— splits continually affecting both major parties via creation of radical splinter parties: Labor since 1961; Conservatives since the mid-1970s; and
— weak center parties—Christian People's Party, Center Party— playing a key role since the 1960s due to their intermediate ideological position.

Minority governments and coalitions are frequent, usually built around the Labor Party on the socialist side and the Conservative Party on the non-socialist side. Coalitions across this dividing line have not been formed since 1945.

Nevertheless, the domestic political alignments are made more complex by important cleavages that do not coincide with the ideological left-right continuum. One of these is the urban-rural conflict, with the values of the modern, industrial consumer society on one side and the values of decentralization, environmentalism, and a simple life-style on the other. Another line of cleavage pits defenders of religious and traditional values against those of secular and so-called nontraditional values.

International position

Until the beginning of this century, Norway was favored by its peripheral geographic location. The remote northwestern coastal position, much of it facing little except water and ice, permitted Norway to maintain relative isolation. International communications passed it by, as did great-power politics. Isolation was aided by historical circumstance. Danish and Swedish dominion kept Norway as a hinterland.

Intermittently, the union with Denmark dragged Norway into unwanted wars, but on the whole Norway's position was rather sheltered. When the union with Sweden was broken off in 1905, it was therefore natural to choose neutrality and seek to continue the previous posture of aloofness. Coordination with the other Nordic neutrals eventually came to play an important part in this policy, which was pursued for the ensuing four decades, interrupted only by World War II.

Ironically, however, roughly since independence, Norway's position has attracted increasing attention and interest on the part of the great powers. Transatlantic trade could conceivably be disrupted from naval bases on the Norwegian coast. Swedish exports of iron ore via the northern Norwegian port of Narvik were of great importance to arms producers in Europe. Coastal seaways and harbors could provide protected passage for hunted vessels over considerable distances. Such factors lay behind persistent and competing greatpower pressures on Norwegian neutrality during World War I and its forced termination by Germany's attack and five-year occupation during World War II.

In recent years, proximity to vital Soviet defense areas has given the area renewed strategic significance. More on this later in this article.

Norwegian profile

Characteristic traits of Norway's international interface follow from the description previously given. A late, and subsequently interrupted, independence is jealously guarded by segments of elite opinion and parts of the press. Foreign influence is sometimes regarded with suspicion, on the left as well as the right. More cosmopolitan attitudes are found in urban areas among business elites and intellectuals, but a nationalistic intelligentsia remains strong.

Sober observers have pointed out that Norwegian foreign politics is marked by an astounding combination of, on the one hand, strong appeals for more international cooperation and, on the other hand, repeated rejections of concrete proposals to involve Norway in the international community. The domestic lines of conflict previously described may help explain this and therefore have a notable foreign policy relevance. These cleavages came powerfully into play in the 1972 referendum on Norwegian membership in the European Community (EC), in which a clear majority of the parliamentary elite was defeated by a groundswell of anti-EC opinion cutting across established party lines. Most parties were split by the issue, which created an unprecedented political trauma in subsequent Norwegian politics. For almost two decades, no one dared to suggest EC membership again. By 1990, polls had started to show signs of a basic change of heart in the electorate, possibly stirred by the dramatic European revolutions of late 1989.

EXTERNAL PRESSURES: THE POLITICAL ENVIRONMENT

Continuing confrontation and adjustment of external and internal pressures shape Norwegian foreign policy. I shall turn first to the external side—the activities and interests of the great powers in the Nordic areas as they apply specifically to Norway.

The United Kingdom, the Soviet Union, the United States, Germany, and—to a lesser extent—France are the major relevant actors. The North Atlantic Treaty Organization (NATO) and the EC have long pooled the interests of the Western powers and are likely to continue to play a coordinating role in the area for the foreseeable future. Nevertheless, the interests of these powers do not always coincide with respect to Norway. Communications—implicit or explicit, in word or deed—from governments or other actors in the international environment, as perceived in Norway, either directly constrain Norwegian governmental behavior or express the actions they want Norwegian authorities to undertake.

Strategic interests of the great powers

How and to what extent can the territory of Norway and the adjacent sea areas under nominal Norwegian control be exploited by one great power against another? As is apparent from the preceding, the answer depends on technology to some extent. With significant technological change, the potential use of a territory may change accordingly. Early in this century, for instance, advances in railway construction allowed strategically important Swedish iron ore to be shipped from Norway, thus introducing a strategic element in northern Norway that had not been there before. Not much later, during World War I, submarine warfare began, thus further increasing the strategic significance of the coastline and coastal waterways.

A more recent example of relevant technological change is the advances in Soviet missile technology enabling submarine-launched missiles to reach the United States from positions farther away, closer to Soviet bases—and closer to Norway. Low-altitude cruise missiles crossing Norwegian, Swedish, and Finnish territory from a launching vessel in the Norwegian Sea en route to targets in the USSR exemplify a current challenge to future arms control regimes.

For the foreseeable future, Norway is likely to continue to have considerable strategic importance. There are several reasons for this. One relates to Norway's position near the direct flight routes for missiles and bombers in a possible war between the United States and the USSR. The Norwegian Sea or the Barents Sea can also be used as a staging area for sea-launched attacks both ways. Another reason derives from the potential use by a great power of Norwegian harbors and airports, in order to gain control over North Atlantic sea lanes or, indeed, other targets in the area, including those just mentioned. Soviet investments in all kinds of military bases on the Kola Peninsula are not likely to be abandoned, even if substantial new steps in disarmament are taken. The importance of these bases to the USSR affects all non-Soviet territory in the vicinity.

Further, the United Kingdom has a continuing long-term interest in naval developments in the area. Britain is concerned for its own security that control is maintained over the Norwegian Sea and the Norwegian coast by itself or allied powers. The specific German interest is likely to be more derivative of the general East-West situation and to focus more narrowly on the southeastern part of Norway.

In sum, compared with the other Nordic countries, Norway's strategic position is marked by a greater symmetry of interests between East and West than in the Finnish case; a greater challenge for a prospective attacker than posed by Denmark and Finland; and a greater uncertainty of alignment in case of a new security regime than Sweden, Denmark, or Finland has.

Economic interests

The world's economic interest in Norway is highlighted by two factors: the international regimes created by governmental organizations, and the expectations of the international business community.

An open national environment for international trade and foreign direct investment is required by the Organization for Economic Cooperation and Development. A chance to participate in the exploitation of the nation's natural resources is a standard expectation on the part of the international business community. Equal competitive conditions are demanded by the General Agreement on Tariffs and Trade and the EC.

Some of these requirements have been controversial in the past and may have far-reaching consequences in the future for Norway. Negotiations between the EC and the European Free Trade Association for adjustment to the new EC internal market regime have demonstrated serious discrepancies.

Given Norway's economic profile, a few primary points of external interest today and for the foreseeable future are likely to be petroleum resources and related industries; industries with especially favorable local circumstances, such as aquaculture or the tourist industry; equal access to government purchasing; access to fisheries in the Norwegian economic zone; and access to the protected segments of the consumer market, for example, fresh fruit and vegetables. Of these, the oil and gas sector represents the densest cluster of foreign economic interest. On the marketing side, Western—including U.S.—and other governments have intermittently leaned heavily on Norwegian authorities for politically motivated sales to—or embargoes of—specific governments.

The regulation of total oil marketing volume is of great interest both to the Organization of Petroleum Exporting Countries, of which Norway is not a member, and to the Organization for Economic Cooperation and

Development's International Energy Agency, of which it is only an associate member. The French government has pressed hard for a package deal in which long-term gas purchases would be linked with other trade conditions. The position of the British government in such matters is always a strong concern, due to the adjacent location of many fields in the North Sea.

On the production side, as one might expect, the international oil industry has demanded equal participation in the exploration and exploitation of resources. The construction industries of Western Europe have wanted to compete for contracts on equal terms and have repeatedly charged Norway with unfair treatment. Governments rarely hesitate to back their own claimants, especially if they consider such charges to be reasonable.

There are continuing pressures on Norway's mainland economy from abroad for liberalizing the remaining restrictions on foreign business activities. While no longer as extensive as during the early postwar decades, these regulations concern conditions for the establishment of foreign-owned corporations, foreign ownership of land, and so on.

Labor power in Norway is expressed in high wage levels and strict labor legislation. International business interests often see a challenge in lowering those wages and standards. Norwegian business sometimes joins forces with them. Immigrant labor is a link in such considerations. Since the mid-1970s immigration has been practically proscribed. In the contin-

uing public debate, issues of labor competition, humanitarian concern, and racism are often mingled.

General political and diplomatic orientation

The broad interests of great powers with respect to Norwegian foreign policy flow from their more specific interests relating to security and economic affairs. A special case worth noting is the rights of signatories to the Svalbard Treaty to participate in economic exploitation of the archipelago's resources. Although all major powers have acceded to the treaty, so far the USSR is the only country besides Norway with concrete investments there. The Svalbard Islands are a demilitarized zone, and all parties to the treaty presumably have an interest in preserving that status.

As pointed out previously, key characteristics of great-power strategic interests in Norway were symmetry and high saliency. This makes stability of Norwegian foreign policy a priority from the great powers' point of view. Of course, all great powers want small states to stay in their place. Nevertheless, concern for the Norwegian case may be above average in Europe.

Stability means a strong great-power preference for minimal change of the basic Norwegian foreign policy course from government to government. It also means a preference for deliberate, incremental, preannounced, and slow change of security policy whenever it does take place. The maintenance of secure territorial control is part of the stability consideration. Before Norway became a member of NATO in 1949, this was a source of worry among the great powers. World War II had demonstrated Norwegian weakness in preventing foreign intrusion. A weakening or dissolution of the NATO regime in the future could well raise such concerns again.

The relative uncertainty—as seen from the outside—of future Norwegian alignment in case of a changed security regime adds special concern to great-power interests. It means an expectation of rapid adjustment of Norway's policy to whatever larger changes are effected in its surroundings by the great powers themselves. The greater the agreement among the great powers concerning such change in Norway's surroundings, the greater the pressure. On the other hand, disagreement between the great powers may occur in the future as in the past and may then place heavy strains on the Norwegian policymaking system. Alignment with one side is a way of reducing the stress and strain resulting from such situations.

NORWEGIAN CONCEPTIONS OF NATIONAL INTEREST

So far we have dealt with the view from the outside. How, then, do Norwegians themselves view their interests, and to what extent do they agree or disagree about them? These questions will be discussed under the headings of "general orientation," "territorial interests," "security interests," and "economic interests."

General orientation

The makers of Norwegian foreign policy must to some extent be expected to heed the general outlook and biases of society and also to be marked by prevailing attitudes themselves. First, a general desire for openness to the West gives the basic tenor of Norwegian foreign policy, shared at all levels of society. Second, one finds a certain skepticism about great-power politics, regardless of who those powers are. There is an undercurrent of a preference for neutrality. Beyond this, economic interests have tended to form the backbone of policy.

Affinity with Britain has historically competed with affinity with Germany, but anglophile tendencies have always been stronger, cemented by interests in shipping and finance. After 1940, antipathies toward Germany were deep and long-lasting, but they have dissipated with the emergence of a more democratic German system, which has also gained great economic importance for Norway.

The United States has traditionally been a more remote partner, broadly viewed with sympathy mingled with some skepticism toward what many perceive as a freewheeling capitalistic system. The U.S. role as great protector, welcomed by a clear majority of Norwegians, has nevertheless been frequently disputed. More important, Norwegian-U.S. relations have only a very limited anchorage in broader economic interests. Thus general ties to the United States, focused on NATO, are weaker than the more concrete ties to Germany, Britain, and Sweden.

Despite the proximity to the Soviet Union, Norwegian relations with that country have never been intense or close. On the political left, the USSR long retained a basically favorable image, which was not generally shared by the Norwegian population. Economic contact has been mostly a regional affair in the North. While relations have never been especially hostile, for most of the Cold War the Soviet posture was widely perceived as threatening.

Norway's foreign policy environment is often described by reference to several partly overlapping circles, extending outward: the Nordic circle, the European—or West European—circle, the Atlantic circle, and the global circle. The ongoing foreign policy debate may at any time be related to the underlying question of the priority to be accorded one or another of these circles.

The Atlantic circle has had apparent priority in official Norwegian foreign policy since 1949—in reality, 1945—when it overlapped with the West European circle. Since the referendum in 1972, when membership in the EC was rejected by 54 percent of the voters, the Atlantic circle has had a more precarious predominance, because the overlap was reduced when Britain and Denmark joined the EC.

Territorial interests

There are no mainland territorial issues between Norway and its neighbors, nor have there been any for centuries. The dispute with Denmark in the 1930s over rights to Greenland must be regarded an oddity. Where control over adjacent seas and seabeds are concerned, however, live issues exist. As these questions affect the coastal population of Norway directly, they are highly salient in domestic politics, with a national spillover to foreign policy.

Disputes regarding the delimitation of economic zones have recently disturbed relations not only with the Soviet Union but also with Iceland and Greenland. In the postwar era, moreover, conflicts over fishing rights have appeared in the well-known Anglo-Norwegian Fisheries Case and in minor though repeated difficulties between Norway and Sweden. Annual agreements with the EC since the late 1970s regarding mutual access to economic zones continue to pose tough bargaining problems every time, yet they have acquired a routine air.

The most difficult issue concerns delimitation of the Norwegian and Soviet economic zones extending into the Barents Sea from their common land border. The USSR asserts the sector principle, Norway the equidistance principle, resulting in a large disputed area that has been jointly administered since a 1977 interim agreement. Oil and gas finds have been made on the seabed on both sides. The Barents Sea is also strategically sensitive to the USSR.

Norway has rejected a proposal for permanent condominium. Emotional overtones complicate the matter, as a key Norwegian negotiator in 1977 later turned out to have been a Soviet agent, while the 1977 agreement itself contains glaring inequities in Norway's disfavor. There is thus very little support in Norway for making the interim agreement permanent.

In a different case, the status of the economic zone and seabed around Svalbard is strongly disputed between Norway and signatories to the Svalbard Treaty. Norway claims these areas exclusively for itself; the treaty signatories claim joint access, as to the archipelago itself.

Security interests

The German attack in 1940 and the subsequent occupation constituted a traumatic experience that left its marks on subsequent policy. After reluctant abandonment of neutrality in 1949, a conscious effort was made to set limits on the implications of the new alliance policy. Soviet concerns over foreign bases were voiced even before Norwegian ratification of the North Atlantic Treaty. The Norwegian government responded with an assurance that foreign troops would not be stationed on Norwegian soil in the absence of threats to peace.

This was the origin of Norway's so-called reassurance policy, supplementing its alliance policy. The Soviet Union was to be reassured that Norwegian ties with the Western alliance were purely defensive and would not be exploited for aggression against the USSR. Later a reservation against acquiring or storing nuclear weapons on Norwegian territory was added, as were various other restrictions on allied military activity in Norway: no allied overflights of Norwegian territory east of 24 degrees of longitude east; no allied vessels in Norwegian territorial waters east of the same longitude; limited duration of allied maneuvers per year; and nuclear weapons assumed not to be present on allied vessels on visits to Norwegian harbors. This policy of alliance with unilateral reservations has been continued by all subsequent Norwegian governments, regardless of political coloring.

It is worth noting that this policy is unilateral, initiated by Norway and not conditional on the assent of any other power in the event of a change. Thus Norway has sought to ensure that its government retains control over decisions should a crisis occur.

This policy has wide support in Norway, although many have criticized it. A main line of criticism holds that the restrictions are not really required for external reasons, that the Soviet Union is not materially affected one way or the other by such Norwegian restraint. The reassurance policy in this view serves not to pacify the USSR but to keep the Norwegian Labor Party together and other dissenting voices regarding NATO membership to a minimum.

Economic interests

It is not easy to depict Norway's international economic interests in comprehensive terms. The oil industry—split into a Norwegian state-owned segment and an international, mostly private segment—is dependent on foreign markets. Yet the Norwegian segment is reluctant to open the development of new oil and gas fields to international competitors.

The Shipowners' Association, the Federation of Industries, and the Association of Commerce are interested in an open economy without protective barriers. Pockets of resistance to this notion were strong in some industries in the first postwar decades, but, though they still exist, they are small today. All of these groups have declared themselves in favor of EC membership by 1990.

The Federation of Labor has been considerably more divided. Many unions fear the loss of jobs, labor immigration, and foreign economic control. Such fears led a majority of workers to vote against EC membership in 1972. During the late 1980s stronger sentiments in favor of EC membership have emerged in parts of the federation.

Agriculture enjoys a protected market and high subsidies. An opening to the outside is bound to take away most of its privileges. In the 1972 referendum campaign, associations and industries connected with agriculture financed most of the opposition to Norwegian EC membership.

Fisheries are in a more ambiguous position. On the one hand, they want—indeed, need—to sell on the external market. On the other, they want to keep access in fishing restricted in the large Norwegian economic zone. They strongly opposed EC membership in the 1972 campaign, and the coastal communities voted heavily against. In 1990 they are more favorably disposed, due to market needs, foreign competition in the domestic frozen-fish market, and declining catches.

DECISION MAKING: STRUCTURES AND PARTICIPANTS

Foreign policy making in Norway is concentrated in a triangle between the Ministry of Foreign Affairs, the Storting, and the Cabinet. If the latter is a coalition, as is usually the case, the Storting assumes a more important role, largely through its so-called Expanded Committee on Foreign Affairs.

The minister of foreign affairs, formally charged with the coordination of foreign policy, tends to assume the actual leading position in the decision-making system. His most important associates in the Cabinet —beyond the prime minister—are the minister of defense and the minister of trade and shipping.

Two additional elements are crucial for understanding how the system works: a fuzzy dividing line between high-saliency issues coordinated by the Foreign Ministry and lower-saliency issues handled by other ministries; and a segmented decision-making process, with a tradition of close and exclusive cooperation in economic and technical affairs between interest groups and ministries.

Regarding the first, the coordinating role of the foreign minister could become an all-consuming task unless some line is drawn between the politically significant and the trivial aspects of foreign policy. Tradition has drawn the line between matters touching broad national interests— foreign policy proper—and issues of narrow sector or technical interest, or international affairs.

With the explosive growth in recent decades of all manner of contacts across national borders, this distinction has tended to lose its meaning. Many ministries are charged with handling international affairs and— aided by the informal and easy contact between ministry officials all over Western Europe—have long carried out their tasks without involving the Foreign Ministry.

The segmented decision-making process derives from the traditional corporatist system, in which groups most directly affected by a prospective decision are invited to take part in its preparation. The system tends to disregard nonorganized interests, such as broad consumer interests, and allows special interest groups privileged access to decision making. The parliamentary link in the decision-making chain has been shown to be less affected by this kind of collusion, but extensive discretionary powers delegated to ministries often leave the Storting out of the process.

In a recent administrative reform designed to improve coordination and reduce segmentation, the Ministry of Trade and Shipping was merged with the Ministry of Foreign Affairs, along with the small Ministry of Foreign Aid, although their ministerial posts were retained. As of 1989, the Ministry of Foreign Affairs is thus led by a troika in which the minister of foreign affairs has the ultimate say.

Still, the wide span of international relations extends well beyond what this reform covers. Moreover, a large number of more specific economic and technical issues cannot be fitted into the broader perspective of a unified foreign policy but have to be resolved on their merits. The expertise in the interest groups continues to be crucial to policymakers, whether their realm is called foreign policy or international affairs.

Domestic actors:
Interest groups

The organized interests in shipping, trade, and industry have been preeminent in defining the foreign economic interests of Norway since before 1905. Lately, the petroleum industry has been added. Periodically, these interests have also provided the predominant basis for the country's foreign policy as such. This influence has usually been wielded through direct contacts with the relevant ministries, as described previously.

This is to say that organized labor, a powerful group in Norwegian politics, has often had to take the back seat, along with other organized interests, in the definition of foreign economic policy. The interests of unions and employers overlap to a considerable extent, however, and labor unions have not been excluded from the decision-making process as such.

The interests of agriculture and fisheries tell a different story. The main domestic conflicts of material interest relating to foreign affairs have usually been between the organizations of industry and trade and the organizations of farmers and fishermen. The battles have concerned proposals for Norwegian entry into various schemes for free trade, customs unions, and common markets, as noted previously.

This general characterization of interest-group influence must be qualified. The business and commercial interest groups are not all-powerful; they have lost important battles to agricultural and fisheries interests, to some extent also to labor interests. The organizations in shipping, trade, and industry have always been largely in favor of Norwegian participation in regional economic integration, most notably the EC. They have repeatedly lost out to the champions of Norwegian self-sufficiency. The reason for such surprising strength on the part of inherently weak economic groups is their alliances with political parties controlling broad parliamentary support.

Domestic actors:
Political parties

With one exception, Norwegian political parties in the postwar era have not put foreign policy issues at the top of their agendas. The Labor Party plays a unique role in that it bridges two of the most important cleavages in the country's foreign policy: the division between supporters and opponents of NATO, and the division between what may be called European-Atlanticists and so-called isolationists. The bridge itself is, of course, the consensus within the party on further development of the welfare state and an active role for government in most areas of policy. Isolationism here and in other parties is expressed in skepticism of foreign influence in Norway generally and in preferences for a combined emphasis on the Nordic circle and the global circle rather than the European and Atlantic circles. The carefully balanced Norwegian NATO policy originates in this party. Ties with the labor unions have always been close, as are the relations with the associations of, respectively, smallholders and fishermen.

The Socialist Left Party, with 12 percent of the voters in 1990, was formed in 1961 as an offshoot of the Labor Party, with campaigns against NATO, against nuclear weapons, and against the European Economic Community on top of its agenda. These issues remain its programmatic basis today, besides more generally socialist causes and environmental issues.

On the nonsocialist side, the Conservative Party strongly favors NATO and European integration. It wants a consistently open economy with minimal restrictions on international business activities. The general policy profile is old-fashioned Liberal and accentuates a social welfare policy to reduce its competitive distance from the Labor Party. Close ties exist with most of the interest groups on the commercial side.

The Progress Party, with 15 percent support in 1990, is a Liberalistic, recent competitor, to the right of the Conservative Party on most issues, especially taxation. It offers no alternatives on foreign policy, except extreme skepticism of foreign aid.

The two parties of the center are ideologically situated between the Conservatives and Labor. The more conservative of these, the Center Party—6 percent in 1990—is largely based on agrarian interests, with which it has strong ties. It is also deeply concerned with environmental issues. In foreign policy it is isolationist, as the term was used previously herein. It comes closer than any other party to being a nationalistic party.

Its close associate, the Christian People's Party—with 8 percent in 1990 —draws its strength from pietist and fundamentalist religious groups. Its emphasis on caring and universal solidarity has given it a special foreign policy profile, based on foreign aid and support for the United Nations. It has long been sympathetic to Israel, though with increasing reservations. Domestically, its social welfare policy places it closer to the Labor Party than to its nonsocialist associates.

CONCLUSION

We can now draw some general conclusions about the way Norwegian policy tends to be made and the likely main course of Norway's future foreign policy.

First, the small-state pattern tends to be reversed in Norwegian foreign policy making. A well-developed democratic and corporatist participatory system makes for a domestically pushed foreign policy. Security policy is a double compromise: a domestic one combined with an external one. Second, in the absence of high great-power tension, economic foreign policy becomes salient. Interest groups have privileged access, making for hard bargaining.

Third, the Labor Party, whether in government or opposition, will continue to play a key role in foreign policy making as long as it continues to bridge the main foreign policy cleavages. The Conservative Party and European-Atlanticist circles in the Labor Party have long made up an implicit foreign policy coalition fundamental to the nation. The EC-membership issue remains the greatest challenge to their future policy-making role. It remains an open question whether a policy of membership is too much for the Labor Party to carry.

Finally, the fundamental security policy agreement between the two largest political parties may have been conditioned by the Cold War. In a more relaxed international atmosphere, with a peaceful restructuring of Europe, it is not clear that the Labor Party—given the opposition within its ranks—will retain its support for a Western alliance, especially if faced with European alternatives inside the frameworks of the Conference on Security and Cooperation in Europe or the EC. The Conservative Party is less likely to leave the Western-alliance position.

ANNALS, *AAPSS*, 512, November 1990

Sweden:
Secure Neutrality

By BENGT SUNDELIUS

ABSTRACT: Sweden's recent record of peaceful external relations is often contrasted with the costly and, in the end, futile attempts during earlier centuries to play power politics through wars and alliances. This experience has served to underline the importance of national defense for a credible neutrality posture. Defense expenditures are considerable. The comprehensive nature of national defense and the economic dimension of security have been stressed. Sweden shares strong economic links with the Western economies. As a result of affluence throughout the postwar era and the recognition of the importance of the Western economic channels for this prosperity, official neutrality has interfered only marginally with the private pursuit of commerce and finance. This liberal attitude toward international exchanges has included items of strategic significance, such as advanced technology, arms, and ammunition. Sweden shares with other Nordic nations an inclination for marked visibility in global issues and arenas, hoping to promote international change both in North-South issues and in East-West negotiations. The classic definition of the Swedish foreign policy doctine is freedom from alliances in peace aiming for neutrality in war.

Bengt Sundelius is director of the International Graduate School of the University of Stockholm. He has served on the faculties of Bradley University and the University of Washington. His books include Managing Transnationalism in Northern Europe; Foreign Policies of Northern Europe; Internationalization and Foreign Policy Management; The Neutral Democracies and the New Cold War; *and, most recently,* The Committed Neutral: Sweden's Foreign Policy.

OVER the last century, Sweden has benefited from the cushioning effects of its Scandinavian neighbors. While these states have been drawn into the pattern of conflict and cooperation in Europe, Sweden has more often remained outside such activities. A policy of splendid isolation has been combined with the quest for international understanding. Possessing relatively strong economic and military attributes, Sweden, a nation of 8.5 million people, could long afford such a stand. The superior resource base, representing almost half of the gross product in the region, has given Sweden dominance in the Nordic arena. In a larger context, however, Sweden is small and defines itself as a leading small state.

Seeing itself as a champion of the rights of small states implies differentiation between the leader and the rest of the pack. This self-aggrandizing image places Sweden outside the group of small and vulnerable nations that must passively adjust to the demands of great-power politics. Swedish governments have never adapted easily to changing realities in the strategic setting. Instead, they have often preferred to attempt to change the world to fit Swedish ideals.

After World War I, Sweden enjoyed an optimal security position. With Germany defeated, the new Soviet state weak, Finland and the three Baltic states independent, and Denmark and Norway strengthened but friendly, it did not have any serious strategic concerns. Within the immediate security environment, Sweden even seemed a major player, resurrecting memories of the grand days of Gustavus Adolphus and Charles XII.

A benevolent policy was adopted, including acquiescence to a League of Nations ruling that granted the Swedish-speaking Aaland Islands to the new Finnish state, against the clear wishes of the inhabitants. Sweden later relinquished its permanent council seat in the League of Nations to the new German member, to enable the latter's participation. Similarly, the various international disarmament schemes of the interwar period found support in Sweden. In 1925 it set an example for other nations by greatly reducing its own defenses. Like many people in another neutral of the interwar period, the United States, prominent Swedes placed great faith in the abilities of statesmen to create a stable and just world order through international law and diplomacy.

By the mid-1930s, these hopes had to be set aside, given the rise of Nazi Germany, the consolidation of the Soviet regime, and the collapse of the League. Joining other small European states, Sweden declared its departure from the collective security system and its return to its traditional defense posture: armed neutrality. During World War II, the government's primary objective was to keep the nation out of a conflict that caused so much suffering in Europe. In this respect, the government was successful, but at the cost of being forced at times to interpret the obligations of neutrality in less than conventional ways. For example, it provided assistance to its war-torn Nordic neighbors, allowed German troop transfers across its territory, and facilitated the return of Allied airmen stranded after missions over enemy territory—all apparent deviations from a strict definition of neutrality. The other neutrals of World War II were forced to accept similar compromises. At war's end, Sweden could not join in the celebrations of the Allies but continued to assist the victims of war. Clearly, Swedish values were served by the victory, but it is an open question whether the Allied cause would have been advanced through Swedish combat participation.

Like the United States, Sweden entered the postwar period from a position of strength. The industrial base was intact and the defense force was formidable. This set the stage for the relative economic and military influence of Sweden over the next thirty years. It joined the United Nations in 1946, after some debate over the compatibility of membership with the policy of neutrality. The second U.N. secretary-general, Dag Hammarskjöld, was recruited from Sweden in 1952. In 1948, an effort was made to keep the Scandinavian region out of the Cold War through a Scandinavian Defense Union outside the blocs. At the time, Swedish military might was still sufficiently impressive that such a defense pact could be regarded as a meaningful choice. When Denmark and Norway opted for membership in the Atlantic Alliance, Sweden returned to its traditional stand of splendid isolation. The resulting formula—freedom from alliances in peacetime, aiming at neutrality in the event of war—remains the cornerstone for Swedish security

policy. Even an altered internal resource base and vastly changed international conditions for armed neutrality have not undermined the domestic support for this doctrine. In the public mind, this posture has spared the country the devastation of war since 1814 and it is not questioned lightly.

CONTEMPORARY SECURITY CONCERNS

It is possible that the Swedish postwar security choice facilitated the Finnish effort to avoid the fate of the other nations along the Soviet border. The creation of a neutral buffer in the North, guarded by Sweden's impressive air force, may have reduced tensions in an increasingly sharply divided Europe. The peacetime utility of the Swedish posture can be readily appreciated when one compares Scandinavia with the record of bloc confrontation in Central Europe. The wartime credibility of armed neutrality is more open to question, because of the fast-developing and unpredictable nature of modern warfare.

Even what has become a comparatively modest Swedish defense force should be sufficient to deter an attack, if one assumes that neither bloc could devote large military resources to a marginal country in a crisis. The cost of entry would be seen as too high relative to the strategic advantages of controlling the territory. Clearly, the level of the armed forces' preparedness and the ability to foresee hostile moves are crucial to the credibility of this policy. Sweden has made a considerable investment in a mobile air force and advanced means of intelligence collection.

During the postwar period the Swedish government has continued to promote, in addition to its commitment to armed neutrality, international understanding and cooperation. Swedish involvement in multilateral initiatives rests on the belief that security can be enhanced both by national defense and by an international milieu less conducive to conflict. This two-dimensional approach to security policy is widely supported at home and has found expression through the concept of active neutrality. Sweden's strong commitment to the United Nations, including its multinational peacekeeping forces; an active role in international development issues; and a vocal concern about superpower armaments and their involvement in local conflicts in the Third World can be understood in these terms.

Closer to home, a major concern has been how to help transform a conflict-prone Europe into a setting of greater stability. Active in the Helsinki process and in the development of confidence-building measures together with the other European neutral and nonaligned states, Sweden recently hosted the Stockholm Conference on Disarmament in Europe. Inspired by the work of the Palme Commission on Common Security, the government has proposed the establishment in Central Europe of a border zone free of nuclear weapons. Similarly, the arms buildup at sea is viewed with concern, and the Strategic Defense Initiative is re-

garded as a destabilizing element in East-West relations. During the 1980s more emphasis was placed on the European setting relative to other regions and to global issues.

Recent developments in the North Atlantic have placed Scandinavia at the center of naval interests. A growing Soviet fleet has operated for some time out of the Kola base complex adjacent to the region. The Soviets have understandably developed an acute concern for the security of the area surrounding the considerable forces they have amassed there. Although presumably not targeted at the neighboring Scandinavian nations, the nuclear weapons located on the Kola Peninsula play a significant role in the broader strategic picture. Thus the North Cape is of great interest to planners of the North Atlantic Treaty Organization (NATO) and to the new American Forward Maritime Strategy. This new element undermines the Norwegian policy of reassurance of the USSR and complicates plans for oil and gas exploration in these waters. The defense of northern Finland and Sweden is affected as well, and this has resulted in an upgrading of local forces.

Traditionally, the U.S. military commitment to European defense has depended on NATO control of the North Atlantic for reliable transoceanic shipment of personnel and supplies. The Soviet Northern Fleet has gradually extended the scope of its operations far into the North Atlantic. Naturally, NATO planners view this development with concern and have urged a greater Allied presence in these waters and coastal areas to counter the Soviet advance. The strategic posturing of both sides has moved closer to Scandinavia, complicating the traditional strategy of keeping the tensions as low as possible in the area. In current war scenarios, the North figures prominently as a potential combat zone in a superpower confrontation. For example, Soviet control of the extensive Swedish air base system could significantly strengthen Soviet ability to fight for dominance of the North Atlantic skies. According to one scenario, the defense of the long Norwegian coastline would be impossible if Norway were cut off through an advance in the Trondheim area.

The strategic role of the Baltic Sea has also changed. The USSR has traditionally promoted the notion of a closed sea, where, as the largest maritime power, it could dominate the waters and shorelines. Sweden and NATO have insisted on the Baltic's status as an international sea open to all states. As a result of the division of Europe in 1945, the Soviets have controlled an immense coastline, stretching from the Finnish border in the east to the West German border south of Denmark and west of Sweden. In recent years, several major ports and naval shipyards have been constructed by the Soviets along the Baltic coast. These serve as major overhaul and construction facilities for the vast Soviet global fleet.

The USSR seems to place great emphasis upon the control of the surrounding waters or at least their denial to other parties. Soviet security concerns may even be intensified by continual NATO surveillance patrols

in the Baltic. The offensive Soviet submarine activities along Swedish coastlines and the increased Allied presence in the Baltic made plain the growing tensions in the area during the 1980s. Since October of 1981, when the famed Soviet Whiskey Class submarine, equipped with nuclear weapons, beached just off the Swedish coast, underwater activities have been a steady source of tension between the Soviet Union and Sweden. In spite of diplomatic protests in 1981 and 1983, all indications point toward continued intrusions. Although the inability to repel such activities may not be considered a serious national security failure, it has clearly left many questions about the credibility of Swedish armed neutrality. This issue has also sparked an intense domestic debate over the proper response to this new type of threat. When one considers these and related developments, it is not surprising that few Swedes view the Baltic as a "sea of peace," as it is sometimes called by Soviet officals.

Innovations in weapons technology have also affected the strategic posture of Scandinavia. A NATO launching of sea-based cruise missiles across the territories of Sweden and Finland may facilitate reaching targets in the USSR and could also create serious political dilemmas for these neutrals. Doubts about the ability or the determination of these governments to resist such territorial violations could motivate preemptive moves by the West. Concerns in the opposite direction may stimulate prelaunch political pressures to allow so-called innocent passage of such missiles. Either way, the pressures on the credibility of Swedish armed neutrality may be greater today than during the postwar years, when the defense force was significantly larger. Allied concern over the region's role in crisis or war may also lead to peacetime demands that would be difficult to reconcile with the domestically popular reassurance policies of Denmark and Norway. The preferred pattern of regional confidence building and stability could collapse as broader strategic interests clash in the North.

These unwelcome developments may even be unaffected by a superpower agreement on force reductions in Central Europe. In fact, one could imagine that confrontation between the blocs would simply shift arenas and increasingly focus on the maritime and air-related dimensions affecting Scandinavian security. Even with a reduction of global and European tensions after the frost of the so-called New Cold War years, the strategic setting of the North could continue a slide toward greater instability. Local security analysts have noted no changes in the regional force structures of the two military alliances comparable to the much publicized developments on the Continent, but continued Soviet interest in the strategic coastline of the Baltic Sea has been clearly evidenced through the recent developments in the Baltic states and through the continued underwater visits in Swedish territorial waters.

Sweden faces a delicate policy dilemma with regard to these events. The submarine operations have generated considerable public debate and critical comments over the last few years. Nothing can be added here to that controversial policy problem. The developments across the waters have reintroduced a classic dimension to the basic policy dilemma. On the one hand, unbending support for the national liberation ambitions of the Baltic peoples would be in line with similar Swedish involvements in more distant regions of the world. On the other hand, the strategic realities of the local area invite caution. Sweden could easily be drawn into a conflict between the central government of the USSR and the independence ambitions of the Baltics. Clearly, such a local confrontation would also affect the larger East-West relationship. Any action or inaction has a direct bearing on the Swedish neutrality posture.

It is an open question whether the end of the Cold War will lead to regional stability or instability in Scandinavia. The strategic and political interests of the major powers could once again, as in 1939-40, converge on a region that fared rather well on the quiet flank of an otherwise inflamed East-West relationship during the previous forty years. So far, the Swedish government has not embraced with any great enthusiasm the demise of the bloc confrontation in Europe. Rather, official statements have more often stressed the valuable stabilizing role of the established neutrality line between East and West at a time of considerable—and possibly unpredictable—

change within the two alliance structures. Alliances may come and go, but Swedish neutrality endures!

THE IMAGES OF NEUTRALITY

Sweden shares with most members of the Atlantic Alliance a democratic ethos, with a pluralistic political and economic system. In this respect, Sweden is a world apart from the predominant political values and social orders of the East European nations. It is also often stressed that the government is not neutral in terms of ideology but merely with respect to national security policy. The neutrality is not one of beliefs but of strategic choice. There is an element of expediency behind the national doctrine. The question is how this support of basic Western values can be combined with the equally firm commitment to neutrality in the political struggle between East and West.

This latent conflict between ideological preference and strategic necessity appears in much of the American scholarship on Swedish foreign policy from the 1920s through the mid-1980s.[1] The neutral strikes many in the West as a free rider. To many in the East, the neutral position may seem an envious one. Throughout the world, it is recognized as a policy of courage. The European neutrals speak more often of strategic necessity than about moral

1. Mikael S. Steene, "Role Model or Power Pawn? The Changing Image of Swedish Foreign Policy, 1929-1987," in *The Committed Neutral: Sweden's Foreign Policy,* ed. Bengt Sundelius (Boulder, CO: Westview Press, 1989), pp. 167-94.

virtue. In one sense, however, a policy that can save people from the sufferings of war or can offer the promise of freedom and democracy may be seen as morally superior to any alternative that would risk these fundamental values.

Partly in response to such normative concerns, key political figures have from time to time stressed the virtues of representing a third, middle position in the East-West confrontation. By keeping a distance from both sides, the Swede indicates a commitment to impartiality in any political conflict between these sets of values. Through such reasoning, the neutral position can be justified in positive terms. It provides a foundation for a unique and valuable mediating role between two alien antagonists. This stand is identified with a vital systemic function and is thus transformed from a strategy of political necessity to a moral imperative. In such a perspective, a neutral democracy is clearly not morally compromised. On the contrary, it represents reason and a concern for the overriding interests of the international community.

Sweden's role as a third party in the East-West context—as mediator, bridge builder, and impartial critic—is widely recognized as having enhanced its national prestige and possibly also its influence on world affairs. By contributing to a more stable environment, with less propensity for conflict, national security interests are also served. In addition to serving such national ends, the role could also be of systemic importance. From time to time, even the superpower leaders recognize this valuable function in a divided world, full of issues that somehow must be managed. To grease the wheels of world politics is to play a vital part, when a breakdown could mean global disaster.

COMMITTED NEUTRALITY

The Finnish scholar Harto Hakovirta has reminded us that credibility and respectability are key resources for successful peacetime neutrality.[2] Drawing on the historical experiences of postwar European neutrality, Hakovirta concludes that

the basic problem of contemporary neutrality lies in its inherent partiality and bias arising from the neutral states' Western values and ties. In terms of value premises and dependencies, this is not neutrality, but Western neutrality, or a paradoxical effort at maintaining a neutral image and label despite Western starting-points and predispositions. . . . In Eastern eyes the credibility of Western neutrality is of course chronically questionable, and this together with the basic Marxian class view tends to lower its respectability, too.[3]

In official policy declarations, the credibility aspect of Swedish neutrality is often explicitly mentioned. It has become part of the official liturgy that the credibility of neutrality must be maintained and, if possible, continuously strengthened. A closer study of Swedish arguments reveals, however, that the respectability aspect of neutrality has just as often been the focus of concern. The potential peace-

2. Harto Hakovirta, *East-West Conflict and European Neutrality* (New York: Oxford University Press, 1988), p. 26.

3. Ibid., p. 249.

time contributions by a North European neutral have been stressed as a way of justifying the Swedish wartime choice.

Certainly, the relationship between these two resources of peacetime neutrality is complex. Often it is assumed that the respected neutral is also the credible neutral. Thus it follows that one should build respectability so as to strengthen credibility. Strategies to strengthen one dimension do not necessarily enhance the other, however. For example, measures to improve respectability abroad may also serve to undermine the certainty that a self-serving neutrality stand will be pursued during an acute crisis affecting shared values. Similarly, clear articulations of the egocentric objectives of neutrality may help to strengthen its credibility, but they also serve to reduce its respectability both at home and abroad.

Obviously, the Swedish government is faced with two potentially conflicting policy requirements. Ideally, the designated policy line should simultaneouly strengthen both the credibility and the respectability components of neutrality. With usual political skill, a conceptual solution for this balancing act has been found in the formula of the committed neutral. This term conveys a clear signal concerning Sweden's unshakable commitment to neutrality, no matter what the cost in other policy areas. The concept also underscores Sweden's commitment to a just world order, the plight of the weak confronting the strong, the principles of democracy, and the value of human rights. Sometimes, it is even inferred that Sweden's contribution in the latter sphere is contingent upon, or at least facilitated by, its unbending neutrality. The two dimensions—credibility and respectability—would appear, then, to be inseparably intertwined and mutually supportive.

The conceptualization of Sweden as the committed neutral also reflects domestic sentiments. To many Swedes, neutrality is a dogma as embedded in the national character as democracy. To question its utility as a security strategy would be political suicide for any aspiring leader. Like the sacrosanct welfare system, this notion offers protection for a people that has been characterized as obsessed with individual security. Neutrality offers the promise of again escaping the perils of conflict even as the surrounding world crumbles. At the same time, the concept does not merely serve as a means toward such a self-centered security objective but is widely associated with the aspirations to international prestige and national pride as well.

The commitment to a just and equitable world order in many ways reflects the salient features of Swedish domestic life. Clearly, the hope for global understanding, nonviolent solutions to security dilemmas, and adherence to principles of international law and organization are inspired by the comparatively tranquil domestic and regional developments of the last century. The quest for global solidarity parallels the ideals of the influential labor movement. The belief in managed market solutions to international economic problems draws upon successful experiences at home that have combined economic growth with shared affluence. The international bridge-building aspirations reflect the dynamics of national consensus formation, whereby sector demands are transformed into broad coalitions composed of leading parties and interest groups. The domestic sources of Swedish foreign policy are obvious and offer one explanation for its international role as the committed neutral.[4]

4. Bengt Sundelius, "Committing Neutrality in an Antagonistic World," in *Committed Neutral*, ed. Sundelius, pp. 8-9, 11-12; the abstract of the present article is drawn from ibid., pp. 3-4.

Finland:
An Image of Continuity in Turbulent Europe

By PAULI O. JÄRVENPÄÄ

ABSTRACT: In the past, Finland was often regarded as Finlandized, or as a country towing the policy line of its large and powerful neighbor. Today it is offered as a model for the newly emerging European democracies. Neither of these role models fits Finland well; the country's historical, political, and economic development would be hard to emulate. In the process of rapid change in Europe, Finland's situation produces an image of remarkable continuity: the domestic situation is stable, the rate of economic growth continues to be high, and the country's international situation is secure. The European situation as a whole continues to be volatile, however. It is in this overall context of rapid change that Finland will have to chart its course. The main policy issues for the 1990s will be European economic integration, the process of the Conference on Security and Cooperation in Europe, and national defense.

Dr. Pauli O. Järvenpää is the national security adviser in the Ministry of Defense, Helsinki, Finland. He also serves as expert member in the Special Mission of Finland to the Conference on Security and Cooperation in Europe, in Vienna, and as secretary to the Parliamentary Advisory Board for Defense Policy in Helsinki. He holds academic degrees from two U.S. universities, Harvard and Cornell, and has published widely in Finnish, Swedish, and English on arms control, strategic questions, and Nordic security.

A S 1989—or the "year of truth," to borrow Timothy Garton Ash's admirable phrase[1]—was drawing to a close in Europe, many turned to Finland in the hope of finding a model for the future. Over the years, "Finlandization" had, against the often desperate protestations of the Finns themselves, become in the West a catchword depicting a small country succumbing to the will of its large and powerful neighbor. Now, in the beginning of the 1990s, this same country is offered as a model for the newly emerging Central and Eastern European democracies to follow. Finnish-Soviet relations have become a model of "stability and predictability" that no less an authority than Soviet leader Mikhail Gorbachev wants to achieve in international relations everywhere.[2]

But it may be that both of these models miss the point. In the postwar period, Finland has charted its own line of policy, which might be hard to emulate. After World War II, there were three factors that contributed decisively to Finland's internal stability and the positive development of its relationship with the Soviet Union: Finland was never occupied, the Finnish political system remained intact, and the entire population of the territories ceded to the Soviet Union—about 12 percent of the total population—chose resettlement elsewhere in Finland.[3] That gave a basis for independent policies that have molded Finland into what it is today.

The country has never been so prosperous as it is today. National income per capita in 1989 was the third highest in the world, trailing only Switzerland and Japan.[4] According to national opinion polls, the Finns feel themselves physically secure. In internal politics, a wide-ranging consensus has emerged across the previously clear dividing line between right and left.[5] To top it all, the government formed after the parliamentary elections in March 1987 is a coalition between the Conservative Party and the Social Democrats, with a Conservative, Mr. Harri Holkeri, as prime minister.

It is against this background that I examine the situation in Finland. If the 1980s were a decade of steady improvements, how will Finland fare in the 1990s? What are the problems, issue areas, and prospects?

1. Timothy Garton Ash, "Eastern Europe: The Year of Truth," *New York Review of Books,* 15 Feb. 1990.

2. President Mikhail Gorbachev, speech at the Finlandia Hall, Helsinki, 26 Oct. 1989. The speech is printed in *Helsingin sanomat,* 27 Oct. 1989, p. 26. See also Richard A. Bitzinger, *Neutrality for Eastern Europe? An Examination of Possible Western Role Models,* P-7622 (Santa Monica, CA: RAND, 1990).

3. Among studies of political development during the Winter War and in its aftermath, Max Jakobson's *Diplomacy of the Winter War: An Account of the Russo-Finnish War 1939-1940* (Cambridge, MA: Harvard University Press, 1961), has become a classic.

4. According to tentative estimates published in *Helsingin sanomat,* 13 Apr. 1990, p. D-1.

5. See, for example, Pertti Alanen and Tuomas Forsberg, "The Evolution of Opinions about Foreign Policy in Finland from the 1960's till the 1980's," *Yearbook of Finnish Foreign Policy 1988-89* (Helsinki: Finnish Institute of International Affairs, 1989), pp. 29-33.

STRATEGIC CONTEXT

Along with the many changes taking place in Europe, there are some important continuities. One such continuity has to do with Finland's strategic environment.

As one astute observer has pointed out, "Many a basic truth is questioned in today's Europe except one—the importance of geography."[6] That observation is particularly pertinent in the Nordic area. Because the Soviet Union is and will remain the geopolitically dominant nation in the North of Europe, physical and military geographies inextricably link the Soviet Union and the Nordic area in a shared security destiny, regardless of political and ideological preferences. At the same time, through its strategic relationship with the Soviet Union, the United States will remain linked to the security of the high North.

The security context of the Nordic area has in the past decades shown great resilience. For countries of the region, the geostrategic framework continues to define the limits and scope of national security policies. Together with Sweden, Finland forms a neutral cushion between the military alliances in an area that will continue to have a high strategic value to both the Soviet Union and the United States. From the end of World War II until the early 1970s, the Nordic region—particularly its northern parts—was a peripheral area of marginal value to East and West. That ended in the 1970s, as the Soviet Union became a major maritime power and transformed the Kola Peninsula into a tight network of naval and air bases.[7] The United States moved to counter the Soviet forces by pre-positioning supplies and improving air bases for reinforcements from the North Atlantic Treaty Organization (NATO) in northern Norway; by promoting a maritime strategy that envisioned a deployment of the U.S. Navy into deep positions close to the Soviet Union early in a crisis; and by starting to deploy great numbers of sea- and air-launched cruise missiles to saturate the Soviet air defenses in the northwestern theater of operations.[8]

That is a familiar story, but from it flow two important conclusions for Finland. First, it would be hard to imagine a situation in the North where Finland alone would be an object of military aggression. More likely, Finland will not be the main target, but it faces military threat from the danger of being caught up in the middle of a conflict—be it a conflict between what remains of the two military alliances in Europe or directly between the two superpowers. Second, in such a crisis, the most likely areas that will have military significance to the opposing parties will be Finland's airspace; Lapland, as a route of attack, be it by air or

6. Rene Nyberg, "On Finnish Security" (Paper delivered at the Graduate Institute of International Studies, Geneva, 14 Mar. 1990), p. 1.

7. For the most detailed discussion of Soviet bases on the Kola, see Tomas Ries and Johnny Skorve, *Investigating Kola: A Study of Military Bases Using Satellite Photography* (London: Brassey's Defence, 1987).

8. See, for example, Norman Friedman, *The US Maritime Strategy* (London: Jane's Publishing, 1988).

land; and southern Finland, with its vital centers of government, transportation, and communications.[9] These areas might be utilized in operations against a third party or might be hit in order to incapacitate Finnish attempts to resist. Were one side or another to calculate that Finnish territory were available to be used on the cheap, that might legitimize the use of force against Finland. It could then be argued that Finland willfully allowed its territory to be used against the third party or that it would not or would not be able to prevent such use.[10]

The Nordic area, despite its strategic significance, has been a relatively low-tension area. Finland has no unsolved problems with any of the other countries in the area. Its relations in the Nordic family are exemplary, and it has made great, successful efforts to build up its relations with the Soviet Union.[11] Finally, Finland has appreciated other Nordic countries' efforts to lessen tensions in the North of Europe, including Norway's and Denmark's voluntary measures to restrict their alliance commitments and Sweden's policy of armed neutrality. These are the most important elements of the framework of Finland's present strategic position.

9. For a lucid discussion of these points, see Tomas Ries, *Cold Will: The Defence of Finland* (London: Brassey's Defence, 1988), esp. chap. 8, "The Two Currents in Finland's Defence Posture," pp. 222-56.

10. See Jan Klenberg, "The Military Doctrine of Finland," Seminar on Military Doctrine, Conference on Security and Cooperation in Europe, Vienna, 17 Jan. 1990.

11. See Roy Allison, *Finland's Relations with the Soviet Union 1944-84* (New York: Macmillan, 1985).

DEFENSE ISSUES

Finland's military planning begins with the premise that, with reasonable effort, it can build up and maintain a military capability to prevent the use of the country's territory for hostile purposes.[12] As in deterrence in general, this form of deterrence declares that although it may not be able to ensure victory in the traditional sense, it can raise the attacker's costs so that they will be disproportionate compared to the attacker's possible gains. In other words, the aggressor will gain, at best, a Pyrrhic victory.

These axioms are widely accepted and have formed the basis for Finland's defense policy in the postwar period. The same premises are likely to form the basis for defense planning in the 1990s.[13] As so often has been the case, the main question for this decade will not be what should be done, or even how to do it, but, rather,

12. The same conviction is presented in *Sweden's Security Policy: Entering the 90's*, Report by the 1984 Defence Committee, Swedish Official Report Series, Report no. 23, 1985. See also *Svensk säkerhetspolitiken i en föränderlig värld*, Swedish Official Report Series, Report no. 5, 1990.

13. A recent analysis of Finland's security in a changing Europe states the following: "The objective of Finnish security policy is to prevent our country from being drawn into a possible conflict, and to prevent conflicts from spreading to our territory. From the military point of view, the crucial factor is that our neighbours and other countries can rely on Finland's capability to control and defend its territory." See Parliamentary Advisory Board for Defence Policy, *An Assessment of the European Security-Political Situation, Its Development Prospects and Its Impact on Finnish Defence Policy* (Helsinki: Ministry of Defence, 1990), p. 22.

how Finland can afford to do what should be done.[14]

Since the early 1960s Finland has spent about 1.5 percent of its gross national product for defense, or about 5.0 percent of the national budget.[15] The figure 1.5 percent excludes such items of expenditure as the Frontier and Coast Guards, which are administered in peacetime by the Ministry of the Interior; civil defense construction; or money spent on economic preparedness. The last item includes, for example, stockpiles of the most vital imports, such as oil, lubricants, and raw materials. Neither does the defense budget include military pensions or social benefits for the families of servicemen. If all these items were counted, the defense share of the gross national product would be a little over 2.0 percent, a still low but somewhat more respectable figure.[16]

Overall growth rates for defense spending have been comparatively high since the early 1970s. The average real increase per year since 1971-72 has been 3.7 percent. There has also been a relatively high teeth-to-tail ratio: acquisition of new military equipment has been allotted about one-third of the defense budget, which represents an increase of about 10

percentage points compared to the spending figures in the late 1960s.[17]

In terms of priorities, peacetime readiness to maintain surveillance and detect violations has occupied the central position both in the tasks of the Defense Forces and in defense planning. This setting of priorities is closely connected to the threat perception that has been the dominant one in Finland; the most central task is to identify and repel any violator of Finnish territory. In peacetime, it is vital to demonstrate that we have full control over our borders and that we are prepared to repel any violations of territory, by force if necessary.[18] In the 1990s, this same set of priorities will guide defense planning. But how are the basic policy guidelines going to be translated into actual purchases of hardware?

As far as the surveillance capability is concerned, several hardware programs are in progress or have just been completed. For example, a program to modernize medium-range

17. Gustav Hägglund, "Finskt försvar inför 1990-talets utmaningar" (Paper delivered at the Swedish Academy of Military Studies, Stockholm, 10 Oct. 1989), p. 5.

18. These priorities are also expressed in the Act on the Defense Forces of 1974. According to the act, the three main tasks of the Defense Forces are the following: the responsibility for the surveillance of the country's land and sea territory as well as airspace in cooperation with other national authorities; the protection of the country's territorial integrity, by force if necessary; and the defense of the country and its legal system as well as the subsistence and the basic rights of the people. See, for example, Finnish National Defense (Helsinki: General Headquarters Information Section, 1988), p. 16.

14. A fuller treatment of these issues is provided by the present author in his "Technology and Military Doctrine in the Future of Finnish Defense" (Paper, Feb. 1990).

15. The Military Balance (London: International Institute for Strategic Studies, various years). See also Pauli Järvenpää, "Puolustusmenot ja niiden vaihtelu eri maissa," Suomalaiset ja turvallisuuspolitiikka, 1986, p. 73.

16. Järvenpää, "Puolustusmenot ja niiden vaihtelu eri maissa," pp. 70-72.

radars has been completed, and new long-range radars have been purchased, to be installed in the early 1990s.[19] Air Force fighters will be replaced soon, starting in the middle of the 1990s, and the surveillance functions of the aircraft will again be heavily emphasized. In particular, all-weather fighters with a good look-down, shoot-down capability will be sought. Electronic warfare capability will also continue to be a vital part of the air defense surveillance task, and it will get special attention in development plans.[20]

Another area that has received special attention for some time in Finland is the detection of submarine operations. In the special hydroacoustic conditions of the Baltic Sea this task is a particularly demanding one. By the late 1960s, the need to reinforce the antisubmarine warfare (ASW) capability in Finland's southern and southeastern waters was recognized, and measures to boost coastal underwater surveillance and ASW capability were taken. This was done by strengthening two areas in particular: the Coast Artillery was given the responsibility for the infrastructure of the fixed command, control, communications, and intelligence (C³I) and listening-device network, while the Coast Guard provides the mobile forces with new ASW patrol boats. In addition, an extended hydrophone surveillance system was constructed, and it now covers all important channels of approach along the Finnish coastline. This Finnish-designed network of listening devices, supplemented by the Coast Artillery's optical and radar surveillance systems, is already operational in peacetime and in full readiness on a 24-hour basis.[21]

In late 1989, along with the fixed network of surveillance systems, there were more than 60 ships and helicopters, 14 of them in the Coast Guard inventory, that had either dedicated or auxiliary ASW capability.[22] This is one way of signaling that serious efforts are made to keep Finland's coastal waters under Finnish control.

While surveillance capabilities and an ability to react quickly to violations of territorial integrity are essential for maintaining the credibility of national control over one's territory, it is the capability to wage an effective defense that forms the linchpin of the Finnish military effort. For this exacting task the combined efforts of all military services are needed, even of those elements of national defense whose main task is surveillance. For the task of deterring or repelling an attack, the on-line items for maritime defense in the 1990s will be a third flotilla of fast-attack boats equipped with missiles purchased from Sweden. Mines are effective weapons in Finnish conditions, and influence mines are now being purchased, following a reinterpretation of the Paris peace treaty stipulations in 1983.[23] Coastal artil-

19. *Jane's Defense Weekly*, 3 Sept. 1989, p. 402.

20. For details, see *Jane's Defense Weekly*, 23 Apr. 1988, p. 767.

21. For a more detailed discussion, see Ries, *Cold Will*, pp. 245-46, 318-42.

22. The author's estimate, based on such public sources as *The Military Balance 1989-90* (London: International Institute of Strategic Studies, 1989).

23. According to Article 17 of the Paris Peace Treaty of 1947, "Finland may not pos-

lery has been modernized, and it will be equipped with the same missiles that are carried by the fast-attack missile boats. Air defense purchases are concentrated on air-to-air missiles for the new fighters and on surface-to-air missiles to provide cover for the ground forces and selected point targets.[24]

The bulk of modernization for the task of repelling an attack is, however, directed at ground forces. The size of the Finnish reserves with basic military training is large by any standard. A total of about 1.1 million men under the age of 60 have received military training through general conscription. It is clear that all of these reservists could not be used —for instance, a portion would be needed to maintain the vital functions of society in a time of crisis.

By the late 1970s it was also becoming very clear that, barring a drastic increase in the level of defense spending, not all of the usable reserves could be equipped to the exacting standards of the modern battle-

field.[25] As a result, in the early 1980s part of the main forces was separated for special attention. Called the fast deployment forces (FDF), it was to be given priority over the rest of the reserves. The number of these troops would be limited to 250,000 men, and they would receive the best equipment. The strength of modern units thus formed would be 2 armored brigades and 11 infantry brigades, called Brigade 90s. The remaining 14 brigades would have older equipment, and they would be less mobile than the Brigade 90s. In addition to these two types of formations, there would be hundreds of independent battalions and companies.[26]

The principal idea in creating the FDF was that a force tailored to the specific requirements of Finnish conditions was needed. The FDF can be mobilized partially or fully, depending on the level of perceived threat, to demonstrate Finland's will and capability to safeguard its national integrity in all possible contingencies. When fully mobilized, the FDF would draw about half of its strength from the ground forces, while the rest of the troops would belong to the other services, including the support troops.[27]

THE ARMS CONTROL CONTEXT

In addition to attempting to build up a viable defense capability, Finland has sought to promote the relaxation of tensions in Europe. Two such

sess, construct or carry out trials with any atomic weapon, any self-propelled or guided missiles or apparatus connected with their discharge (other than torpedos . . .), sea mines or torpedos of non-contact types... submarines or other submersible craft, motor torpedo boats, or specialized types of assault craft." The restrictions concerning missiles and influence mines have been removed. In 1963 "defensive" missiles were permitted, and in 1983 influence mines were allowed. See, for example, Ries, *Cold Will*, pp. 177-78, 257.

24. For point air defense, the Crotale NG missile system, built by the French Thomson-CSF company in cooperation with American LTV Missiles and Electronics, is being purchased. See Gerard Turbe, "Crotale NG Multi-Sensor Guided Missile System," *International Defense Review*, June 1989, pp. 783-85.

25. See *Report of the Third Parliamentary Defence Committee*, Committee Report no. 1, Helsinki, 1981.
26. See Mauri Mikkola, "Maavoimavoittoinen järjestelmä," *Ruotuväki*, 4 June 1989, pp. 24-25.
27. Ibid., p. 24.

policies will be discussed here. First, Finland has initiated regional security arrangements. Second, it has been able to provide technical competence in certain fields related to arms control and disarmament.[28]

The establishment of nuclear weapons free zones is an arms control measure that represents a geographical approach to solving some of the security problems created by the existence of nuclear weapons. The Nordic area is one geographical region where a zonal idea might work. The Finnish proposal for a nuclear weapons free zone in Northern Europe was first presented in 1963, by Urho Kekkonen, then president of Finland. The ideas were reintroduced and broadened in another speech by President Kekkonen in May 1978 in Stockholm.[29]

What is most interesting in the Finnish proposal is not so much its present-day practical feasibility but its long-term security-political goals. First, the Nordic region adjoins strategic areas of immense importance. Those areas have, for example, been mentioned as a potential target for what has been termed warning shots by using nuclear detonations. It has also been argued that military operations in the North could lead to nu-

clear war through a process of rapid escalation from conventional to nuclear warfare. "Inadvertent nuclear war," to use Barry Posen's term, could occur in the high North.[30] It could occur because, in the sea area surrounding northern Scandinavia, it would not be easy to make a sharp distinction between conventional operations against conventional targets, on the one hand, and conventional operations against nuclear-capable targets, on the other. Military logic might, in a tense crisis, then take us down the "slippery slope of escalation"—to use the term Thomas Schelling coined long ago—without anybody really wanting to escalate.[31]

Again, the actual fact of what might happen in a real situation is less relevant here than the principle involved. It is impossible, of course, to know in detail what a real crisis would look like. What is undeniable is that it would be impossible to distinguish various weapons for targeting purposes—for example, submarines that carry submarine-launched ballistic missiles from submarines that are not so equipped.[32] Also, communications in deep crises would probably be hampered, and decision makers would have to make their crucial decisions in a relatively short period of time under great uncertainty. Inad-

---

28. For a more complete discussion, see Pauli O. Järvenpää, "Finland," in *The Missing Link: West European Neutrals and Regional Security*, ed. Richard E. Bissell and Curt Gasteyger (Durham, NC: Duke University Press, 1990), pp. 42-58.

29. A speech by President Urho Kekkonen at the Swedish Institute of International Affairs, Stockholm, 8 May 1978, reprinted in English in *Yearbook of Finnish Foreign Policy 1978* (Helsinki: Finnish Institute of International Affairs, 1978), pp. 64-66.

30. Barry Posen, "Inadvertent Nuclear War? Escalation and NATO's Northern Flank," *International Security*, 7(2):28-54 (1982). See also Desmond Ball, "Nuclear War at Sea," *International Security*, 10(3) (Winter 1985-86).

31. Thomas Schelling, *The Strategy of Conflict* (Cambridge, MA: Harvard University Press, 1960), esp. "The Threat of Inadvertent War," pp. 188-90.

32. See Ball, "Nuclear War at Sea."

vertent escalation could indeed result from any military operation in the North.

Whatever might be the actual outcome of such a crisis in the Nordic area, it is clear that it is in everybody's interests to keep tensions there at the lowest possible level. A nuclear weapons free zone established in the region would lower incentives for unintended escalation. It would be important to know in those crucial moments of very severe crisis that at least one geographic area would not be the site of escalation.

In peacetime, a nuclear weapons free zone would serve as a sort of political firebreak, or as an area contractually free of nuclear weapons. It is true, of course, that nuclear weapons might be introduced into the proscribed area in war, and a nuclear weapons free zone might, in any case, be targeted by nuclear weapons from far outside the zone.[33] But such objections do not invalidate the scheme, since they do not really address the predicament for which the Kekkonen proposal was designed. It was meant, in language familiar from the Conference on Security and Cooperation in Europe (CSCE), as a "confidence-building measure," which would have the purpose of lowering incentives for introducing the use of nuclear weapons in situations where it is in everybody's interests not to cross the nuclear threshold but where the adversaries fear preemption by the other side.

It certainly would be in the interests of nuclear powers to help deter a desperate gamble on preemption in the northern regions of Scandinavia and the adjacent waters. From the viewpoint of the Nordic countries, it would be important to know that there would be no pretexts for the nuclear states to introduce nuclear weapons, their launchers, or their support systems into the area. A nuclear weapons free zone would, therefore, capitalize on a common interest, shared by all countries in the Nordic area and other states with security interests in the wider geographical region of Northern Europe.

With the likelihood that the use of nuclear weapons will decrease in Europe, the subject of nuclear weapons free zones no longer creates the kind of interest in the Nordic area that it did in the early 1980s. But a working group of officials, appointed by the Nordic governments in 1987, is examining the preconditions for such a zone in the Nordic region. From the Finnish point of view, it is still important to guarantee the existing nuclear-weapon-free status of the area.[34]

A highly advanced industrial society like Finland can perform some special functions on other questions of arms control. Yet, a small country has to be selective and carefully choose areas of interest, in order to maximize its impact. Finland has focused on research on ways to verify chemical agents in the last twenty years.

33. See Johan Jørgen Holst, "The Challenge from Nuclear Weapons and Nuclear Weapon-free Zones," *Bulletin of Peace Proposals,* 1981, no. 3.

34. See Parliamentary Advisory Board for Defence Policy, *Assessment of the European Security-Political Situation,* p. 12.

As verification has been one of the greatest obstacles to the conclusion of a comprehensive ban on chemical weapons, the Finnish Ministry for Foreign Affairs established a project on the verification of chemical disarmament in 1971. Experimental work, initiated in 1973, has centered on the development of analytical techniques required for verification. The goal of the project has been to create a verification capability that would cover all verification needs: nonproduction, destruction of stockpiles, and alleged use. A technical capacity has been developed and the necessary field equipment has been acquired for the verification of chemical agents. The Finnish goal is to create a chemical-weapons-control capability on a national basis, which, if the need arises, could be put to international use. This project has permitted Finland to be present as an observer at the sessions of the Conference on Disarmament in Geneva.

Another case worth mentioning here is a seismological verification capability being created in Finland, in cooperation with several other countries. In 1976, the Geneva Committee on Disarmament set up an ad hoc group of governmental experts to explore the possibility of international cooperation in the detection and identification of seismic events. Finland has participated in that expert group and is also participating in the network of seismic verification stations that has been built up around the world. Today, the network consists of some 50 stations located in different parts of the globe. There are two registering multipoint stations in Finland, as well as two single seismographic stations that belong to the international network. Such a system of verification of seismological events is of utmost importance if an agreement is reached on a comprehensive nuclear test ban treaty.[35]

The special significance of the Finnish contributions to arms control outlined here does not, of course, stem from any lack of technical know-how or a shortage of resources on the part of other countries to carry out such arms-control-related research by themselves. The others, however, may often be reluctant to do it in such a way that the findings would be openly available. Neutral countries like Finland, by contrast, are able to enter the picture with high-caliber research in some very specialized areas of verification; that way, the kind of information that otherwise might end up in the vaults of the great powers' ministries of defense becomes open to all. It is only through such technological research capabilities and imagination and political agility that opportunities to find areas of contribution—cornering specialized markets —can be exploited.

ECONOMIC ISSUES

On their way to the 1990s, the Finnish people have acquired, without much conscious self-analysis, a new image of themselves. They no longer feel that *"on maamme köyhä,*

35. For a good discussion of the problems, see Farooq Hussein, "The Future of Arms Control, Part IV, The Impact of Weapons Test Restrictions," *Adelphi Paper,* Spring 1981, no. 165. See also C. Paul Robinson and Les Paldy, "Substantial Progress in Nuclear Testing Talks: Verification Protocols Nearing Completion," *NATO Review,* Feb. 1990, no. 1, pp. 17-19.

siksi jää" ("poor is our land and will stay so forever"), as they moan in their national anthem, which was composed in the 1840s. On the contrary, as recent opinion polls show, they feel themselves fortunate and privileged to be living in Finland.[36]

One factor contributing to that new image is the newly acquired sense of wealth and prosperity that the Finns now feel. From its position in the 1940s as a badly damaged and impoverished country paying off enormous war reparations, Finland has gradually become a capital-exporting country, and about 120,000 people now work for Finnish multinational companies all over the world. At the same time, Finnish investments abroad amounted to over $10 billion in the 1980s.[37]

This process of the internationalization of Finnish industries and capital is reflected in Finland's attitudes toward economic integration. Until recently, Finnish integration strategy could be expressed in two concepts: adaptation and exclusion.[38] It has been the need to adapt to the most important market area and the fear of exclusion from it that have driven Finland's approach to European integration. These same elements form, of course, the basis for Finland's integration strategy in the 1990s, but now the policy is more one of active participation and less of passive adaptation.

The new strategy is two-pronged. First, Finland seeks to strengthen national structures and national industries, through its own efforts, to meet future challenges. These are best met by promoting a highly competitive national economic structure. One way to do that, as the Finnish government's white paper of November 1988 recognizes, is to "achieve as far as possible the same competitive advantages for Finnish companies as other companies in Western Europe enjoy."[39]

Second, in its approach to negotiating with the European Community (EC), Finland relies heavily on the European Free Trade Association (EFTA) card. The aim is not to apply for membership in the Community but to create with the EC what in the 1984 Luxembourg meeting came to be called a European Economic Space (EES). For the EFTA countries, including Finland, the EES promises to be a particularly interesting concept, since it offers the benefits of economic integration with the EC in an 18-nation area with few foreign policy problems even for the neutral EFTA countries. For Finland, the EES presents a suitable way of advancing its own interests and of strengthening EFTA. Although the EC countries have

36. In an opinion poll conducted in 1989, more than 8 of 10 agreed with the statement that it is "a good fortune and privilege to be born a Finn." *Finnish Gallup Reports*, Mar. 1989.

37. *Helsingin sanomat*, 21 Apr. 1990, p. 75.

38. See Esko Antola, "The Finnish Integration Strategy: Adaptation with Restrictions," *Facing the Change in Europe: EFTA Countries' Integration Strategies*, ed. Kari Möttölä and Heikki Patomäki (Helsinki: Finnish Institute of International Affairs, 1989), pp. 55-63.

39. Pertti Salolainen, Minister for Foreign Trade, *Report to Parliament by the Goverment on Finland's Stance on the Economic Integration of Western Europe*, 1 Nov. 1988, reprinted in *Facing the Change in Europe*, ed. Möttölä and Patomäki, pp. 63-66. The quote appears on p. 64.

generally been less enthusiastic about the EES than have been the EFTA countries, the Community has taken a positive interest in the concept. The Community view was expressed by Mr. Martin Bangemann, then president of the Council of the European Community, as follows: "It is our task to create a large and dynamic European Economic Space out of the EC and the EFTA countries. Our cooperation will give an even broader base to the European economy."[40] It is in this context, strengthening Europe in the world economic competition with the United States and Japan, that the EES looks most interesting to the EC countries. It is also in this context that the EFTA countries could travel the "third way" to European economic integration, as the president of the European Community Commission, Mr. Jacques Delors, has called it.

In its November 1988 white paper to Parliament, the Finnish government was firm on the question of Finland's membership in the EC: "Membership in the EC is incompatible with Finland's policy of neutrality, thus she has no intention of seeking a membership of the Communities."[41] Discussion of a possible Finnish membership is no longer as taboo as it was just a few years ago, however. One reason for the change in the climate for discussion is the fear that the EFTA card is not being played seriously enough by the other EFTA countries. If Switzerland and Sweden follow the Austrian example and seek full EC membership, Finland does not want to be the only one left out. There are other reasons as well. The difficulties in Soviet-Finnish trade—some relating to the nature of the barter trade, others to the general disarray of the Soviet economy at the moment—have made Western Europe an indisputably major market for Finland. In 1986, still more than 20 percent of Finnish exports ended up in the Soviet Union. By 1989, that figure had decreased to 14.5 percent.[42] In Soviet-Finnish trade, oil, oil products, and natural gas continue to be the most important import commodities.

The changed Soviet attitude toward European economic integration has also altered the atmosphere of the EC debate in Finland. In all earlier instances of integration, Finland has been very careful to extend the same trade privileges to Soviet goods as it has received through Western integration. For example, having granted most-favored-nation treatment to the Soviet Union in the bilateral trade agreement of 1947, Finland in 1961 extended it the same tariff privileges as to Finnish EFTA partners. Similarly, in 1973 the concessions made to the EC countries through the agreement between Finland and the European Economic Community were also granted to the Soviet Union. Furthermore, in 1973 Finland concluded agreements of trade liberalization with most of the other members of the European Coun-

40. *Helsingin sanomat,* 13 Mar. 1990, p. D-1.
41. Möttölä and Patomäki, *Facing the Change in Europe,* p. 65.

42. *EFTA Trade 1986* (Geneva: European Free Trade Association, 1987), tab. 8; *Helsingin sanomat,* 13 Mar. 1990, p. D-4.

cil for Mutual Economic Assistance.[43] Now that the Soviet Union and other East European countries are actively seeking to improve their economic relations with Western Europe, the increasing integration of West European neutrals with the economies of the EC countries seems to raise few eyebrows in East European capitals.

PROSPECTS

In the beginning of the 1990s, a general overview of Finland's situation in Europe produces an image of remarkable continuity. No fundamental changes of policy direction are in the offing, and the nation appears to be more at ease with itself than ever. One is almost inclined to agree with a seasoned observer of the Finnish scene that "Finland has become, politically, one of the most boring countries in Europe, probably second only to Switzerland."[44]

This certainly holds true for Finnish domestic politics. One would be hard put to find a source of great discontent in the society even over a time span of a decade. In general terms, the same is true of the strategic environment. As in the past, it seems to be in the best interests of the superpowers to try to keep the Nordic area a region of calm and stability. At the same time, however, there are processes at work that will keep strategic interest focused on the northern parts of Europe. The driving force behind this interest is modern technology: the growing vulnerability of the nuclear ballistic missile submarines, the renaissance of the air-breathing leg of the strategic triad, and the great proliferation of cruise missiles.[45] They all have a common denominator: all these developments are prone to increase the relative importance of the high North.

Paradoxically, emerging arms control agreements might have some unexpected results from the point of view of Northern Europe. In fact, instead of making it easier to cope with the long shadow of military power, they might produce specific problems, which may result in drawing Northern Europe further into potential tensions in superpower strategic relations.

Furthermore, the eventual outcome of the talks in Vienna on conventional forces in Europe might not be such an unmitigated blessing for Northern Europe.[46] Since the eventual outcome is unknown, firm conclusions cannot be drawn. The conventional-forces agreement will, of course, greatly improve the international climate, but there is a strong possibility that the shape of the re-

43. See the discussion in Allison, *Finland's Relations with the Soviet Union 1944-84*, pp. 112-26.

44. Max Jakobson, "Relazioni est-ovest un punto di vista Finland" (Paper delivered at the Centro di Studi per la Conciliazione Internazionale, Rome, 5 Nov. 1987), p. 21.

45. See, for example, R. James Woolsey, "U.S. Strategic Force Decisions for the 1990's," *Washington Quarterly*, Winter 1989, pp. 69-83.

46. For details of the emerging CFE agreement, see *CFE-negotiation on Conventional Armed Forces in Europe* (Washington, DC: Arms Control and Disarmament Agency, Office of Public Affairs, Mar. 1990).

maining military forces will be leaner but meaner in the areas geographically close to the Nordic neutrals.

NATO is already openly talking about its plans for harmonization. A plan by the Supreme Headquarters Allied Command Europe to shuffle hardware between the alliance partners after an eventual Vienna accord was announced in September by the Supreme Allied Commander Europe, General John Galvin. Under this scheme, a NATO ally with an advanced weapons system that it is reluctant to scrap could transfer the hardware to prevent its destruction under quotas dictated by the Vienna agreement. There are also certain signs that the Soviets are preparing to exchange older equipment for modern hardware within their forces. What we might be faced with is not the old, largely discredited sausage theory but a more modern application of qualitative sausage theory, with, after deep cuts in the numbers of weapons systems, the quality of the remaining systems radically improved on the alliances' flanks.[47]

In terms of defense issues, the most challenging question facing Finland can thus be formulated as follows: How can a neutral country steer a reasonable course between two formidable alternatives, between the Scylla of high requirements for national defense and the Charybdis of soaring prices of modern high-

47. The "sausage theory" refers to an idea that when one squeezes a sausage in the middle, the meat gets packed toward the ends. In other words, when armaments are thinned out in Central Europe, the relative weight of the flanks will increase.

technology weapons systems? Finland is, of course, not the only country facing that predicament. Rapid advances in weapons technology will be one problem complicating defense planning in all countries, large or small. It is, however, a particularly vexing problem for a country that has traditionally minimized rather than maximized its military spending.

In foreign policy, the issues of European economic integration and the CSCE process will most likely dominate the political scene in Finland. It is particularly important to underline the fact that, within the CSCE process, Finland has been able to contribute to the neutral and nonaligned view. On all major issues these countries have been able to cooperate. It has not always been easy and compromises have been necessary, but it has happened. Although the national viewpoints can be expected to gain importance, when the negotiations get closer to the core of each country's special security concerns, we can expect that the cooperation between the European neutral and nonaligned countries that has marked the CSCE process will continue. It is also possible that the number of countries involved will grow, with the addition of such countries as Czechoslovakia and Hungary.

In sum, during the past year momentous changes have taken place in the Soviet bloc. These developments might create a completely new security and political constellation in Europe. In that process of change, Finland's position seems to be well established and stable. However, the

European situation as a whole continues to be highly volatile. In the past, a consistent foreign policy and a viable defense capability have been the trademarks of Finland's national security policy. These same policy tools can be expected to serve the country well, even in a rapidly changing international situation.

Continuity and Change in Icelandic Security and Foreign Policy

By GUNNAR GUNNARSSON

ABSTRACT: This article addresses the security policy of Iceland and also foreign economic policy in terms of the changes its development may imply for Iceland's external relations. Iceland has concluded that there is no reason to change its security arrangement during the present transitional period in East-West relations. Looking further ahead, it appears fairly certain that if NATO remains intact, Iceland will want to stay in it. For the short term, there is no reason to believe that Iceland would want to make any changes to its defense agreement with the United States. Iceland's participation in the undertaking to establish a European Economic Space will, if negotiations succeed, imply a substantial change in the country's foreign policy and lead to much closer integration with Western Europe. The question of European Community membership is, however, not on the agenda and is not likely to be soon, but, in the longer run, it cannot be excluded. During the postwar period, Iceland has consistently pursued good relations with Western Europe and the United States. However the external situation will evolve, Iceland will prefer a policy that aims at a balanced relationship with both.

Gunnar Gunnarsson has been working as an adviser in the Ministry for Foreign Affairs in Reykjavík since 1989. He is on leave from the University of Iceland, where he has been assistant professor of international politics since 1987 and was lecturer in international politics from 1978 to 1987. He has also been director of the Icelandic Commission on Security and International Affairs. His publications have been in the fields of Icelandic security and foreign policy, naval strategy, arms control, and European security.

WITH a population of around 250,000, Iceland is by far the smallest of the Nordic countries. Socially and economically the country is, however, quite comparable. The last century has been a period of rapid social and economic change during which Iceland has developed from a poor country of farmers and fishermen into a modern society with a high standard of living. Its economy is highly dependent on foreign trade, with fish, the main export product, accounting for up to three-quarters of exports.

In one respect Iceland differs from most other states in the international community; it does not have armed forces. The basic framework of Icelandic security policy—membership in the North Atlantic Treaty Organization (NATO) and a defense agreement with the United States concluded in 1951—should be viewed in that context. The present period of transition in East-West relations away from the Cold War and the process of restructuring the European security order obviously raises questions about the implications for the future of security policy.

Another dimension of change bears on Iceland's foreign economic policy. During the last decade Iceland's dependence on trade with the European Community (EC) has increased substantially relative to the past, in particular after the entry of Portugal and Spain in 1986. Iceland became a member of the European Free Trade Association (EFTA) in 1970 and entered into a free-trade agreement with the EC in 1972 and is now participating in the EFTA-EC process of creating a European Economic Space. Success in these negotiations would involve a much greater integration of the country in Europe. Although EC membership is not on the agenda, it cannot be excluded in the long run.

The importance of fishing for the economy has given high priority to a policy of securing control of the rich fishing grounds around the country. Thus Iceland extended its fishing zone to 12 miles in 1958, to 50 miles in 1972, and to 200 miles in 1975. These measures caused serious political disputes, in particular the cod wars with Britain. Securing control of fishing grounds has been one of the three major issue areas in Icelandic foreign policy since World War II. The country has succeeded in acquiring the control it has aimed for. The issue now belongs to the past, except for certain claims made by Iceland in northern waters on the basis of the Law of the Sea Convention.

For the present and the near future, the issue areas of security policy and foreign economic policy remain important. This article focuses mainly upon the former but also addresses foreign economic policy in terms of the changes its development may imply for Iceland's external relations.

THE FORMATIVE YEARS OF
SECURITY POLICY

NATO membership and the Defense Agreement with the United States of 1951 have justifiably been described as the cornerstones of Icelandic foreign policy. A short historical background of the formation of Iceland's security policy is thus in order as perspective for the country's present policies.

In 1918, when Iceland gained independence from Denmark, a policy of eternal neutrality was declared. This policy was founded not least on the intense nationalism that identified neutrality with sovereignty.[1] But it was also based on the evaluation that distance from other countries provided some measure of security. This had proven to be the case during World War I, when the area of conflict did not extend to the shores of Iceland. An additional factor was that the Atlantic Ocean was dominated by the British Royal Navy, providing for indirect protection.

Technological developments, in particular the rise of air power, had changed these conditions by the start of World War II. On 10 May 1940, a month after Germany had occupied Norway and Denmark, Iceland was occupied by Britain. The occupation was in large measure a preventive action by Britain, which feared that Iceland would be seized by Germany. This fear was not unfounded, as it is known that Hitler proposed the capture of Iceland after Norway had been occupied.

The British occupation was not unexpected. On the same day that Denmark was occupied, the Icelandic government received notification from Britain that it had decided to prevent the seizure of Iceland by German forces. In accord with its policy of neutrality, Iceland's government formally protested the occupation. At

1. Thor Whitehead,"Icelandic Security Policies 1945-1951" (Paper delivered at the Nordic Historical Conference, Reykjavík, Aug. 1987). This section is partly based on that paper.

the same time, however, it issued a plea to the Icelandic population to regard British troops as guests, explaining that the occupation was a precautionary measure. In 1941, when British troops were needed elsewhere, the Icelandic government suspended neutrality and, at the request of Britain, asked for military protection by the United States, which at that time had not yet entered the war.

The war brought about a great change in the lives of Icelanders. Its social impact may be indicated by the fact that when the number of troops reached its peak, in 1943, there were about 50,000 troops while the Icelandic population numbered only about 140,000. An economic boom based on Allied expenditures and high market prices for exported fish products followed in the wake of the war. The large residual valuta reserves enabled Icelanders to start on a major program to modernize the fishing industry in 1945.

The war brought the strategic importance of the country to light. Its importance for Allied control of the North Atlantic was a decisive factor in the war. Furthermore, serving as a bridgehead between the North American and European continents, Iceland greatly facilitated the transit of combat and transport aircraft to Europe.

Based largely on the war experience, the United States concluded even before the end of the war that there would be a need for military facilities in Iceland in the postwar period. A proposal put forward by the United States in the autumn of 1945 for a long-term lease, lasting 99 years, on bases met with definite opposition in Iceland and was turned down by the government. In 1946 the so-called Keflavík Agreement was concluded, by which the United States acquired the right to use Keflavík airport to support its presence in Germany. On the basis of the agreement, about 600 U.S. civilian employees operated the Keflavík airport until the Defense Agreement was concluded in 1951.

When the republic was established in 1944, a return to neutrality was the prevalent concept in Iceland with respect to postwar security policy. It was hoped that membership in the United Nations would guarantee security. By the time the Keflavík Agreement was signed, the picture was less clear. The concept of neutrality was still attractive to many but not as much as in the past. The agreement reflected this change and constituted the first step to align with the Western powers.

A further step toward closer ties with the West was taken with the reception of Marshall aid in 1948, and in 1949 Iceland became a founding member of NATO. The decision to enter NATO was closely connected with the same decisions made by Norway and Denmark. Icelanders had been concerned about the plans to form a Scandinavian Defense Union in early 1949. They did not think that Iceland could enter such an alliance, as the latter would not have the capacity to provide security for the country, due to the distances involved. At the same time, Iceland was concerned about isolation from the Scandinavian countries. It is very

doubtful that Iceland would have entered NATO if Denmark and Norway had not. Other major factors involved were the previously mentioned realization that distances did not provide for any degree of security because of developments in military technology and the uncertainty of the international situation in the immediate postwar years.

Iceland entered NATO on the precondition that membership would not entail a commitment to stationing foreign troops or military facilities during peacetime. The Defense Agreement of 1951 between Iceland and United States was entered into after a gradual change in threat perceptions on the part of the political elite in Iceland, which also corresponded with a change in popular attitudes. The main reason for this was the perception of a dangerous world situation created by the Korean War.

All the major decisions that paved the way from neutrality to alignment with the West caused political controversy in Iceland. Membership in NATO was much more controversial than the Defense Agreement; the latter did not meet as much opposition as the discussion of U.S. proposals for bases in 1945-46. There is a likely twofold explanation. On the one hand, neutrality no longer had the support it did earlier, probably due to the international situation at the time. On the other hand, Americans had been stationed in the country for several years after the war on the basis of the Keflavík Agreement of 1946, and this had not caused the problems that many had initially feared.

STRATEGIC CONTEXT
AND DEFENSE

The strategic importance of the country has increased rather than diminished since World War II. Iceland's strategic importance can be seen in its central position in the Atlantic. The North Atlantic has, since the beginning of the 1960s, become an increasing focus for the central strategic interests of the superpowers. This is mainly a result of two major developments: the advent of the ballistic-missile submarine and the expanded Soviet naval capabilities deployed to the Northern Fleet on the Kola Peninsula.

Strategically, the North Atlantic area may be seen as being split into two main regions, the area north of the Greenland-Iceland-United Kingdom gap (the GIUK gap) and the area south of the gap. The northern region—the Norwegian Sea and the Barents Sea—has become a focal point of the strategic interests at stake. This reflects its position as a major operating area of ballistic-missile submarines, while also being the principal domain of Soviet naval power in the Atlantic.

The main sea lines of communication across the Atlantic are in the southern region. Depending on the duration of a war in Europe, the sea lines could play a role similar to their role in the first and second world wars. Their defense has thus been of major concern to NATO, in order to secure reinforcements and resupply operations from the United States to Europe. As assessed by NATO, the Soviet Northern Fleet is the principal threat to the sea lines—in particular

its attack submarines and bomber force. It is primarily in that connection that Iceland's strategic position should be viewed. The GIUK gap constitutes a choke point through which the Soviet navy would have to pass for operations in the Atlantic. NATO strategy would aim to prevent Soviet transit by erecting an air, surface, and subsurface barrier in the GIUK gap. It can be argued that Iceland's central position in the gap places it in a unique position as a basing area for the conduct of sea control operations in the Atlantic. Its location allows antisubmarine warfare and air defense forces to operate with a high degree of efficiency in covering large areas of the seas in the North. Such importance is attached to Iceland in this respect that it has widely been seen as the linchpin in the defense of the North Atlantic.[2]

On the basis of the Defense Agreement of 1951, the United States has responsibility for defense of the country. With the exception of a small base with approximately 100 personnel located at Höfn, on the southeastern coast, the U.S. military presence in Iceland is concentrated at Keflavík. There are radar facilities at Höfn, but these are operated by Icelandic personnel. The military personnel at Keflavík number around 3000, mostly from the U.S. Navy and Air Force. Antisubmarine warfare and air defense are the base's primary missions. Submarine and surface surveillance are carried out by a squadron of eight Orion P-3C mari-

2. See Bert H. Cooper, *Maritime Roles for Land-Based Aviation*, Report no. 83-151 F (Washington, DC: Congressional Research Service, 1983).

time patrol aircraft, aided by localization data on submarines from a system of listening devices in the GIUK gap. A Dutch maritime patrol aircraft has also been stationed at Keflavík since 1985. Air defense consists of 18 F-15 fighter bombers, aided by ground-based radars and by two aircraft with airborne warning and control systems. During crisis or war, Iceland would be reinforced with fighter aircraft and antisubmarine-warfare aircraft as well as U.S. Army units responsible for ground defense.[3]

THE CONDUCT OF SECURITY POLICY AND CURRENT ISSUES

Although security policy has been supported by the majority of the Icelandic population during most of the postwar period, it should be borne in mind that dependence on a U.S. base for the defense of the country has, from a political point of view, not been considered either a particularly desirable or a permanent solution. It is a choice based on the lack of other realistic alternatives. The only alternative security arrangement considered to be open to Iceland, unarmed nonalignment, has not been regarded for some time as a policy that could secure the country's independence.

At the same time that security policy has enjoyed majority political support, it has been controversial in postwar Icelandic politics. The focus

3. On the Keflavík base, see Gunnar Gunnarsson, *The Keflavík Base: Plans and Projects* (Reykjavík: Icelandic Commission on Security and International Affairs, 1987); Albert Jónsson, *Iceland, NATO and the Keflavík Base* (Reykjavík: Icelandic Commission on Security and International Affairs, 1989).

of the controversy has, in contrast to 1949, essentially been on the Keflavík base rather than NATO membership. Icelandic governments have twice declared—in 1956-58 and 1971-74—that they intended to terminate the Defense Agreement. The policy was not carried out in either instance, apparently due to lack of consensus within the coalition governments concerned once they had taken office. It should be noted in this context that a gradual lessening of the controversy has been evident during the 1980s. In particular, the Keflavík base has been a remarkably low-key issue since 1985.

The most notable aspect of Icelandic security policy has been the effort to reduce friction concerning the issue in domestic politics. The principal approach has been to try to reduce the visibility of the American presence in Iceland. Thus American base personnel have their homes in the base area with strict rules regarding movements outside it. In 1978, when the restrictions were eased, it was clearly demonstrated that the restrictions are a necessary measure. The protests that followed extended to the whole political spectrum and resulted in the reinstatement of the previous order within a week. Furthermore, on the basis of a bilateral agreement with the United States, since 1974 restrictions have been put on manpower levels, limiting the number of base personnel to around 3000.

The rather unpleasant measure of having strict rules with respect to the movement of base personnel outside the base area may best be understood in view of the fact that Iceland has a population of 250,000. If one includes the families of those serving in the Iceland Defence Force, there are around 5000 Americans living at the Keflavík base. In proportion to its population, this would compare with 85,000 people being stationed in Norway and 5 million in the United States! The potential social impact seems rather obvious and was also a cause of friction during the period 1951-54, when the restrictions on movement did not apply.

The base television station used to be an issue of substantial controversy, as its signal could be received throughout the southwestern part of Iceland, where more than half the population lives. It was for some years the only television station available to Icelanders, who did not acquire television of their own until 1966. From the late 1960s, the base television was gradually restricted, and in 1974 it was completely confined to the base area.

As to military aspects of the base, the ban on stationing nuclear weapons on Icelandic soil deserves a special note. This restraint has not been as well known outside Iceland as have the nuclear weapons policies of Denmark and Norway. Statements on the issue have, however, repeatedly been made by all Icelandic foreign ministers since 1964, and it was reiterated in a resolution by the Althing, the legislature, in 1985. The policy with respect to nuclear weapons also extends to port visits by warships. This is not comparable, however, to the policy of New Zealand, as Icelandic authorities assume that the policy is respected by its NATO allies

and thus do not require a confirmation that ships do not actually carry nuclear weapons.

A matter that caused some friction in this respect during the last decade was the U.S. policy neither to confirm nor to deny the presence of nuclear weapons anywhere. Documents and statements by U.S. authorities have, however, definitely confirmed that there are no nuclear weapons stationed in Iceland, and hence it can be assumed that the policy has been respected. A comparable policy on chemical weapons was announced by the Icelandic government in 1986.[4]

With regard to military and defense matters, Iceland has been inactive rather than active in the conduct of security policy. This is probably due, to a large extent, to the unarmed status of the country and the general attitude of Icelanders, who tend to regard military affairs as something strange and alien—a phenomenon that may be explained by the fact that the country has been largely disarmed since the sixteenth century.

This attitude has been undergoing a change in the last decade, and since 1985 it has been the policy of Icelandic governments to become more actively involved in NATO, in particular with regard to military affairs. An example of this is that new radars in the country are being manned by Icelandic personnel. An increased involvement of this kind opens up the question of whether Iceland might

4. For further information on Icelandic nuclear weapons policy, see Gunnar Gunnarsson, "Icelandic Security Policy," in *European Security beyond the Year 2000*, ed. L. Reychler and R. Rudney (New York: Praeger, 1987).

eventually establish an armed force. That seems doubtful, to say the least. On entering NATO, one of the reservations made was that membership would not entail an obligation to establish an armed force. A proposal put forward and debated during the 1950s to establish a home guard seems to have had no chance of being adopted. Since then, the issue has not been debated and does not seem likely to arise.

In the field of arms control, arms control at sea has been receiving increased attention by Icelandic governments in recent years. The interest in this issue has been particularly pronounced by the present Icelandic government, which took office in the autumn of 1988. According to Foreign Minister Jón Baldvin Hannibalsson,

It derives from the geostrategic location of the country that if there is any one area of arms control that is more important to Icelanders than others, it is arms control at sea. Our interests in this area are so obvious that they hardly need any extensive explanation. The core of our interests in the sphere of disarmament is clearly to promote military stability and lower levels of armaments in northern waters and to reduce the danger of nuclear accidents and the damaging consequences they can have for marine biology.[5]

PUBLIC OPINION

Security policy is no longer the controversial issue in Icelandic politics that it used to be. As a result of the policy toward the Keflavík base, the cultural aspect of the American presence has not been very noticeable

5. Address by Minister for Foreign Affairs Jón Baldvin Hannibalsson to the Althing, Mar. 1990.

in debates during recent years, and it can no longer be regarded a major issue in Icelandic politics. Instead, military aspects of the base became prevalent in debates during the last decade. This has not, however, had any comparable effects on policy, which may partly be explained by the fact that the cultural issue has resonance far beyond those opposed to the security arrangement. Since 1985, or after major decisions were taken with respect to increasing the air defense capabilities of the base, national security policy has been relatively unnoticeable in public debates. Instead, international or regional security issues—particularly arms control—have become more important, with the effect that the political parties have had to take a stand on an increasing number of topics in security affairs compared to the past. In short, the debate has been expanding in scope, with the result that the traditional issues of NATO membership and the Keflavík base are now much less in focus.

Opinion polls taken after the general elections in 1983 and 1987 show that 80 percent of those stating an opinion support NATO membership. There are, however, some significant differences with respect to attitudes toward the Defense Agreement. In 1983, 64 percent of those stating an opinion supported the base while 36 percent were opposed to it. In 1987, 55 percent supported the base and 45 percent were opposed to it. The fundamental change is not increased opposition to the base but that the proportion of those who express the view that the base makes no difference has increased from 15 percent to 26 percent. The reasons for this change are unclear, but a possible explanation might be friction in U.S.-Icelandic relations during the last few years over transatlantic transport for the base and attempts by the U.S. government to ban whaling. Similarity with opinion poll results during the 1975-76 cod war with Britain supports this hypothesis.[6] Another possible explanation is simply that, with reduced internal conflict on the issue of the base, many people who primarily supported the base out of party loyalty no longer see any particular need to do so and thus express their indifference to the issue.

THE IMPLICATIONS OF EXTERNAL DEVELOPMENTS

The developments and changes that have been taking place on the political landscape of Europe, and their impact on East-West relations in general, obviously raise questions about implications for Iceland's security policy. Assuming that NATO will remain intact, Iceland will definitely want to stay a member. Another question is whether there is a reason for Iceland to change its policy with regard to the Defense Agreement with the United States. The issue was addressed in the yearly report of Foreign Minister Jón Baldvin Hannibalsson to the Althing in April 1990. The report notes that the collapse of communism and the disinte-

gration of the Warsaw Pact imply that the political preconditions for Soviet use of armed force against Western countries hardly exist now. Several factors have led, however, to the conclusion that Iceland should not change its policy. Among these are uncertainty about further political developments during a period of transition in East-West relations and the continued importance of the sea lines of communication and trends in Soviet naval developments in the North that do not indicate diminishing capabilities. It is also noted that the security system in Europe will probably undergo a substantial change in the years ahead, with political arrangements gaining importance over military arrangements. Defense arrangements would, though, continue to play a substantial role in the security structure.[7]

In the new political climate and conditions of East-West relations, calls for changes in the security arrangement that Iceland has opted for have not, as of this writing, been very noticeable in the political debate in the country. To be sure, the traditional opponents of security policy, most of whom are on the left of the political spectrum, have called for the abrogation of the Defense Agreement on the basis of a different international situation. This has clearly not found much resonance in the public, nor, for that matter, has it been a very insistent demand—one indication that the base issue has become less controversial during the last decade.

6. See Olafur Th. Hardarson, *Icelandic Attitudes towards Security and Foreign Affairs* (Reykjavík: Icelandic Commission on Security and International Affairs, 1985); idem, *Icelanders and Security Affairs* (Reykjavík: Icelandic Commission on Security and International Affairs, 1989).

7. *Foreign Affairs, Report of Minister for Foreign Affairs Jón Baldvin Hannibalsson to Althing* (Reykjavík: Ministry for Foreign Affairs, 1990), pp. 48-50.

A further question is whether the United States may wish to close down the Keflavík base. Knowledgeable sources in the United States indicate that this seems unlikely. The Keflavík base has been regarded as one of the more important U.S. bases abroad. Defense of the transatlantic sea lines will remain important in the years ahead and will even increase following the reduction of U.S. forces in Europe. The Soviet Northern Fleet will, in all probability, remain a formidable military force. Therefore the United States seems likely to retain an interest in having a military presence in the country. One is, however, bound to ask whether larger defense projects, such as an alternate airfield, which the United States has been interested in building in Iceland, will continue to be seen to be as relevant as in the past.

THE EUROPEAN ECONOMIC SPACE

The changes in Europe with bearing on Icelandic security and foreign policy are not limited to the implications of developments in Eastern Europe. They also include the process of closer political and economic integration of Western Europe. More specifically, the EFTA countries—Norway, Sweden, Finland, Switzerland, Austria, and Iceland—and the EC have recently begun the process of establishing what has been termed the European Economic Space (EES).[8]

8. On Iceland, EFTA, and the EC, see Gunnar Helgi Kristinsson, "Iceland: Vulnerability in a Fish-Based Economy," *Cooperation and Conflict*, 22:245-53 (1987); idem, *Iceland and Western Europe* (London: Royal Institute of International Affairs, forthcoming).

The EES idea has its origin in a statement delivered by the president of the EC Commission, Jacques Delors, in January 1989 in which he offered EFTA a "more structured partnership with common decision-making and administrative institutions" in the economic, social, financial, and cultural sphere.[9] The EES would aim at the unhindered movement of persons, goods, services, and capital within its boundaries. It would thus provide the EFTA countries access to the single market, but would not constitute a customs union like the EC or include a common agricultural policy. The EES would presumably also entail closer cooperation in education, research and development, environmental protection, and social policy.

As noted, Iceland is heavily dependent upon fish exports, which account for up to three-quarters of export earnings. The three main markets for fish products are Western Europe, the United States, and Eastern Europe. The EC market has been taking a much larger share of the exports, up from 16 percent in 1972 to over 60 percent in 1989. In spite of a free-trade agreement between Iceland and the EC that includes fisheries products, certain fish products are still subject to tariffs. Attempts to have this changed have failed because of the EC policy requiring access to resources in exchange for access to markets—that is, fishing rights within Iceland's 200-mile zone. Iceland's policy is to deny foreign fishing vessels access to the 200-mile zone. This has been inevitable, in

9. Jacques Delors, "The Main Lines of Commission Policy," mimeograph (Strasbourg: European Community, 17 Jan. 1989), pp. 31-33.

view of the limits put on the yearly catch in order to preserve the fishing stocks. These limits subject Icelandic vessels to severe restrictions with respect to the amount of fishing. In short, Icelanders cannot afford to give foreign vessels access to the fishing zone as long as they do not have enough for themselves. They have therefore not been willing or able to grant any rights to the EC.

The EFTA countries reached an agreement on free trade in fish products in 1989. A primary aim of Icelandic participation in the EES negotiations scheduled to take place in 1990 is to obtain free trade in fish products within the EES without having to grant the EC access to the fishing grounds.

The Icelandic perspective on the EES is not only about fish, however. The meaning of the EES for Iceland should be understood in the broader sense of much closer integration into Europe than has been the case in the past. That is the main reason why the EES undertaking has been described as "probably the most demanding challenge the Icelandic Government has faced since the founding of the Icelandic Republic in 1944."[10]

EFTA has sometimes been described as a waiting room for EC membership. While for the time being the question of membership is really not relevant, as the EC has clearly stated that it is not ready to consider new members until later this decade, the description may be true to some ex-

10. Jón Baldvin Hannibalsson, "20 Years in EFTA—The Challenges Ahead," *EFTA-Bulletin*, Apr. 1989-Jan. 1990, p. 17.

tent. Austria, an EFTA member, has already applied for EC membership. Other members, such as Norway, may follow suit. Icelanders are not considering membership in the EC at present, but neither have they excluded that possibility in the long run.

The EES as currently envisaged certainly implies a substantial change in Icelandic foreign policy, but, it need not affect security policy or Iceland's close political relationship with the United States to any meaningful degree. Membership in the EC would, however, be a different matter, particularly in light of the process toward increased political cooperation among EC members. It seems premature to speculate in detail about the issue, as the question of EC membership is not on the agenda and is unlikely to be for the next several years.

CONCLUSION

Iceland has concluded that there is no reason to change its security arrangement during the present transitional period in East-West relations. Looking further ahead, one can easily state with a relatively high degree of certainty that Iceland will want to stay in NATO if it remains intact—which seems more likely than not. Calls for the abrogation of the Defense Agreement with the United States have not been very insistent in the country as of this writing. For the short term, there is no reason to believe that Iceland would want to make any changes in that respect. It is not useful to make predictions for the longer term, as it will very much depend on external factors and their impact upon attitudes in the country.

Iceland's participation in the EFTA-EC undertaking to establish a European Economic Space will, if negotiations succeed, imply a substantial change in the country's foreign policy and lead to a much closer integration with the countries of Western Europe. It does not, however, affect security policy in a way that EC membership would. Although the question of EC membership is not on the agenda and is not likely to be in the next few years, in the longer run it cannot be excluded.

A final note bears on U.S.-Icelandic relations. It has been a consistent pursuit of Iceland since World War II to foster good relations with Western Europe as well as the United States. Thus from a political point of view, NATO membership and the Defense Agreement with the United States have been regarded as preferable to an arrangement that would depend exclusively on either the United States or Europe. There is a rather strong sense in Iceland that it would be very unfortunate to come up against a situation in which the country would have to make a choice between Europe and the United States. It is therefore safe to assume that, whichever way the external situation will evolve, Iceland will prefer a policy that aims at a balanced relationship with the United States and Europe.

ANNALS, *AAPSS,* 512, November 1990

The United States, the Changing Europe, and the Nordic Region

By GREGORY FLYNN

ABSTRACT: The United States has adopted a cautious approach toward the changing strategic situation in Europe and the requirements of a new European order. The evolution of the Northern region will reinforce this American predisposition because military shifts will be slower to materialize here than elsewhere in Europe. The countries of the region will be more affected by the dramatic changes in political atmosphere between East and West, which will reinforce a general tension between European and American policy over constructing the new Europe, with the former concentrating more on longer-term possibilities and the latter concerned with nearer-term risks.

Gregory Flynn is a senior associate at the Carnegie Endowment for International Peace in Washington, D.C., and former deputy director of the Atlantic Institute for International Affairs in Paris, where he resided from 1976 to 1987. He is author and editor of numerous works on European security and East-West issues, including The West and the Soviet Union: Politics and Policy; NATO's Northern Allies; Public Images of Western Security; *and* The Public and Atlantic Defense.

THE changes that have taken place over the past year have profoundly altered the security environment in Europe. Europe has been the center of the postwar order, the principal point of confrontation between the two superpowers and between the economic and political systems they have represented. With the collapse of the Soviet external empire, the movement of Eastern Europe toward democracy, and the acceleration of efforts to dismantle the military postures that have guaranteed the European stalemate for the past 45 years, that order is now history. There is no way of reimposing the structures that have dominated the postwar era.

What will replace the postwar order, however, remains uncertain. There is no guarantee that the transformations under way in the states of Eastern Europe will successfully produce a prosperous and stable clone of Western Europe. There is even greater uncertainty about the future shape and character of the Soviet Union itself. But the strategic challenges in the coming years will not under any circumstances simply be an updated version of the dilemmas that have dominated the last four and a half decades.

With all of the attention to the dramatic changes in Central Europe, particularly the reunification of Germany, relatively little is heard of how the changes under way will affect security in the Nordic region. Not that it was ever a subject that attracted the interest of a large community beyond the borders of the area. But the security arrangements of the region were special during the Cold War in a variety of ways, and these are already being affected by emerging conditions. The moves by the Baltic republics toward independence from the Soviet Union naturally give added interest to what may indeed be an expanding region.

This article treats U.S. attitudes toward the changing European strategic situation and the types of dilemmas that system change poses for U.S. policy and military strategy. It then looks briefly at the specific elements of strategic change, or lack thereof, in Northern Europe and their influence on the European equation. It concludes with some thoughts on how the Northern region will affect and be affected by U.S. policy.

It is my basic thesis that the strategic situation in the Northern region will, for the near and medium term, be heavily conditioned by the new political atmosphere between East and West but that the military shifts will be slower to materialize than elsewhere in Europe. This will tend to reinforce the American predisposition toward caution in appraising the strategic requirements of the new order. The result will be to reinforce the general tension between European and American policy over constructing the new Europe, with the former concentrating far more on longer-term possibilities and the latter concerned with nearer-term risks.

THE UNITED STATES AND THE SHIFTING EUROPEAN PARADIGM

Like most of the states of Europe, the United States has had difficulty adjusting to the speed and scope of change on the Continent. Events of the past year have called into question most of the basic assumptions that have guided Western policy over the postwar period. While this represents a transformation that the West always claimed was necessary, there was never a serious belief that it would be possible. Indeed, it was difficult to accept that the system had truly begun to change until regimes in the East began to fall and there was no Soviet military intervention.

Initially, U.S. policy heavily accented preventing illusions about how far change would go; the emphasis was on potential reversibility. This created an understandable lag in addressing the problem of what happened if change continued, when the problem was no longer one of creating change but channeling and adjusting to its consequences. By the late summer of 1989, however, reality began to impinge.

Such a period of system change left the West ill prepared to deal with its consequences because it reversed the Cold War relationship between what was desirable and what was possible. For over four decades, thinking about what was desirable in Europe had been constrained by what was possible. Because structural change had been impossible for so many years, concepts about desirable alternative security arrangements remained general and abstract. In the new situation, however, many things became possible, and the task became to identify what was truly desirable. The United States in particular had never really addressed the question of what kinds of change were truly desirable in Europe or what types of

structures would provide a more durable long-term framework for security on the Continent. For the first time, the United States now had to begin to contemplate what the new strategic challenges would be and the most appropriate ways of meeting them.

As the Bush administration has confronted these issues, one basic concern has been an overriding determinant of its policy response: the fear that existing security structures will be undermined before a viable new system can be erected. Moreover, there remains a conviction that a core ingredient of the new system must be Western cooperation. Beyond that, the administration's general approach to the new Europe, as portrayed most clearly in Secretary of State James Baker's speech in Berlin on 12 December 1989, is based on a belief that stability in Europe will require governments with legitimacy and that a legitimate and stable European order will help, not threaten, Soviet security interests. Because an undivided Europe will not automatically be peaceful and prosperous, however, a great deal of attention must be paid to the institutional arrangements that will form the new architecture for a new era. Those arrangements must confirm the U.S. role in Europe's future.

Four broad strands of policy characterize U.S. diplomacy toward the changing Europe over the past year. The centerpiece of American Eurodiplomacy has been its policy toward Germany. The role of the new Germany will heavily determine the viability of security arrangements on the Continent, and partnership with

Germany will remain the key ingredient in U.S. strategy for dealing with the Soviet Union. The result has been unequivocal support for German reunification from the moment the German question was reopened in the late summer of 1989. This has also produced the emphasis on finding a way for the united Germany to remain a member of the North Atlantic Treaty Organization (NATO). A neutral Germany would be both a less reliable ally in dealing with future Soviet power and potentially a loose cannon on the deck in a new European order, creating fear and uncertainty among its neighbors.

The primary object of U.S. diplomacy in Europe, as well as globally, remains the Soviet Union. While the United States was relatively slower than its allies in accepting that changes in Soviet diplomacy were fundamental and had far-reaching implications for Europe and the superpower relationship, by the autumn of 1989 the United States was engaging Mikhail Gorbachev in a wide-ranging dialogue over the issues that had traditionally been at the heart of superpower tensions. If Washington came to believe that Gorbachev was serious in his reform intentions, however, it has remained essentially skeptical about his chances for success and for survival. The possibility exists that the Soviet Union will effectively transform itself into a more responsible member of the international community, and it is a goal of American policy to help it achieve this new status. But even under the most optimistic of circumstances, the Soviet Union will become a partner that also remains the primary U.S. geostrategic adversary. Under more probable scenarios, the Soviet Union will continue to be a nonbenign source of threat to U.S. security interests, even if the world does not return to conditions of tight bipolarity.

The European dimension of U.S. policy toward Moscow has been a central element in its larger strategy of not making life more difficult for Mikhail Gorbachev while attempting to capture benefits from changes already manifest and encouraging those that are considered still desirable. The most important facet has been a publicly announced decision not to exploit events in Eastern Europe in a way that would threaten Soviet security interests. This has been accompanied by a continuing push for democratic and economic reforms to solidify the region's reemergence into mainstream Europe. The Bush administration has also attempted to capitalize on Soviet desires for unwinding the military confrontation in the center of Europe through proposals that reduce the levels of superpower troops on the Continent but in a way that emphasizes the difference in status between occupation forces and those present by invitation.

The third major strand of U.S. diplomacy has reflected a critical shift in psychology toward Western Europe's playing a larger role in determining its own destiny. This has traditionally been an avowed U.S. objective but one that has always harbored a rather serious schizophrenia. In the past, Washington was always uncomfortable when the states of Western Europe began to move beyond economic integration to coordinating policies on various security and foreign policy issues, especially if greater assertiveness developed over issues in conflict with prevailing opinion in the United States. Early in the Bush administration, however, a conscious decision was made to support fully further efforts to strengthen the European Community as in the U.S. security interest, particularly in a world where the United States was inevitably going to feel less capable of sustaining old levels of engagement abroad.

This strand of policy predated considerably events in Eastern Europe, and already in the spring of 1989 there was substantial evidence of the new attitude. But the perspective was strengthened by the events unfolding on the Continent during the summer and fall. Moving Western Europe toward new levels of unity was critical to enhancing the European Community's role as a key stabilizing force on the Continent, as a continuing means of anchoring Germany in the West, and as pole of attraction for the states of Eastern Europe. The expectation that this would occur led to the passage in the Baker Berlin speech about the need for new mechanisms to manage the U.S. relationship with the Community of the future. Rather than an attempt at gaining a U.S. seat at the table, as it was quickly interpreted to be, this was a reflection of the belief that new conditions would require a new type of partnership to manage the issues the United States and the Community would jointly face. Manifestations of the new U.S. attitude are to be found in U.S. support at the

July Summit of Seven for the European Community's assuming the coordinating role for aid to Eastern Europe from the 24 member states of the Organization for Economic Cooperation and Development. In addition, although not widely known, each time President Bush has been in Brussels, he has been careful to spend time alone with Jacques Delors, president of the European Commission.

The final main strand of U.S. diplomacy toward a changing Europe has been its belief that NATO remains the key to Western security, at least for the foreseeable future. The Alliance provides the indispensable guarantee that the evolutions under way in Europe will threaten no state's security interests. For the Bush administration, NATO is the forum where Western nations must cooperate to negotiate, implement, and verify agreements between East and West, as well as the means to hedge against reversals in the East. The Conference on Security and Cooperation in Europe is a forum that can be used to push further the Western agenda in Eastern Europe and the Soviet Union, particularly on issues such as providing guarantees of regular and free elections, but it is not an institution that can perform the job that NATO currently performs.

The emphasis on NATO stems from a basic concern about how easily the new order in Europe will be built. Under the best of circumstances, it will take time to dismantle the military vestiges of the Cold War, and it is still totally unclear what role military forces will play in the new Europe. The most likely outcomes for the Soviet Union will leave it the preponderant power on the Continent, and the other states of Europe will need and want a guarantee against that power, even if all of this transpires at lower levels of military force. American presence will continue to be necessary to offset even this form of Soviet power, and NATO is believed to be the only viable basis for a link of this kind between Europe and the United States. Pan-European solutions will not be able to substitute for NATO in performing these functions. Moreover, NATO also continues to provide a means for integrating Germany into a military command structure, which guarantees that its neighbors' worst fears could not be realized.

These four strands of policy add up to a cautious U.S. approach to the changing strategic situation in Europe. There is a willingness to take advantage of opportunities that present themselves, especially in the arms control arena, but a heavy concentration on what has not yet changed. There is a clear desire to see the relationship between East and West continue to improve and the levels of military force continue downward, but there is concern about how easily this will be accomplished and how many obstacles may lie in the road. Above all, there is worry about the future of the Soviet Union and how difficult the process of transforming the internal empire, the political system, and the economy will yet be.

At the same time, the Bush administration is clearly conducting policy on the assumption that the future will not be the same as the past. At a minimum, the Soviet Union will be a more normal power; that is, the ideological factor that gave the Cold War its essence has been eliminated by the bankruptcy of communism. Even if a future authoritarian Soviet regime continues to call itself Communist, there will be no continuation of the ideological competition that gave military power and East-West confrontation its special meaning over the past four and a half decades. Even if the Soviet Union remains the primary American geostrategic adversary, military power will play a lesser role in their relationship.

The consequences are already visible in the debates between Congress and the administration—and beyond—over the U.S. defense budget. Under all plausible scenarios, the United States will be spending less money on defense and will be less engaged around the globe. Under the probable scenarios, there will be considerably less need for the number and the variety of weapons systems currently on the drawing board. Each of the armed services will have its roles and missions questioned by the changes under way. The real question, however, is not primarily one of numbers and missions but one of strategy.

The entire body of deterrence theory and nuclear strategy that was developed over the postwar period was based upon a world in which there was a sharp dividing line between two camps and a relatively clear identity of stakes. As a result, there was a commonly accepted relationship between military power and the types of conflict situations that could emerge, even if the likelihood of conflict was frequently contested. Force postures were developed around discrete packages of military options, and since the 1960s these had been bound together in a seamless web called flexible response. The concept was applied in a way that linked both conventional and nuclear power, and created possibilities for selective use of nuclear weapons.

It is this corpus of military thinking that is also challenged by the strategic changes under way in Europe and in the superpower relationship. There is no developed body of thought about how to threaten the use of force in order to deter in a world where the international framework does not define supposedly clear stakes. In Europe, the more united and fluid environment that is emerging is not one that will be conducive to building and maintaining escalation ladders. We do not yet know what force postures will be appropriate to controlling the emerging types of conflict potential on and around the Continent. It is far too early even to hazard a guess about how the United States will come to grips with these questions, except to say with some difficulty.

THE NORDIC AREA IN
THE NEW EUROPE

The Nordic area was special during the Cold War. While it did not witness the same type of military confrontation that existed in Central Europe, it had a critical strategic significance for both East and West. The greatest concentration of military power in the world ultimately came to be located within the region, with the Soviet submarine-launched ballistic missile base in Murmansk and their use of the White Sea as a staging ground. The Soviet border with Norway was not heavily armed, nor was that with Finland, but the passage along the Norwegian coast from the Kola Peninsula to the North Sea was one of the key strategic areas for both sides. The Baltic was more closely related to the Central Front and its potential war scenarios, with the Danish straits providing a key choke point for the West to prevent the Soviets from using their fleet to challenge Western supply lines and for the Soviets to prevent the West from penetrating more easily to the Soviet heartland.

Politically, the region has been even more special. Norway and Denmark are charter members of NATO, but Sweden and Finland are neutrals. This buffer-zone configuration has produced a particular political dynamic generally referred to as the Nordic balance. Norwegian and Danish restraint helped guarantee Soviet restraint against the two neutrals, and vice versa. The sharpness of the confrontation between East and West was tempered almost from the beginning by a subtle but firm combination of deterrence and reassurance.

The changes under way in Eastern Europe and the Soviet Union have had their most immediate effect on the strategic situation in Central Europe, not the flanks. The virtual disintegration of the Warsaw Pact in all but name has made the traditional scenarios of a Soviet frontal assault on the West with the aid of its allies unthinkable, even if the military structures have not yet been dismantled. That, however, will naturally have implications for the likelihood of war in Northern Europe and eventually even for the strategic calculations of the region.

At the heart of Soviet toleration of this dramatic alteration in the USSR's security situation is a deepseated shift in Soviet security thinking. The Soviet Union clearly no longer feels that in order to guarantee its security it is compelled to prepare today for the same kind of war as it has over the past several decades. If total control over the Eastern European glacis is no longer necessary, then the Baltic area also must be further receding in strategic significance. While it would remain the quickest surface route to the Soviet heartland for the United States, the scenarios of all-out war between East and West that make this contingency a high-priority concern have obviously been discounted significantly by the Soviets in recent years. This is what permits the Kremlin even to consider the idea of allowing the Baltic states to become independent, although it is difficult to believe that this will come to pass without adequate guarantees of Soviet access to the ports that now house the Soviet Baltic fleets.

Independent states in the Baltic republics would signify a completion of the shift in Soviet calculations about potential war in Europe. For the Northern region, it would imply a significant enlargement of the buffer zone, and for the foreseeable future a probably irreversible demotion of the Baltic in the European military calculus. It is still far too early to assess the emerging political dynamics of the region as it is enlarged to include all the littoral states, but in such a world, regional considerations would probably be subordinate to the broader all-European framework that would be emerging and that would be the focus for most states' diplomatic energies on issues of security. The traditional character of the Nordic balance would have lost most of its meaning because of the transformed political environment.

This tendency will be strengthened by the continued reinforcement of the European Community as the primary source of dynamism and stability on the Continent. Already, the states of the European Free Trade Association have negotiated new arrangements to make sure they are not excluded from post-1992 Europe, and it is assumed that at least Norway and Sweden will be applying for full Community membership within the next few years. The Community is also a critical magnet for the states of Eastern Europe, even if their opportunity to become full members must await a complete transformation of their economies. Rather than slowing down European integration, therefore, the revolutions of the East and the reunification of Germany are actually giving further political impetus to the process. This can only reinforce the emerging position among the Nordic states to be full partners in building the new Europe.

At the same time, there is little change in the strategic significance of the Kola Peninsula and little prospect thereof. The Soviet submarine-launched ballistic missile fleet, while less central than that of the United States, will nonetheless continue to be a key ingredient of Soviet nuclear posture for the foreseeable future. The sea lanes linking the White Sea to the North Sea will thus continue to be a critical strategic zone for both superpowers, even if the overall tension in their relationship continues to attenuate. This will remain the case unless and until the sea leg of the superpowers' nuclear arsenals were to come under a regime that severely limited its size and importance, something that Soviet thinking on command and control would seemingly welcome but that would require a complete reversal of U.S. priorities.

THE UNITED STATES AND THE NORTH IN THE EMERGING EUROPE

Future American attitudes toward the emerging Europe will be heavily conditioned by concern about the future of the Soviet Union. The nature of the state that emerges from the process of transformation within the internal Soviet empire will determine in a major way what the future European order will look like. That process is in its early stages, and we cannot yet know how much of the problem and how much of the solution the Soviet Union will provide to the new Europe.

The Bush administration's approach to this crucial set of imponderables embodies a fundamental skepticism about how difficult and protracted the transformation will be. Even if there is now wide acceptance of the intent on the part of Mr. Gorbachev to carry out a new revolution on Soviet soil—and this is not uniformly accepted—the burden of proof remains on the Soviets to succeed before the United States will be comfortable entertaining the idea that the Soviet Union could be a viable partner in managing the future security of Europe. Even though there has been a clear decision not to try to make life more difficult for Mr. Gorbachev, and to engage him on issues of clear mutual interest such as arms control, there also remains a need to demonstrate that the Soviet role in postwar Europe has not been legitimate in American eyes and that there is no symmetry between the American and Soviet positions in Europe today. While there is some sensitivity to the fact that American policy, and Western policy more generally, may influence the outcome in the Soviet Union, there are limits beyond which the Americans cannot go psychologically before the process of democratization in the Soviet Union has advanced further and become visibly more durable.

This approach contrasts rather sharply with the basic approach of states in Western Europe and especially that of the Federal Republic. For reasons of history, most of the states of Europe are more comfortable than is the United States with the Soviet Union as more than simply the focus of the European security system. There is currently a predisposition to hold open the prospect of equal partnership with the Soviets in a new European order as a means of influencing positive elements in the Soviet Union working for transformation of the domestic system. The burden of proof is placed on the Soviet Union to fail in its efforts to reform and to become a more responsible European actor before it would be considered primarily a threat to acceptable order in Europe and thereby become the principal object of the new security system.

This general difference in perspective is already having significant consequences for the position on specific issues taken by the United States and its allies. The most important area is the institutional framework for the new order, with the Europeans more willing to look toward creating pan-European institutions and the United States more concerned with the military tasks that will remain to be performed under all likely scenarios and convinced that NATO will remain the most appropriate place for these tasks to be coordinated. In some ways the difference of focus is one of time frame, with the European states contemplating future possibilities and the United States focusing on nearer-term risks. But the consequence is also different answers about how best to manage the transition from the present to the future.

The evolution of the Nordic area will probably reinforce this divergence over the short term because military changes will come more slowly here than in the center of Europe. In absolute terms, the likelihood of war may be further decreased because of political developments in Europe, but, in relative terms, the Northern Straits will remain a central interest of both the United States and the Soviet Union. Moreover, the U.S. predisposition to use NATO as the primary vehicle for engagement

will also be strengthened by the current Norwegian government. The Norwegian coastline makes the country a key strategic asset in any potential conflict that could involve the superpowers. The Norwegians, who increasingly do want to be part of Europe, continue to see their traditional link to the United States as the only ultimate means to guarantee their security interests.

Norway will also remain a key to American strategy in another crucial way, even in a Europe with significant force reductions. Assuming a major draw down of U.S. forces in the context of the talks on conventional forces in Europe, the West will be concerned with what is necessary to offset inherent Soviet geographical advantage on the Continent. Probably the primary consideration about the residual American force posture in Europe will be its capacity for timely regeneration to higher force levels in case of necessity. Great emphasis will be put on pre-positioned equipment and lines of communication in order to make an American capacity to intervene plausible if conditions in Europe deteriorate dramatically, and Norway will be important for each. The issue of pre-positioned stockpiles of equipment and ammunition has always been sensitive in Norway, and defining and maintaining a force posture that will be sustainable in the prevailing political environment could prove to be difficult, despite Norwegian concern about Alliance links with the Americans.

If strategic military calculations about the Nordic region will tend to reinforce American caution about the emerging European environment, the changing political landscape in the region could also play a major role, perhaps a decisive role, in determining the ultimate American outlook toward the new European order. The future of the Baltic states will fundamentally influence American assumptions about future Soviet possibilities. If the Baltic states succeed in their peaceful drive for independence, this will remove important doubts in the Bush administration and the U.S. Congress about the real opportunities for integrating the Soviet Union as a more responsible actor in the international community. If, however, Gorbachev retrenches on the issue of independence—above all, if he uses force—the American predisposition not to view the Soviet Union as a legitimate partner in addressing Europe's security needs will be reinforced. Predictably, this will accentuate differences between the Allies and pose a major test both for U.S. policy and for the West's ability to meet the challenges of a changing Europe.

The Soviet Union and Northern Europe: New Thinking and Old Security Constraints

By ROBERT W. JANES

ABSTRACT: This article argues that the interdependence and traditional stability of Northern Europe make it an excellent arena for the Soviet foreign policy of New Thinking. For most of the postwar period, the situation in the Nordic region, according to the Soviet perspective, has been satisfactory if not ideal. In the 1980s, the U.S. naval response to the Soviet strategic buildup on the Kola Peninsula brought increasing instability to the region, a major challenge to Soviet foreign policy. New Thinking attempts to manage current problems through a comprehensive set of security, economic, and environmental initiatives. The article concludes that New Thinking was probably oversold, as Soviet foreign policy has had little success with the intractable security issues in the region. Soviet diplomacy in Northern Europe presents insights into Gorbachev's policy of a common European home, however.

Robert W. Janes is finishing a doctorate in political science at the University of Maryland. His dissertation examines security and economics in Soviet foreign policy toward Finland. He received a master's degree in international affairs from Columbia University. He has contributed to Problems of Communism *and* International Journal.

IT would seem that New Thinking, the foreign policy line under Gorbachev, would have a natural compatibility with the Nordic region. In addition to jettisoning the ideological accretions of the Brezhnev era, New Thinking promotes interdependence and humanistic values in international relations. Perhaps its most important feature, given traditional Soviet means of ensuring security through threateningly massive military buildups, is reasonable sufficiency in defense matters. All of these features have strong correlates in the Nordic region. Not only is there a high degree of cooperative interdependence and social welfare values, but there has also been a tradition of military restraint, often referred to as the Nordic balance. These connections have not escaped the attention of Soviet analysts; they have been quick to assert the relevance of New Thinking in the application of Soviet policy to the region.[1] Two questions are addressed in this article. First, how has New Thinking fared in dealing with the problems and possibilities that the Nordic states present to Soviet foreign policy? Second, what is the region's role in the further elaboration of New Thinking in Soviet policy toward Europe?

For Soviet policymakers looking north, the Nordic region has always been a crossroads where strategic regional and bilateral considerations meet. It is certainly a distinct region of Northern European states, one in which the Soviet Union has at times claimed membership, as a fellow northern country. After World War II it quickly became an area of strategic interaction, through which U.S. power would be projected during conflict. But equally important, it represents a subsystem of Europe; the implications of Soviet policy in either Eastern or Western Europe cannot easily be separated from the Nordic area. Finally, there are rich histories of bilateral ties to most of the Nordic countries that continue to influence Soviet perceptions.

The characterization of Northern Europe as a multidimensional arena for Soviet policy needs to be stressed. The chief issue for Soviet planners, of course, entails the strategic forces based on the Kola Peninsula, which constitute a major share of Soviet nuclear reserves. Defending these forces, however, must occur regionally, most likely off the coast of Norway, quite possibly by making use of the territory of Finland or Sweden. Regional military considerations also include the Baltic, the northern flank of the Central European front.

The cultural and political homogeneity of the Nordic region provides for a high level of cooperation and interdependence. These are industrially advanced countries whose historical ties and geographical proximity to the Soviet Union make them attractive prospects for economic relations. Regionally, cooperation offers considerable potential for technology transfer. Bilaterally, trade ties are strongest with Finland, something the Soviets would like to duplicate with Sweden and Norway.

The political dynamic between the Nordic area and the rest of Europe presents another dimension of Soviet

1. See, for example, Yuri Komissarov, *Bezopasnost' i sotrudnichestvo* (Moscow: Mezhdunarodnye Otnosheniya, 1989), p. 32.

policy toward the region. Through the Nordic nuclear weapons free zone (NWFZ) proposal, Moscow has campaigned to keep the Nordic security environment tractable. It also sought, however, to influence European perceptions more widely during the tense period preceding deployment of intermediate-range nuclear forces (INF). Current efforts at a so-called common European home also suggest this kind of interaction: Soviet policy promotes a Northern Europe that will supply, in the words of Gorbachev, the "roof" to the common home. The connection, at least in the Soviet view, is more than rhetorical, especially with regard to successful relations with Finland. Soviet-Finnish relations are frequently referred to as the model for contemporary relations with Europe: "new thinking in practice."

STABILITY AND REACTION

Even though the concept of a Nordic balance has been frequently denied by Soviet scholars, it merits attention, since it captures unique security postures in the region. In its most basic form the Nordic balance theory states that the diverse alignments in the region produce stability and low tension. Denmark and Norway are members of the North Atlantic Treaty Organization (NATO) but have adopted self-imposed prohibitions on the basing of foreign troops and nuclear weapons in peacetime. Sweden maintains an armed neutrality with a westward tilt. Finland is also neutral, but has a special treaty arrangement with the Soviet Union.

These diverse positions limit and balance superpower involvement in the region.

In the Soviet view, U.S. involvement cannot enhance the region's stability. The self-imposed Danish and Norwegian restraints are indeed appreciated and are cited as examples of realistic foreign policies. The Soviet explanation for stability in the region, however, focuses primarily on the friendly and cooperative relationship with Finland. The "Paasikivi-Kekkonen line," Finland's postwar policy, puts good relations with the Soviet Union at a priority and accommodates Soviet security concerns. Finland has sought to engender Soviet trust, a policy pursued very actively during the long tenure of President Kekkonen. One lasting example of this has been the promotion of the NWFZ.

More than anything else, the Friendship, Cooperation and Mutual Assistance (FCMA) Treaty negotiated in 1948 has been the basis for Soviet confidence in Finland. The treaty obliges Finland to defend its territory against aggression aimed at the Soviet Union, if necessary with the aid of the Soviet Union. Soviet leaders still count the FCMA Treaty as an active element in maintaining peace and security in the north. Its continued relevance derives in large part from the advent of cruise missiles in the late 1970s, when fulfilling the treaty obligations shifted from defense against a primary threat of ground attack to defending Finnish airspace. Most recently, in his October 1989 speech in Helsinki's Finlandia Hall, Gorbachev reasserted the relevance and current value of the treaty as "an inalienable component of security in Northern Europe."[2]

Because Finland has taken care to ensure that the Soviet Union has a nonhostile and reliable neighbor on its border, it is a linchpin for Soviet security concerns in Northern Europe. This is reinforced by the fact that for most of the postwar period the region has not been confronted with stability-threatening crises and has thus not been a high-priority area for the Soviet Union. As Orjan Berner, the current Swedish ambassador to Moscow, has suggested, the Soviet attitude has been one of "positive vigilance combined with steady pressure in order to maintain and, if possible, improve a fairly satisfactory situation and to insure against any negative developments arising from internal or external sources."[3]

More concretely, this has meant keeping Denmark's and, especially, Norway's integration into NATO to a minimum, as well as keeping Swedish neutrality from tilting too much toward the West. The chief Soviet concern regarding Sweden continues to be its possible technological dependence on the West and the prospect of Sweden's being drawn into the U.S. military-industrial complex in an effort to maintain the high technological level of its forces.[4] Soviet relations with Denmark, despite the latter's NATO membership, have been fairly smooth. Danish policies have not proven to be major irritants to Moscow. Attitudes about Star Wars and resistance to paying for deployment of intermediate-range missiles in the 1980s put Denmark at odds with Washington, factors obviously appreciated by Moscow.

Soviet relations with Norway stand in contrast with the relative calm that has persisted in Soviet-Danish relations. Despite a period of good relations earlier, Norway's increasingly close involvement in NATO throughout the 1980s has brought it into conflict with Moscow. By virtue of geography, Norway will occupy a central place in any conflict in the north of Europe. Soviet critics of Norwegian policy argue that extensive agreements with the United States for prestocking matériel, coupled with increasing joint exercises, creates de facto foreign bases on Norwegian soil. In a crisis the United States will be in a position to make Norway abandon its nonnuclear pledge: "elementary logic suggests that everything will be decided in Washington."[5]

It is clear that through much of the postwar period a modus vivendi existed, despite periods of tension. By the 1980s the region had become the focal point of a burgeoning military standoff centering on the Soviet Northern Fleet based on the Kola Penin-

2. *Pravda*, 22 Oct. 1989 (FBIS-Sov 22 Oct. 1989).

3. Orjan Berner, *Soviet Policy toward the Nordic Countries* (New York: University Press of America; Cambridge, MA: Harvard University, Center for International Affairs, 1986), p. 108.

4. See, for example, Sergey Morgachev, "Military and Military-Industrial Circles in Sweden," *Mirovaia ekonomika i mezhdunarodnaia otnosheniia* (hereafter *MEMO*), Apr. 1989, no. 4, pp. 121-27 (JPRS-UWE 23 Aug. 1989, pp. 36-41).

5. Yuri Lavrov, "The North European Variant of Security Policy," *MEMO*, Nov. 1989, no. 11, pp. 112-20 (JPRS-UWE 2 Mar. 1990, p. 41).

sula. With 60 percent of the Soviet strategic submarine (SSBN) fleet stationed there, including all of the most modern Soviet submarines, the Typhoon class, defending Kola is a Soviet strategic priority. In the 1970s it became clear that the Soviets had adopted a bastion strategy—keeping such submarines in northern waters instead of on patrol off the U.S. coast. The Northern Fleet would also have the task of attacking NATO sea lines of communication during war.

As Steven E. Miller has noted, once such a large strategic force was based at Kola, it naturally served as a magnet, drawing the U.S. fleet northward.[6] In the 1980s the United States responded to the buildup with a maritime strategy that aggressively sought to attack the Northern Fleet in its home waters. During wartime, domination of the Norwegian Sea would be a strategic priority both for NATO forces attacking Kola and for the Soviet Northern Fleet defending it. Even with its forward deployment, the U.S. fleet still has the traditional role of protecting the sea lines of communication. Air bases in Norway, particularly in the northern half of the country, would play a key role in any battle for the Norwegian Sea. Soviet seizure of these bases would probably involve an attack across northern Finland and Sweden combined with amphibious operations with forces based on Kola. The spillover from strategic to regional confrontation would be inevitable.

6. Steve Miller, "The Maritime Strategy and Geopolitics in the High North," in *The Soviet Union and Northern Waters*, ed. Clive Archer (New York: Routledge, Chapman, Hall, 1988), p. 226.

MURMANSK TO HELSINKI

By the mid-1980s Soviet policy in the North of Europe had clearly become unproductive. In the face of a worsening security environment, Soviet diplomatic initiatives, such as promoting the NWFZ or accusations that Norway and Denmark were deviating from their self-imposed restraints, had failed. Although by then the NWFZ campaign had achieved a permanent place on the agenda in Northern Europe, concrete results were as distant as ever: it could do little to slow, much less reverse, the Soviet Union's increasing vulnerability in the high North.

Gorbachev responded to this situation with a regional diplomatic offensive, launched in a speech in the city of Murmansk, on 1 October 1987. He presented an array of initiatives that tied together security, economic, and environmental issues in the region. These represented the application of New Thinking to Northern Europe, the chief feature of which was its comprehensiveness, or "all-embracing" quality.[7] This meant that security, economics, and environmental concerns were all part of a unified cooperative package. The Murmansk speech signaled the start of a two-year period when Sweden, Norway, and Finland would be the recipients of greatly renewed Soviet diplomatic attention.

Diplomatic efforts following the Murmansk speech had considerable success. In January 1988 Prime Minister Ryzhkov visited Stockholm and

7. Yuri Deryabin, "Echoes of Murmansk," *International Affairs* (Moscow), June 1988, no. 6, p. 39.

Oslo, the first high-level Soviet visit since the early 1970s. An early sign of Soviet interest in improving relations with Sweden was a shift in position on the issue of demarcation of the Baltic. For two decades the two countries had been in dispute over where to draw the line marking off zones of economic interests between Sweden and the coast of Lithuania. Ryzhkov's trip produced an agreement in principle, resulting in an agreement signed in April. The Soviet Union also became forthcoming on the fate of Raoul Wallenberg, the Swedish diplomat who had disappeared in the custody of the Soviet army at the end of World War II.

A chief purpose of Ryzhkov's January 1988 trip was to take advantage of improving relations in order to promote economic ties. In this regard, the all-embracing philosophy of the New Thinking approach has obvious advantages in Northern Europe. There is considerable economic advantage for the Soviet Union in northern cooperation. It has resource-rich areas in the north but considerable difficulty in exploiting them. Sweden, Norway, and Finland all produce equipment and have technical know-how well suited to the climatic demands of the region. This is especially true of Norwegian offshore oil-production capabilities, which could be valuable in exploiting Barents Sea reserves.

In the case of Sweden, however, actual economic relations have remained quite limited, a problem exacerbated by the disruptions and economic downturn associated with *perestroika*. The substantive results of the economic dimension of Ryzhkov's visit were extremely limited. Both sides acknowledged at the end of the visit that there was much room for growth in the economic relationship.[8]

Since the 1970s, Soviet-Norwegian relations have been complicated by a dispute over the delimitation of economic zones in the Barents Sea, involving approximately 45,000 square nautical miles in the waters north of the Soviet-Norwegian border. In 1978 both sides accepted as a temporary measure the Grey Zone agreement, largely in order to protect cod and other fish stocks. Norway is dissatisfied with the agreement, claiming with some justification that it favors the Soviet Union. The Norwegians regard the issue as a major impediment to further progress in other areas. Soviet policy seems to want to move around the immediate dispute and, using the conceptual framework of the Murmansk speech, to enfold the problem into a broad range of cooperative efforts. Accordingly, the complexity of the problem calls not only for patience but the development of trust and confidence. As Ryzhkov put it, "The simple drawing of a line on a geographic map will not now find a balance of these interests or strengthen security and stability."[9] Thus, in his press conference in Oslo, he proposed a joint-partnership zone, with both countries contributing to cooperative ventures on a fifty-fifty basis. This would have obvious economic advantages from the Soviet point of view. Norway has taken it

8. *Pravda*, 14 Jan. 1988 (FBIS-Sov 14 Jan. 1988).

9. *Pravda*, 16 Jan. 1988 (FBIS-Sov 20 Jan. 1988); Komissarov, *Bezopasnost' i sotrudnichestvo*, p. 114.

under consideration but continues to call for further negotiations on the delimitation question.

New Thinking provides some tactical advantage for the Soviet Union in the Barents negotiations. In terms of international legal standing, the longer the Soviet Union can demonstrate effective cooperation under the Grey Zone agreement, the more Norway's case weakens.[10] In other words, New Thinking's pursuit of cooperation would erode the Norwegian negotiating position. This is, no doubt, why the Norwegians continue to insist that, whatever merits broader cooperation might have, the delimitation issue must be solved before further progress is attempted. In his speech at Finlandia Hall, Gorbachev suggested that it was time to try again to resolve this issue, although there has been no substantive change in the Soviet position.

Ecological issues have a strong emotional appeal in the Nordic states, and the environmental component of the Murmansk initiatives doubtless has its propagandistic side. This is, however, a rapidly growing area of concern and of ideological change within the Soviet Union. The Kola Peninsula shares a delicate ecosystem with Lapland, and there have already been joint Finnish-Soviet meetings on environmental problems on Kola. Whatever concrete results Soviet foreign policy theorists expect from environmental cooperation, they hope it will bolster the content of New Thinking: Northern Europe helps fill out the ecological dimension of the common European home.[11]

Although the cooperative aspects of New Thinking—comprehensive relations, including economic and environmental ties—are a necessary condition for peace and security, they are not sufficient. As Gorbachev noted at Murmansk, broad economic cooperation may be the ultimate goal, but mutual security is the first step. The security initiatives proposed at Murmansk were split between furthering the traditional NWFZ approach and a new emphasis on confidence-building measures. It became clear following the speech that the confidence-building approach, instead of being merely a second prong to Soviet arms control efforts, became the central focus of regaining stability and security in the North.

The importance of such measures results in part from the side effects of the INF agreement of December 1987. To compensate for missiles taken out of Europe, the United States and the Soviet Union have increased the number of intermediate missiles deployed on submarines. Nordic analysts have been quick to note that already the Soviet navy has deployed SSN-21s on submarines in the sea to compensate for removal of SS-20s from Europe.[12] The growing military significance of the region puts a premium on confidence building, a perspective emphasized in the secu-

10. Robin Churchill, "The Soviet Union and Jurisdictional Disputes in Northern Waters," in Soviet Union and Northern Waters, ed. Archer, p. 52.

11. Mikhail Amirzhdanov and Genrikh Cherkasov, "Our Common European Home," International Affairs (Moscow), Dec. 1988, p. 33.

12. Julian Isherwood, "Scandinavians Say Soviets Used Hole in INF Treaty to Cover Ground Targets," Armed Forces Journal International, Sept. 1989, p. 28.

rity approaches of the Nordic states as well. If anything, Soviet officials and commentators have expressed more concern about such compensation than the West has. The shift in accentuation from NWFZ to confidence-building proposals was quite clear during Ryzhkov's January 1988 trip to Oslo, when a list of specific confidence-building measures was put forward. This was the first high-level statement on the issue since the signing of the INF agreement. The key ideas proposed to limit naval and air exercises—one every two years—and restrict antisubmarine warfare activity in certain areas. This reflects the underlying objective of strengthening SSBN bastions in the Barents Sea, and, furthermore, it reflects concern over the possibility of permanent stationing of naval forces in the region.[13]

At a luncheon speech during President Koivisto's visit to Moscow in October 1987, one week after his Murmansk speech, Gorbachev said that not only do the NATO countries wish to maintain the same level of military confrontation, but, "moreover, the waters and airspace of the North Atlantic and the adjoining seas are being chosen as a sphere for such confrontation."[14] The occasion of Gorbachev's comments was not taken as being unrelated to the subject: a subtle reminder to the Finns of their obligations under the FCMA Treaty to defend their airspace.

A number of concessions regarding the NWFZ were included in the Murmansk speech. Gorbachev promised to eliminate from the Baltic six Golf-class diesel submarines, which carry a total of 18 nuclear missiles, if a zone were established. He also noted the possibility of including areas of Soviet territory in the zone. In the post-INF period, the zone proposal was not so much less important as less urgent. The likelihood of its ever being put in place, although never high, became even lower. In part, this is because now that Norway was at the center of an accelerating arms spiral, it was less likely than ever to weaken its ties to the United States and NATO, as would happen if it joined such a zone.

The Soviet Union has been implementing the unilateral reductions in the Baltic hinted at in Murmansk. At the time of his visit to Helsinki, Gorbachev announced the removal of two submarines from the Baltic and the destruction of their missiles. He promised the liquidation of the remaining four by the end of 1990. He further claimed that medium- and short-range missiles are no longer on alert duty in areas adjoining Northern Europe and no tactical missiles are deployed so as to be able to reach Nordic countries.

Although these measures are naturally welcome, they generally fail to impress Scandinavians. The Golf-class submarines were extremely old—one dated from 1959—and bound for retirement soon in any case. Thus these measures are taken to be militarily insignificant, especially in the face of the continuing Soviet naval buildup, which included the launching of a second aircraft carrier of the Kiev class and a second cruiser since the

13. Komissarov, *Bezopasnost' i sotrudnichestvo*, p. 28.

14. *Pravda*, 7 Oct. 1987 (FBIS-Sov 7 Oct. 1987).

Murmansk speech.[15] This may reflect continuing building and deployment of vessels started as a response to U.S. maritime strategy.

Regional diplomatic efforts dealing with security questions are basically constrained by the strategic interests of the superpowers. The inadequacy of the Murmansk initiatives and New Thinking in coping with these problems was evident in Gorbachev's Finlandia Hall speech, when he noted Nordic concern about Kola. He went on to say that these forces would have to be dealt with on a "global scale," in other words, through strategic negotiations with the United States. As Shevardnadze's April 1990 visit to Washington demonstrated, naval arms control remains the most intractable point in the U.S.-Soviet negotiations. No matter how effective New Thinking is in Northern Europe, the global level will continue to be decisive.

NEW THINKING, NEUTRALITY, AND EUROPE

Gorbachev's effective style of public diplomacy may have oversold the claim to New Thinking in the Murmansk initiatives and the subsequent acceleration of Soviet policy. The strong regional orientation and the public diplomacy of the arms control concessions have obviously found a receptive audience among Nordic populations. The geostrategic realities of the region, however, severely limit realization of the confidence-building elements, while at the same

15. Julian Isherwood, "Norwegians Eyeing Soviet Naval Buildup in Kola Region," *Armed Forces Journal International*, Mar. 1989, p. 44.

time they guarantee a continuation of military policies already at work. Thus, in its own ambitiousness, New Thinking has produced a credibility problem in the region: is it an actual departure from previous Soviet policy or merely more effective packaging?

As an elaboration of New Thinking, the post-Murmansk diplomatic offensive deserves to be judged in the broader context of policy toward Europe. Although New Thinking is global in its perceptions, it has found very immediate and thorough expression in Gorbachev's concept of an "all-European home." It should not be surprising, given the urgency with which Gorbachev brought *perestroika* to Soviet foreign policy, that some of its theoretical aspects would gain definition as events unfold. Northern Europe serves Gorbachev well as an arena for marshaling the conceptual points in the emerging Soviet image for Europe. The speech in Finlandia Hall during his visit to Helsinki encapsulates the two-year diplomatic effort in Northern Europe. It is also a point of departure for tying the Nordic states to the common European home. In effect, this amounts to building the roof for the house first, since it seems easiest—and, in the process trying to work out the blueprint for the rest of the edifice.

In his Finlandia Hall speech, Gorbachev called for the 1992 Conference on Security and Cooperation in Europe (CSCE) to be a meeting of leaders of all 35 member states. The main thrust in the speech was refocusing the CSCE toward a range of Soviet objectives, not the least of which is establishing confidence-building regimes. Underlying this is a strong orientation toward a small-state perspective. Gorbachev notes their contributions, especially those of Northern Europe, within the CSCE process as well as those of the neutral and nonaligned countries. These points are reinforced in the communiqué of the visit, which, one Soviet analyst says, "sets out in bold relief the role of the so-called small countries of Europe in strengthening fresh approaches to security and cooperation in Europe."[16]

The revitalization of the Helsinki process coincides with a desire to de-emphasize bloc politics. The structure of the CSCE is based on equality of all members and consensus decision making. It has a "democratic character" that increases the influence of neutral and nonaligned actors and of small and medium-sized states, and, one way or another, this includes all the Nordic states as well.

Antibloc rhetoric is not new to Soviet policy toward Europe; it has always promoted divisiveness within the Atlantic alliance. The disintegration of the East bloc, however, has certainly given the Soviet Union new and stronger motivation to reduce the collective power of Western political and economic groups. NATO may currently be having some identity problems, but Moscow is still confronted with a number of cohesive structures in the West that look as if they will be focused around a united Germany. With the Soviet Union shorn of its own defensive and diplomatic glacis

in the East, promoting the politics of many small states within the common European home may be the best answer to changing political structures in Europe.

CONCLUSION

It is easier to give intellectual underpinnings to a foreign policy line such as New Thinking than to achieve results in the changing environment of contemporary Europe. Beyond this obvious point, it is too early to draw conclusions regarding New Thinking and Soviet policy in Northern Europe. One reason is the continuing secession crises of the Baltic republics, which represent an acid test for New Thinking. The Soviet response will be closely watched in the Nordic states, given historical links across the Baltic. It will also greatly affect how recently stated Soviet respect for neutrality will be judged, especially since the Soviet Union wants to promote a concord of small states cooperating on equal footing in the context of the CSCE.

A second reason is that ideologically or, at least, theoretically, Soviet attitudes toward neutrality and security are still evolving in Northern Europe. The policy of putting faith in local neutrality is not easily reconciled with the presence of U.S. power. It greatly depends on how much confidence the Soviets have in New Thinking, which seeks to solve problems politically and economically without resort to military measures. How likely are the traditional and more sure-handed methods of dealing with insecurity to resurface in the complex politics of the Nordic region?

16. Yury Deryabin, "Milestones in the Year of Europe," *International Affairs* (Moscow), Feb. 1990, no. 2, p. 59.

ANNALS, *AAPSS*, 512, November 1990

The Changing European Security Context and the Nordic Region: A View from Germany

By HELGA HAFTENDORN

ABSTRACT: The situation in Europe is changing so fast that any statement, however carefully made, is bound to be overtaken by events. This is especially true for the structures of European security and for the evolving process of German unification. Europe might enter a period of military stability and political change. The peaceful revolution in East Germany and the call by its people for speedy reunification have forced the question of the future of the two German states back on the international agenda. The long-term prospect is for an expansion of a somewhat more loosely knit Western system of collective security to which a unified Germany would belong. The impact on the Nordic region would be significant: instead of providing a Northern support for the Atlantic Alliance, the Nordic region would become a halfway house between East and West or a building block for an all-European security structure in which it could find a congenial home.

Helga Haftendorn is professor of international relations at the Free University of Berlin and president of the International Studies Association. She earned her Ph.D. at the University of Frankfurt and has taught at Hamburg University, the Armed Forces College of Hamburg, Georgetown University, and Stanford University. She has published widely on German and American foreign policy and on international security affairs. Best known in the United States is her book Security and Détente: Conflicting Priorities in German Foreign Policy *(1985).*

THE political situation in Europe is changing so fast that any statement, however carefully made, is bound to be overtaken by events. Instead of making a prognosis, the scholar is well advised to stick to identifying factors of change, describing trends, and evaluating their likely impact on the Nordic region.

THE CHANGING EUROPEAN SECURITY CONTEXT

At the beginning of the 1990s, major elements of the postwar European security system are in rapid transition. The two most far-reaching results of World War II were the division of the Continent into two hostile ideological systems and military alliances, and the political and military presence in Europe of the Soviet Union and the United States. Today, that division, as well as the military presence of the superpowers, is undergoing significant changes. The East-West conflict is deideologized as well as demilitarized. The dramatic changes in the East also herald the disintegration of the once solid Communist bloc; they open up the prospect for close cooperation between the countries of Eastern and Western Europe.[1] The influence of the two superpowers upon the evolution of Europe is diminishing. The German question, thought laid to

1. For reasons of parsimony, the term "Eastern Europe" refers to the (former?) Soviet bloc, including the German Democratic Republic; while "Western Europe" denotes all countries west of the system's divide, and it includes the Northern region as well as the southern flank of the North Atlantic Treaty Organization.

rest by anchoring the two German states firmly into opposing military alliances, is back on the agenda.

Within ten years, the superpower relationship has changed from confrontation and containment to détente and cooperation. Well into 1989, the Iron Curtain looked as solid as ever before in its postwar history, backed up by a struggle, though a mellowing one, of power and of ideology between two contending political systems. It started to fall in the summer of that year: first went the barbed wire at the Hungarian-Austrian frontier; then the divide became permeable to fugitives from Communist oppression and economic mismanagement in East Germany; and on 9 November the wall in Berlin crumbled. At the same time all of Eastern Europe—except Albania—experienced a largely peaceful revolution; with the slogan "We are the people," its population claimed the civil rights it had been deprived of for forty years. Eastern Europe is now realizing its own *perestroika* and is moving down the road toward democratization. It is too early to tell where this road will eventually lead, but it is evident that major changes are under way that will significantly alter the political structure of Europe. Will the European political elites—East and West—be able to cope with a challenge as enormous as the present one?

The superpowers are reappraising their global roles and commitments. Secretary Gorbachev's top priority is *perestroika,* a sweeping reform of the political and economic system of the

Soviet Union, to make it more competitive in world affairs. The encouragement of democratic forces in Eastern Europe should transform the East European glacis of the Soviet Union from a burden into an asset. But it is still open to question how lowering the costs of empire could result in a new political order that would work to the political and economic benefit of the Soviet Union itself. The United States, for its part, is asking whether and how some of its European burden can either be better shared with its allies or devolved over time. This is all a consequence of over-extension of resources, of a sense of overcommitment, and of decline as a superpower,[2] and it is also a reaction to the reduced danger of Soviet military attack.

The Soviet-American rapprochement has led to a reactivation of the long-dormant arms control process. The December 1987 Double-Zero Agreement, concerning intermediate-range nuclear forces (INF), removed all ballistic nuclear missiles with a range of more than 500 kilometers. Both the process of the Conference on Security and Cooperation in Europe (CSCE) and the search for ways to reduce conventional forces in Europe have received new impetus. The Ottawa understanding to limit U.S. and Soviet troops in the central region to 195,000 men each will result in significantly lower force levels. Together with the results of the negotiations on conventional forces in Europe,[3] it

will lead to a predominantly defensive military structure. Military stability will be enhanced to the extent that both the risk of surprise attack or inadvertent military confrontation and the temptation to use military means for political ends are minimized.

In Europe, the danger of a military conflict between East and West is at an all-time low. The alliance systems that have guaranteed peace and military stability in Europe for more than forty years are losing function and importance. For the Soviet Union, the Warsaw Pact (WTO) was an instrument of military coordination and control; unlike the Atlantic Alliance, it never was a community holding shared values and goals. It now is disintegrating. For the first time in its existence, the WTO, at its meeting of 17 March 1990, publicly disagreed on so important an issue as the future military status of a unified Germany. The WTO is, however, complemented by an overlapping system, still intact, of bilateral ties between the Soviet Union and the WTO countries.

The Atlantic Alliance, in the words of Lord Ismay, its first secretary-general, had a threefold political function: "To keep the Soviets out, the Americans in, and the Germans down." The end of the Cold War has deprived it of its containment function; with a reorientation of U.S. foreign policy toward a greater degree of unilateralism and less entanglement, its coupling function is under duress; while its function to keep the Germans down is no longer accepted by a Fed-

2. Paul Kennedy, *The Rise and Fall of the Great Powers: Economic Change and Military Conflict from 1500 to 2000* (New York: Random House, 1987), p. 515.

3. The Conference on Conventional Forces in Europe has a mandate from the Vi-

enna CSCE to negotiate reductions in the conventional forces in Europe.

eral Republic that has for forty years been an exemplary democratic state and that expects to be treated on a par with the other members of the alliance.

The military function of the North Atlantic Treaty Organization (NATO) has been to deter an attack on any member of the alliance and, should deterrence fail, to defend all alliance partners against any aggression, especially those on the Central Front. The strategy of flexible response served as an instrument of coupling the defense of Western Europe to that of the United States, as it also controlled the risk that the United States would be drawn into a nuclear conflict against its will. With the strategy of flexible response losing credibility, with nuclear deterrence between the United States and the Soviet Union increasingly being transformed into a security partnership, and with threat perceptions largely gone, NATO's military role is declining.

Accordingly, a number of countries are reorganizing their military forces, partly for budgetary reasons, partly to restructure them into instruments of balance and reassurance. While NATO is changing into a forum for political coordination between Western Europe, the United States, and Canada, the West European countries are strengthening their joint coordination as well as their common identity; their goal is building a so-called European pillar within NATO.

Past policy has been based on the assumption that military stability went together with political stability[4]

4. This has been the basic assumption of the Harmel Doctrine and German *Ostpolitik*.

—interpreted as territorial stability and political status quo. This has changed. In the 1990s, Europe may be entering a period of increased military stability, while political stability might be reduced by ethnic strife and social unrest and by the reemergence of territorial conflicts. A major task will thus be to manage change while maintaining political stability.

THE GERMAN QUESTION ON
THE INTERNATIONAL AGENDA

A factor of uncertainty in the European situation is the evolution of the German question. The peaceful revolution in East Germany and the call for speedy reunification by the masses on the streets of East Berlin, Leipzig, and Dresden have forced the question of the future of the two German states back on the international agenda.

People in West Germany, as in most other parts of Europe, have been caught largely by surprise by the events in Eastern Europe and in the German Democratic Republic (GDR). West Germans had all but given up on the unification of their country, the claim to it safely enshrined in the preamble of their constitution. In the shadow of the Berlin Wall, they successfully adapted to their role as economic superpower. Cynics claimed that the western half of the country did not require the eastern half for its pursuit of happi-

See "The Future Tasks of the Alliance. Report of the Council. Annex to the Final Communiqué of the Ministerial Meeting, December 1967," *The North Atlantic Treaty Organization: Facts and Figures* (Brussels: North Atlantic Treaty Organization, 1984), pp. 289-91.

ness and prosperity.[5] The Kohl government, however, never failed to remind its compatriots that there was unfinished national business, but it was presented as a problem of freedom withheld from the other Germany rather than as territorial unity denied to both. While public opinion polls continued to record high levels of support for the idea of reunification, the prosperous West Germans were less prepared to pay for it in economic and political terms. The German people had adjusted to the division and considered it a virtue and the most acceptable form of Germanness to the rest of humankind, provided the East Germans would one day enjoy the same liberties as their more fortunate brothers in the West.

While West Germany was enjoying the blessings of a democratic society and harvesting the fruits of economic integration, East Germany's case for contentment was as brittle as West Germany's was solid and strong. As amputated heirs to a large empire, the western half lived down the pains of dismemberment remarkably well, while the eastern half looked more and more like a terminal patient, hemorrhaging, with ever diminishing prospects of recovery.

As a society forced to live under the Communist dictate, East Germans had found consolation in the idea of the one German nation, which was their claim to a better life after totalitarian rule, though nobody in the GDR had an inkling that this day was so near. The constitutional premise of West Germany's Basic Law that it was an inalienable right of the Germans to unite and to live in an undivided nation had, over the years, a powerful impact upon the psyche of East Germans, stiffening their resistance to the scheme of a socialist German nation. Thus German unity quietly served to corrode the legitimacy of the Honecker regime, leaving it with no justification other than enforced socialism. That, in turn, led Professor Otto Reinhold, the chief ideologue of the Socialist Unity Party (SED), to make his famous comment that a GDR without socialism had no legitimate purpose for existing. But it was not its shaky legitimacy that pulled the rug from under the Honecker regime; it was the Socialist brother abandoning an ally that had foolishly misread the writing on the wall. After his visit to East Berlin on the occasion of the GDR's fortieth anniversary, Gorbachev commented that "he who is late will be punished by history."[6]

East Germany was in the midst of a peaceful revolution when the Berlin Wall fell on 9 November 1989—not by intent but rather in consequence of a careless remark by SED spokesman Günther Schabowski. When a border guard was asked from whom he received the order to open the gates, he asked, "Which order? It was not orders that came but masses of people."[7] The political leaders in the two German states were in a similar po-

---

5. I owe these and the following ideas on German *Befindlichkeiten* ("sentiments") to Thomas Kielinger, editor in chief of the *Rheinischer Merkur*, and his presentation at an Atlantik Brücke/Armonk Institute German-American Jewish Conference, Bonn, 8-10 Feb. 1990.

6. Ibid., in *Atlantik-Brücke e. V.*, Rundschreiben nr. 3/1990, p. 8.

7. West German Television, 10 Nov. 1990.

sition: they were overwhelmed by events. Neither by political experience nor by national instinct were they prepared for so enormous a task as fitting together the two halves of Germany.

Initially, the new guard of SED leaders in East Germany wanted to reform their system by democratizing and liberalizing it. The Kohl government in its turn proposed a *Vertragsgemeinschaft* (close cooperation based on treaties), eventually leading to a German confederation. The people in the GDR, however, had lost their patience with the SED regime and, with the slogan "We are one people," forcefully demanded unification—or left the country by the tens of thousands. By the end of 1989 it was evident that only the prospect of unification could prevent the complete collapse of East Germany. The results of the elections of 18 March 1990 in the GDR underline this trend.[8]

A first step will be the construction of a currency union between the two German states. It will be complemented by an economic and social union, to provide for the necessary economic adjustments and their social acceptability, and will lead to an economic union. Cooperation in a great number of other sectors, already begun in early 1990, will intensify. This process will have all kinds of repercussions for both the cohesion of East Germany and the domestic situation in West Germany. If care is not taken, the first democratically elected political authorities in the GDR, especially at the local level, could be discredited; while, with the costs of unification higher than previously imagined, political opposition against it might increase in West Germany. The present situation, with its high number of East German immigrants and various kinds of financial subsidies, calls for speedy solutions.

Normally, unification would have been a long and cumbersome process of adjustment, but, due to the high public expectations in the GDR, it has had to be accelerated. Public opinion in West Germany—1990 is an election year—will add further pressure. All political parties except the Greens have welcomed unification, but they differ in their estimate of whether it should be through long and careful assimilation or a single act, to be taken sometime in 1990. Given the initial popular enthusiasm about the prospect of unification, political leaders have been reluctant to spell out either the financial and economic costs or the international risks of this process.

The rapid unfolding of the prospect for unification has caught the West between its commitment to self-determination and its interest in a stable European balance. Reunification of Germany will only be acceptable to its neighbors if care is taken that this process will not endanger peace and stability in Europe. The allies of both German states have declared their support for the German desire to unite; they have, however, counseled proceeding with pru-

8. In the elections of 18 Mar. 1990 in the GDR, the Christian Democrats and their allies of the Demokratische Allianz, scored an impressive victory, with 48.15 percent of the popular vote. They were the political forces most closely associated with economic and political reunification.

dence and caution. The Four Powers with special rights and responsibilities concerning Germany as a whole —the United States, Great Britain, France, and the Soviet Union—have demanded that negotiations between the two German states be joined by talks with the Four Powers. At the Ottawa foreign ministers' meeting, the term "two plus four" was coined for this process.[9] Finally, all European states shall be consulted at a CSCE Summit Conference in November 1990.[10]

A core problem will be the political and military status of a unified Germany. The Soviet Union is determined in its neutralization, while the United States has voiced its expectation that Germany will remain a member of NATO.[11] GDR Defense Minister Hoffmann has suggested that each part of Germany remain in its respective alliance but reduce the size of

their combined forces to 300,000.[12] The Bonn government proceeds from the assumption that West Germany would continue to be a member of the integrated military organization of NATO but that its reach would not extend to the territory of the GDR.[13] It also assumes that Allied forces, though reduced in numbers, would for a transitional period remain deployed on German territory—Western forces in the Federal Republic, Soviet forces in the GDR. The Ottawa agreement on a ceiling of 195,000 American and Soviet troops in the central region—which is, for this purpose, essentially identical with the territory of Germany—points in this direction. It also indicates that the Four Powers are exercising authority to deploy troops in Germany on the basis of their original rights as occupation powers, not subject to negotiation with a unified Germany.

The Soviet position on the German question has been quite equivocal; it has ranged from Gorbachev's remark in early December 1989 in a talk with French President François Mitterrand that on the day after the unification of the two Germanies he would be replaced by a Soviet general at the helm of the ship of state, to his statement less than two months later, when welcoming GDR Premier Hans Modrow in Moscow: "When I used to say that history will decide the German issue, then this is what is going to happen. Already one can see that

9. See "Communiqué of the Meeting of the Foreign Ministers of the Federal Republic of Germany, the German Democratic Republic, France, the United Kingdom, the Soviet Union and the United States of America in Ottawa, February 13, 1990," *Bulletin der Bundesregierung*, 20 Feb. 1990, p. 215.

10. The CSCE process started in 1973, with the Helsinki Conference on Security and Cooperation in Europe; its result has been the Helsinki Final Act of 1975. See Luigi Vittorio Ferraris, *Report on a Negotiation: Helsinki— Geneva—Helsinki 1972-1975* (Leiden: Sijthoff, 1979). So far there have been review conferences in Belgrade, Madrid, and Vienna. The Vienna meeting gave a mandate to a Conference on Conventional Forces in Europe, charged with negotiating reductions of conventional forces in Europe.

11. See "Address by Secretary of State Baker before the Berlin Press Club, December 12, 1989," *U.S. Policy-Information and Texts*, 13 Dec. 1989, pp. 35-44.

12. See "Hoffmann: In den Bündnissen bleiben," *Frankfurter Allgemeine Zeitung*, 26 Feb. 1990, p. 3.

13. See "Sicherheitspolitische Fragen eines künftigen geeinten Deutschland," *Bulletin der Bundesregierung*, 21 Feb. 1990, p. 218.

history is taking its first corrective steps."[14] So far, the bottom line has been that under no circumstances will Moscow tolerate membership of a reunified Germany in the Western alliance, even without NATO troops on East German territory. The WTO ministers, however, have been divided, with Czechoslovakia, Poland, and Hungary arguing against neutral status for Germany. Will Gorbachev stick to his line? What price will he try to exact, and what price will the Germans—or the United States—be prepared to pay?[15]

It is still not decided whether the denouement of the process of German unification will be a political arrangement by the Four (custodial) Powers with the Germans, a peace treaty between Germany and its former war enemies, or a new European order of peace blessed by a CSCE summit. The West German government has supported the two-plus-four process and has voiced opposition to a formal peace treaty. There is little it could gain from it, and it could lose much. It would singularize Germans vis-à-vis their former wartime enemies and stimulate various constraints and claims, especially for reparations. A sine qua non under any arrangement, however, will be formal recognition of the finality and legitimacy of the Polish border. A united Germany will have no problem formally recognizing all existing borders.

The process of German unification, if successful, will change the European situation more than any other event since the end of World War II and the onset of the Cold War. The necessary adaptive processes on the part of other European states will add a new, dynamic dimension to European politics and might well lead to original solutions, but it might also hold serious challenges and risks to postwar European stability. Among the uncertainties are the future of the members of the former Communist bloc—will they maintain their bonds to a democratized Soviet Union, form a *cordon sanitaire,* or associate with Western Europe? Will Germany continue to follow a policy of Western integration, or will it be lured by the economic opportunities opening up in the East and act as a halfway house between West and East? How will Europe's relationship with the superpowers evolve?

Any new European security structure will have to give a place to a politically dynamic and economically vital Germany of 80 million, accepting the pride and self-esteem of a proven democracy apprehensive of new international constraints but also coping with the concerns unleashed by the process of unification. Germany can be expected to balance opportunities with commitments and to play an active role in the reconstruction of Europe.

14. See Hans-Peter Riese, "Die Geschichte hat sich ans Werk gemacht. Der Wandel der sowjetischen Position zur deutschen Frage," *Europa-Archiv,* 45(4):117-26 (Feb. 1990).

15. A very real price will be paying for the Soviet troops continuously stationed on East German territory as well as for the devolution of the former East German trade with the Soviet Union.

WEST EUROPEAN INTEGRATION, ATLANTIC ALLIANCE AND ALL-EUROPEAN COOPERATION

The dramatic changes in the center of Europe have an impact on the European Community (EC) as well as on the Atlantic Alliance. Will the emergence of an economically and politically strong Germany speed up the process of European integration and union, or will attention be distracted by the new opportunities in Eastern Europe, with the consequence that the integration of Western Europe stagnates?

German policy is based on the assumption that the EC will be the most effective stabilizer in a process of rapid change. Above all, a united Germany should find its permanent moorings in a strong and vital EC that would respond to the desire to contain a resurgent Germany combined with a German need to reassure its partners.

By 1993 the EC will have completed economic and monetary union and will have gained in attractiveness tremendously. Its litmus test will be whether the Community remains wide open vis-à-vis West and East and does not allow itself to become a fortress Europe. Neither should transatlantic relations be burdened by a new series of chicken or steel wars, nor should those countries of the European Free Trade Association that express a desire to become members of the Common Market be denied entry to it. Most of all, the EC should be open for association with the Central and East European countries— Hungary, Czechoslovakia, and Poland —once they have adopted market economies. They need to benefit from Europe's prosperity and should not be left out in the cold. It would be disastrous if the European divide, this time not military and ideological but economic and social, would be moved just a few hundred miles east, from the Elbe to the Oder River, but still run through the center of Europe.

Only recently have Chancellor Kohl and President Mitterrand pledged their countries' support for the Community's further evolution toward political union. Though one might ask for squaring the circle, the Community should further proceed, with both enlargement and community building. As in the past, when the Common Market rested on a different organizational set up from the European Political Cooperation, different institutions could deal with different tasks. While the economic and monetary union would be the prime integrator, the political union, probably limited to those European countries that are prepared to cede sovereignty to the Community, would develop into a strong European pillar on which, together with the North American pillar, the Atlantic Alliance could safely rest. For this purpose the European political union would need a common defense policy, which could use article 30 of the Single European Act as its point of departure.

With more internal unity and increased economic and political weight, Western Europe could lead a more assertive policy vis-à-vis the United States and assume a larger role in international affairs. One of NATO's major problems has been the unequal distribution of power and influence between the United States and its allies, notwithstanding the professed equal status of all members. In cases of disagreement, the influence of the other alliance partners has been limited to a veto or leaving NATO integration. Over time, the differences in status have been leveled somewhat, but the dominance of the North American nuclear superpower, as well as the weakness of the nuclear have-nots, has remained.

To give the European members a greater voice in NATO affairs and to take account of opposition to giving the EC a security role, the Atlantic Alliance could be further Europeanized. This presupposes that the Europeans are prepared to assume greater responsibilities for their defense. No doubt, NATO will change significantly regarding function and force posture as well as military doctrine with the abatement of the Soviet military threat. Important tasks will be the reintegration of the French into an alliance framework and, to provide for some residual nuclear deterrent, the establishment of a joint command for the independent nuclear forces of both France and Britain. With likely reductions of U.S. forces, American influence will decrease, and conceivably the next Supreme Allied Commander Europe might be a European. Such a European NATO, however, would face the twofold problem of dispelling Soviet concerns about a radical shift in the European balance of power due to German membership in the Western alliance and coupling the United States to the political future of Europe.

Despite the Europeanization of NATO, the political architecture of Europe will remain incomplete if the Soviet Union and other East European countries are left out, though skepticism prevails about creating a new European collective security system or transforming the CSCE into an all-European security structure. Such an arrangement would be too unwieldy to be effective, as any one country could prevent agreement. Given the negative experiences with both the League of Nations and the United Nations, it is doubtful whether such a system would have the capability for peacekeeping.

Skepticism concerning a new European security system would negate the usefulness of the CSCE process. The latter would be best suited to integrating the East European countries and the Soviet Union into an all-European security framework, however loosely knit. In strengthening the CSCE process and preparing for its institutionalization, the different functions should be identified and distinguished.

For creating some overarching European security structures, basket I would provide a suitable point of departure. Under its roof a European Security Commission could operate that would be charged with the verification of an accord on conventional forces in Europe and other arms control agreements. Another institution could be a European Crisis Management Center for the exchange of information on crisis situations, to coordinate crisis-management strategies, and possibly to oversee the deployment and operation of multinational European peacekeeping forces. Regular meetings of high officials from member countries—if necessary, on the level of foreign ministers—or a small secretariat could be additional elements of networking and continuity.

Basket II provides an agenda for a European Economic Commission, if members prefer not to revitalize the U.N. Economic Commission for Europe. The European Economic Commission would be charged with assisting with the economic reform of Eastern Europe and other less developed areas of Europe. Another idea would be the establishment of a code of good conduct and self-restraint for Western investment in Eastern Europe. The commission could be complemented by a European currency union to cooperate with the European Monetary System if the convertibility of European currencies has been achieved. Another useful institution would be a European Environmental Commission, to be entrusted on a continued and transnational basis with safeguarding the human environment.

If democratic reform in Eastern Europe and the Soviet Union is successful, these countries might wish to become members of the Council of Europe. In implementing the goals specified in basket III the council would look after the social, cultural, and humanitarian development of Europe. At some stage or another, its members might also wish to broaden the functions of its assembly to provide for a European Parliamentarian Assembly. But this would not be a first step; in a pragmatic process institutions would follow functions to be fulfilled rather than vice versa.

The configuration of a new European security system should be designed to cope with the most likely potential threats to European security and stability: domestic instability, ethnic and nationality conflicts, and spillover from Third World crises. Also, William of Occam's advice should be heeded: *"Entia non sunt multiplicanda praeter necessitatem."*[16] Thus a suitable and realistic European system would consist of a combination of elements of the EC, the North Atlantic Alliance, and the CSCE process. In building such a new European security system, preference should be given to a pragmatic step-by-step approach instead of waiting for grand designs to become true.

THE IMPACT ON THE NORDIC REGION

Though influenced by the overall European security structures, the Nordic region is a mini-cosmos of its own, not a flank. Iceland, Denmark, and Norway are members of NATO with, however, very different statuses. Iceland has no military forces of its own but is host to a large U.S. military base at Keflavík; Denmark and Norway allow neither military bases nor nuclear weapons on their soil in peacetime. Sweden is militarily neutral, and Finland is nonaligned, bound by special treaty relations to the Soviet Union. This system of calibrated defense options has been called the Nordic balance.[17]

16. The translation is "Without necessity, entities should not be multiplied." I owe this reference to Gwyn Prins, "Report on a Discussion: Preparing for CSCE," mimeograph (Cambridge Global Security Programme, 22 Mar. 1990), p. 3.

17. See Arne Olav Brundtland, *The Nordic Balance* (Oslo: Norsk Utenrikspolitisk Institutt, 1981).

The five countries cooperate closely with each other in the Nordic Council (Nordiska Radet) and participate in a number of other joint Nordic institutions, ranging from a passport union to the Nordic Research Council. They also vary in their patterns of economic cooperation.

Because of the different geostrategic position of each country, threat perceptions differ as much as defense policies. Denmark's defense is tied to the Central European theater; its navy has the special mission of denying a potential attacker the control of the Baltic Sea approaches. Norway controls the North Atlantic lines of communication for both the United States and the Soviet Union. In case of military conflict, it would be a valuable prize for the Soviet Union, which could move its naval and air bases some 1000 miles forward from the Kola Peninsula to northern Norway. Neutral Sweden's defense posture is directed at preventing any military invasion or other violation of Swedish territory. Finland's military forces are mandated by the Finnish-Soviet Treaty of Friendship, Cooperation and Mutual Assistance of 1948 to prevent military transit by a third party and to safeguard Finland's independence.[18]

In the past twenty years the Northern region has acquired a significant strategic importance in the overall balance of forces due to the naval buildup of the Soviet Union.[19]

18. For an excellent overview of security and defense in the Nordic region, see Falk Bomsdorf, *Sicherheit im Norden Europas. Die Sicherheitspolitik der fünf nordischen Staaten und die Nordeuropapolitik der Sowjetunion* (Baden-Baden: Nomos, 1989).

19. See *NATO's Defense of the North*, ed. Eric Grove (London: Brassey's U.K., 1989).

The Soviet navy was transformed from a coastal force with limited capabilities to a blue-water navy with global ambitions. Of special importance is the Soviet Northern Fleet based at Murmansk, the only base on Soviet territory with direct access to the open seas. The Soviet Union has deployed a large number of both nuclear and conventional submarines as well as surface ships, air force components, and INF missiles on the Kola Peninsula. Besides posing, with its strategic nuclear submarines, a direct strategic threat to the United States, the Northern Fleet constitutes the main challenge for NATO's transatlantic communications and its capability to reinforce the European forces in a crisis. In a war, northern Norway would be a valuable forward base for the Soviet Union from which the strategic link between the defense of Western Europe and that of the United States could be broken up. Neither present Scandinavian military forces nor available NATO reinforcements are a match for the Soviet military power in its northwestern territory.

In the 1980s, the military threat to the Nordic countries was increased by a second factor, the deployment of INF in Europe and of sea-launched cruise missiles in the Northern seas. Though with the December 1987 INF treaty the land-based INF have been removed, sea-launched cruise missiles still abound, in the absence of naval arms control.

All Nordic countries have complemented their defense policy with an active policy of détente and arms control. Each of the three core countries has developed its own programs.

Norway's is based on the concept of *avsrekking og beroligelse* ("deterrence and appeasement"), implying deterrence of the Soviet Union but at the same time reassuring it about the defensive character of Norway's military policy. In the 1980s *skjerming*, preventing horizontal escalation, was added as a third function of Norwegian security policy.[20] Sweden's security policy rests on the two pillars of "a strong military defense combined with an active peace and disarmament policy." It is characterized by a "combination of stability, activity and flexibility."[21] Denmark has held fast to the Harmel formula of defense and détente.[22]

All Scandinavian countries have actively promoted negotiations on European arms control and confidence building. The Swedish contri-

bution has been most visible. Sweden not only hosted the Stockholm Conference on Confidence Building Measures and Disarmament, but its late socialist premier, Olof Palme, reminded the world on many occasions that any nation's security required the "common security" of all. At one stage or another, mostly under social-democratic rule, the Nordic countries have embraced the renewed Kekkonen proposal for a nuclear weapons free zone, "to some outlining a nuclear sanctuary in a potential conflict between the superpowers" but, to most, "intended to add a confidence-building impetus to the Nordic efforts to relaunch détente and dialogue between East and West."[23]

The success of the INF negotiations and the prospects for further arms control agreements on strategic and conventional weapons systems have mitigated the military threat to the Nordic region less than in the central region. Naval arms control has not even started. Nor has the United States been prepared to consider constraints on its maritime forces and, with them, on its ability to project power globally. Nor have the Vienna negotiations on the reduction of conventional forces in Europe affected the Soviet bases on the Kola Peninsula. After Gorbachev's visit to Finland, the Soviet Union announced plans to reduce its Northern Front forces to 40,000 men and 1200 tanks. Land-based INF have been dismantled, and Moscow has assured Sweden that it will not deploy shorter-range nuclear forces in the adjoining territories. Consequently, the de-

20. See John Kristen Skogun, "Norsk sikkerketspolitikk i brytningen mellom allianse og nöytralitet," in *Norsk utenrikspolitikk*, ed. Johan Jørgen Holst and Daniel Heradsveit (Oslo: NIIA, 1985), pp. 35-37; Johan Jørgen Holst, *Norsk sikkerhetspolitikk i strategisk perspekiiv* (Oslo: NIIA, 1976), vol. 1; Bomsdorf, *Sicherheit im Norden Europas*, pp. 77-82.

21. See Bo Huldt, "The Strategic North," *Washington Quarterly*, 8(3):99-109 (Summer 1985); "Report of the Defense Committee on Security Policy and Defense Planning" (Press release [unofficial translation], Stockholm, 23 Jan. 1990), p. 1.

22. For the Danish concept, see *Dyvig-Rapporten. Danmarks sikkerhedspolitiske situation i 1980'erne, med kommentarer og debat*, ed. Det sikkerhedsog nedrustningspolitiske Udvalg, 1985; *Rapport fra Udredningsgruppen om Sikkerhedsog Nedrustningspolitik*, ed. Forsvarskommissionen AF 1988, 1989; see also Martin O. Heisler, "Denmark's Quest for Security: Constraints and Opportunities within the Alliance," in *NATO's Northern Allies*, ed. Gregory Flynn (Totowa, NJ: Rowman & Allanheld, 1985), pp. 57-112.

23. Huldt, "Strategic North," p. 104, fn. 19.

fense policies of Norway and Sweden—the countries most immediately affected by the strategic naval threat—have changed little. Norway has been one of the few members of NATO that has met the goal of increasing its defense expenditures by 3 percent net. Sweden is developing the JAS, an advanced fighter aircraft, and plans to introduce a new main battle tank into its army and to modernize its navy.

Denmark is in a somewhat different situation. It profits from the climate of détente on the Continent, but even if it did not, for domestic reasons it could not be expected to increase defense expenditures. Denmark is moving toward a unilateral modification of military posture, from a contribution to forward defense to one of territorial defense. With the dispersion of the United Kingdom Mobile Force earmarked as reinforcement for Denmark's defense, its defensive posture has been further weakened.

Due to their contrasting threat perceptions, Denmark and Norway also evaluate the role of the Atlantic Alliance differently. Denmark seems to be in favor of transforming NATO into an instrument of political consultation, and it supports all efforts to strengthen the existing all-European ties such as the CSCE process. Norway, for its part, would like to see NATO continue as it is, and adamantly opposes loosening its coupling link with the United States. Though favoring greater European defense cooperation—for example, within the Eurogroup or the Independent European Program Group—both are reluctant to become members of the Western European Union, which they consider a French ploy to weaken NATO. Denmark would probably resign itself to becoming a member if NATO dissolved, while Norway, instead of relying on a West European Defense Community, would probably rather conclude a bilateral defense agreement with the United States.

The realization of the Common European Market in 1992 holds interesting prospects for the Nordic members of the European Free Trade Association. An agreement for association is about to be signed, and both Norway and Sweden may apply for full membership in the next few years. But it is their trade pattern and the economic attractiveness of the Community, not the prospect of becoming part of a strong and viable political union, that draws the Scandinavian countries to Brussels. The Danish policy of footnoting many an EC agreement underlines this judgment.

Liberalization in the Soviet Union and Eastern Europe holds both promise and concern for the Nordic countries. With a greater autonomy of the Soviet provinces, historically close political, economic, and cultural relations with the Baltic states may be revived. In the seventeenth and eighteenth centuries, Sweden ruled large parts of Poland and East Germany, while the name of Estonia's capital, Tallin—meaning "pearl of Denmark"—is a reminder of the former Hanseatic connection. While the Baltic states may look to the Nordic countries for support and inspiration, the latter have been cautious to support moves toward independence from Moscow. The Nordic countries value prospects for liberalization in

Eastern Europe but are afraid of a destabilization of the USSR and the resulting dangers to peace and stability in Europe.

World War II and wartime German occupation have left deep scars on both Denmark and Norway, influencing these countries' positions on the German question. But, 45 years after the war, a new generation has grown up in both countries. Political and economic ties have developed with the Federal Republic and, to a lesser extent, also with the German Democratic Republic. The Nordic countries came forward very quickly to support the process of German unification, but especially Denmark and Norway have cautioned that it should only take place after careful consultation within the institutions of the EC, NATO, the Council of Europe, and the CSCE and in tandem with a process of all-European cooperation.

The new developments in European security could, to some extent, uncouple the Nordic region from the center of Europe. The processes in the center of Europe might take on a dynamic of their own and marginalize Scandinavia and its interests. NATO and the EC may not be expanded and strengthened but, instead, modified to accommodate a unified Germany. Much energy may be spent in such adaptation, with little left for either enlargement or transformation into a political union. As a result, relations between Scandinavia and Western Europe might loosen. The Nordic region could become either more inward looking or more all-European in its perspective. Under the stewardship of Norway, it might wish to strengthen its relations with the Anglo-Saxon countries, while Finland and to a lesser degree Sweden could provide a bridge to Eastern Europe and the Soviet Union. The latter might look to them for assistance in circumscribing the room for maneuver for independent Baltic republics. Instead of providing a Northern support for the Atlantic Alliance, the Nordic region could become a halfway house between East and West or, in the long term, a building bloc for an all-European security structure in which it would find a congenial home.

From the Outside Looking In: The Nordic States and the European Community after 1992

By M. DONALD HANCOCK

ABSTRACT: Recent moves within the European Community (EC) toward closer economic, financial, and social union compel Scandinavian political elites to rethink their nations' ties with the EC. Denmark has been a member since 1972, but the remaining Scandinavian countries remain highly ambivalent toward the Community—the Norwegians because of a deeply rooted tradition of isolationism and the Swedes and the Finns because of their foreign policies of neutrality. Seeking to steer a middle course between extreme domestic viewpoints on optimal ties with the EC, Sweden, Norway, and Finland are likely to achieve de facto membership on the basis of unilateral and multilateral steps toward greater economic harmonization.

M. Donald Hancock is professor of political science and director of the Center for European Studies at Vanderbilt University. He specializes in comparative political analysis, with particular emphasis on modern Germany, Sweden, and the United Kingdom. He is the author of Sweden: The Politics of Postindustrial Change *and West Germany: The Politics of Democratic Corporatism *and is a contributing coauthor and coeditor of a forthcoming volume entitled* Managing Modern Capitalism: Industrial Renewal and Workplace Democracy in the United States and Western Europe.

T HE Nordic states maintain a deeply rooted ambivalence toward the European Community (EC). On the one hand, politically, culturally, and economically, Scandinavia is inexorably linked with Western Europe. Borrowing extensively from British and Continental patterns, Sweden, Norway, Denmark, and Finland have emerged in this century as exemplary political democracies and advanced welfare systems. Since the mid-1930s, the Nordic countries have also achieved—to varying degrees—among the world's highest standards of living on the basis of efficient domestic capitalist economies and extensive trade and financial links with advanced industrial nations in Europe and elsewhere.

On the other hand, Denmark alone within the Nordic region, acted on economic imperatives in 1972 to become a full member of the EC. The remaining Scandinavian nations, in contrast, remain consciously, even stubbornly, removed from the Community. In part, this is due to a combination of historical and cultural factors, including the greater geographic separation of Sweden, Norway, and Finland from the rest of the Continent and a strong sense of national identity and pride on the part of their citizens. Foreign policy calculations have also played a major role in shaping Scandinavia's relations with postwar regional organizations and the European integration process. Traditions of neutrality—voluntary in the case of Sweden, and based on treaty obligations with the Soviet Union in the case of Finland—precluded Swedish and Finnish involvement in Western security arrangements and all forms of regional supranational cooperation at their inception. Norway joined Denmark in becoming a founding member of the North Atlantic Treaty Organization in 1949, but a majority of Norwegians voted against membership in the EC in a wrenching national referendum in the fall of 1972.

Ongoing economic and institutional changes within the EC confront Scandinavian political elites with the need for major policy adjustments in the years ahead. Given the increasing importance of trade and financial transactions with the EC, can any or all of the three nonmember Nordic states continue to remain outside the Community? Conversely, is membership compatible with Swedish and Finnish neutrality? Under what conditions can the membership issue be reopened in the case of Norway? This article addresses these fundamental issues in light of evolving economic relations between Scandinavia and the EC and the public debate on the implied consequences of 1992 for the region's economic future.

THE POLITICAL BACKGROUND

The Nordic countries initially avoided the necessity for a hard choice between intergovernmental and supranational cooperation when they joined Britain, Austria, Switzerland, and Portugal in creating the European Free Trade Association (EFTA) in 1959. With this step Scandinavia linked forces with all of their principal European trading partners —except West Germany—in the parallel elimination of tariffs and other constraints on industrial trade. Alongside their economic cooperation within EFTA, the Nordic states also pursued extensive cultural, legal, and labor market collaboration within the Nordic Council, which was founded in 1952.

A potential policy dilemma confronting all of the Nordic states arose in 1961, when Britain submitted its initial bid for membership in the European Economic Community. Danish government and industrial leaders promptly indicated their interest in membership as well, whereas the governing Social Democrats in Sweden unequivocally declared that Sweden's policy of neutrality precluded that country from following the British lead. The prospect of Finnish neutrality was wholly precluded on the basis of that country's 1948 treaty of mutual assistance with the Soviet Union. The issue proved moot in light of President de Gaulle's veto of the British initiative, but it resurfaced at the end of the decade when the Hague summit of 1969 opened the way for formal negotiations on membership between the European Commission, Britain, Ireland, Denmark, and Norway.

Swedish Prime Minister Olof Palme was initially receptive to the possibility that Sweden might join the Community after all if appropriate safeguards could be incorporated in a treaty of accession to protect Swedish neutrality. He pursued this theme in a series of public speeches and quiet diplomacy in various European capitals during the year 1970. By 1971, however, skeptical voices

within the ranks of the Social Democratic Party and among leading members of the opposition Center and Liberal parties—though not the Conservatives—convinced Palme that membership was not a valid option. Too many influential Swedes worried that such a step would compromise the credibility of Sweden's traditional policy of neutrality and therefore increase the possibility that the country could become directly involved in a future war. Reinforcing such concerns about Sweden itself was the simultaneous fear that a departure from neutrality would endanger neighboring Finland's political and economic independence in relation to the Soviet Union.

Thus Palme abandoned his earlier flirtation with prospective membership in favor of negotiations with the European Commission on a free trade agreement between Sweden and the EC. Such a formula promised access to the expanded Common Market for Swedish industry—though not Sweden's agrarian sector—without involving Sweden in binding policy decisions that might restrict the capacity of political elites to maintain a policy of nonalignment. Caution rather than affirmation seemed wholly vindicated as Sweden witnessed the intense partisan conflicts that accompanied the ratification debate on EC membership in Denmark and Norway in 1971 and contributed to the subsequent advent of increased electoral volatility in both countries.

Denmark's ultimate acceptance of membership and Norway's rejection of it resulted in a split in Nordic ranks on the EC issue. The political and economic effects of regional division were largely blunted, however, by continued Scandinavian cooperation within the Nordic Council and the conclusion of free trade accords in 1972 between the Community and Sweden, Norway, and Finland. Thus both Sweden and Norway, whose leaders enjoyed greater freedom of foreign policy choice than the Finns, were able to avoid the painful consequences of choice by pursuing a compromise solution that offered substantial economic benefits with no direct political obligations.

THE MOVE TOWARD CLOSER EC UNION

The Community's expansion in 1972-73 presaged the onset of an extended period of international economic crisis triggered by successive oil-price shocks later in the decade. Consequently, political and economic elites in the Nordic states, like their counterparts in other industrial democracies, became necessarily preoccupied with efforts to restore growth and full employment while seeking to minimize inflation. Through the early 1980s the overriding necessity of managing domestic consequences of stagflation therefore diverted the attention of national policymakers from regional processes of economic integration.

With the gradual recovery of the international economic system from the early 1980s onward, the EC entered a new phase of expansion and policy innovation. In June 1983 EC members reaffirmed closer regional cooperation in the form of the Solemn Declaration of European Union, and they embarked on concrete measures to achieve the completion of an internal market by the end of 1992 on the basis of the Single European Act of 1986.

The growing momentum toward greater economic and social union within the Community seemed potentially threatened by sweeping political and economic reforms that had culminated by 1990 in the restoration of pluralist democracies throughout Eastern Europe and prospective German unification. Yet, as recent decisions within the EC have indicated, the political and economic upheavals in Eastern and Central Europe have by no means sidetracked subsequent steps toward further integration. The EC's Council of Ministers affirmed at its Strasbourg and Dublin summits of 1989-90 the creation of a common European monetary system, a European bank, and eventual political union. Further reflecting the emergence of a more closely integrated Community was the council's endorsement in principle in December 1989 of a Charter of Basic Social Rights, which is designed to protect workers individually as well as collectively in relation to employers. Once implemented, the Social Charter will serve as a moral and legal basis for the harmonization of social policies within the EC.

The culmination of these policy initiatives is likely to be the emergence by the mid-1990s of an economically united EC with increasingly centralized political authority shared jointly by the Council of Ministers and the European Commission. The underlying force compelling such an outcome is a joint European commitment—shared not the least by the Germans themselves—to bind a unified Germany firmly in the social and security fabric of Europe as a whole.

IMPLICATIONS FOR THE NORDIC STATES

The prospect of more comprehensive West European economic, financial, and institutional unity by the mid-1990s has compelled Scandinavian political leaders, industrialists, and trade unionists once again to examine their national and regional ties with the EC. The principal reason, as before, is the overwhelming importance of trade links with the EC. Since the initial round of the EC's expansion in 1972-73, the EC has consistently contributed the major share of Swedish, Norwegian, and Finnish imports. Simultaneously, it serves as the principal market for the export of Nordic industrial goods. The long-term trend is toward even closer economic ties between the Scandinavian countries and the Community as the relative importance of intra-EFTA trade declines.

Within Scandinavia, the prospect of a single European market has galvanized elite political and economic opinion, particularly in Sweden. Following extensive administrative deliberations and informal consultations with representatives of the leading organized interest groups, the Swedish cabinet submitted a formal policy paper in December 1987 that outlined a strategy of intensified cooperation both within EFTA and be-

tween EFTA and the EC. The general goal of such an action program is the attainment of a common market uniting the 18 member states of the two regional organizations. Specific objectives include "increased movement of goods, services, people, and capital in Western Europe as well as the maintenance of full employment and social security."[1] Once again, however, the government excluded the possibility of full EC membership by Sweden in the foreseeable future on the grounds that such a move would be incompatible with the country's policy of neutrality.

The government's policy paper served as the basis for protracted interparty consultations between members of the parliament's Foreign Affairs committee during the winter and early spring of 1988. The most enthusiastic supporters of closer ties with the EC were Moderate Unity (Conservative) deputies, who urged that the question of Swedish membership remain open and advocated, as an interim step, negotiations to achieve a joint EFTA-EC customs union. In contrast, the Social Democrats, the Liberals, and the Center endorsed a less ambitious agenda, stressing repeatedly the continued irreconcilability between full membership and neutrality. Ultimately, the latter view prevailed when the committee adopted a joint resolution affirming that "Swedish membership is not a goal for forthcoming discussions [with the EC]."[2] An overwhelm-

1. *Från Riksdagen och departementet*, 15 Jan. 1988, nr. 2, p. 13.
2. *Från Riksdagen och departementet*, 3 Mar. 1989, nr. 8, p. 2.

ing majority of the members of the national parliament endorsed the committee's position following a plenary debate in May 1988.

The response in Norway has been more muted, largely because of widely shared fears among political and economic leaders that a new debate on prospective membership could reopen wounds dating from the 1972 referendum. Contributing to a reluctance to reopen the issue is the continuing strength of Norwegian isolationism, a cultural trait dating from a deeply rooted schism between traditional agrarian and working-class groups, on the one hand, and the country's industrial and shipping elites, on the other. Among the principal policy actors, only the Conservatives openly favor full membership.

Finnish government officials are the most circumspect of all Nordic spokespersons on the EC question. Whether Finland can ever countenance ties with the Community that are closer than an industrial free trade agreement will obviously depend on the further course of political reform in the Soviet Union, including the Baltic republics.

PROSPECTS

Accordingly, the Nordic states have affirmed a linkage strategy that seeks to steer a middle course between the extremes of full membership—which many Conservatives and industrialists would prefer, especially in Sweden and Norway—and an overtly critical stance toward the EC, as Communist leaders and the Greens have urged. Through a carefully orchestrated process of unilateral policy adjustments—including the liberalization of domestic financial markets and tax laws, notably in Sweden—and multilateral negotiations on the creation of a European Economic Space that would encompass both the EC and EFTA, Nordic leaders will seek during the present decade to achieve comprehensive harmonization of their countries' economic relations with the more closely integrated EC. The result would be the expansion of existing economic and financial ties in the direction of de facto Nordic membership—a move that would preserve the appearance of Swedish and Finnish neutrality and assuage Norwegian isolationism while avoiding the economic pitfalls of a policy of self-isolation.

Book Department

INTERNATIONAL RELATIONS AND POLITICS

ELDERSVELD, SAMUEL J. *Political Elites in Modern Societies: Empirical Research and Democratic Theory.* Pp. xviii, 69. Ann Arbor: University of Michigan Press, 1989. No price.

This book is made up of three talks that Samuel Eldersveld delivered during the 1986-87 session of the Distinguished Faculty Lecture Series in Ann Arbor. Eldersveld concentrates on four themes: the linkages between socioeconomic position and political power; the cohesiveness-versus-pluralism of elites as an organizational force; ideological consensus as compared to disagreement among elites; and the relative commitment of elites to democratic as compared to hierarchical norms. His examination of these questions is enriched by a perspective that looks at elite politics from two complementary angles: across levels, from local to national, and across countries, including both First and Third World settings.

The first of the questions, involving the connections between economic and political power, seems to be the most readily answered. Everywhere the correlation is positive; the two dimensions of power tend to go together. Nevertheless, despite the apparent universality of this tendency in capitalist and indeed in social democratic societies, a question remains about the strength and the substance of the relationship. Detroit, where the local political leadership has become more elitist in the sense that elected officials of middle-class provenance have grown in number relative to those from working-class origins, no doubt differs from, say, cities in the interior of South America, where *políticos* tend to be closely aligned with a landed class—even if the correlation is close to the same in both cases.

The empirical findings become more varied and their theoretical implications even more complex as Eldersveld moves beyond this initial stage. The organizational cohesiveness of elites remains a contested topic in democratic systems. What is striking about the debate, aside from its substantive importance, is the almost complete lack of replication of the studies—most notably, Robert Dahl's analysis of New Haven—that confronted theory with data in the first place. A similar deficit afflicts the study of elite ideologies. In contrast with research on political attitudes in mass publics, it is rare to encounter systematic investigation of elite orientations over time.

It is with cross-national comparisons that elite studies have generated differential patterns of great interest. Eldersveld documents the tendency of American elites to espouse a populist political rhetoric while remaining faithful to an ideal of economic stratification that is plainly hierarchical in comparison to the more egalitarian structures that many European elites claim to favor. Part of this difference may be due to the legitimacy that Americans are inclined to give to the ideal of mobility within the social pyramid. Such flexibility, to the degree that it exists at all, can operate without reshaping the pyramid itself.

In the space of less than eighty pages Eldersveld covers considerable ground. Two qualities in particular recommend his book. Eldersveld does a commendable job of reviewing several decades of research about political elites, and anecdotes about his days as a Democratic Party activist and mayor of Ann Arbor add charm to the presentation of empirical results.

PETER McDONOUGH

Vanderbilt University
Nashville
Tennessee

GREENAWALT, KENT. *Speech, Crime and the Uses of Language.* Pp. viii, 349. New York: Oxford University Press, 1989. $45.00.

Greenawalt concludes this work with the basic premise that "for encouragements to specific crimes, the level of constitutional protection should depend on their general value and harmfulness in various contexts." He ends as he begins. This book is about free speech, what constitutes it, and the interpretation of the First Amendment and its application.

"The constitutional guarantee of freedom of speech reflects the important political principle that government should not suppress the communication of ideas." This principle, Greenawalt tells us, constitutes a cornerstone of liberal democracy. The book delves into free speech both as a political principle and as a constitutional standard in this country. He has divided the work into three parts. The first deals with the political principle of free speech, the justifications for freedom of speech, and the communications to which free speech is applicable. Part 2 discusses the relationship between free speech and criminal liability. The third part talks of the "conclusions from American constitutional law." Greenawalt suggests standards for protecting individual liberty. What free speech is under the First Amendment of the Constitution is the objective of this work. One single test, the author indicates, cannot exist to make this particular determination.

Greenawalt develops justifications for freedom of speech. He talks of a "minimal principle of liberty," that is, the government has no right to prohibit people from speaking out unless there exists a positive reason to do so. He deals also with the various ways language is utilized and the factor that some uses of language have no bearing on issues of free speech.

There is much discussion of major First Amendment cases such as *Brandenburg* v. *Ohio* and their implication for freedom of speech. Greenawalt informs the reader that "deciding exactly what threats should be made criminal is harder than deciding what offers should be made criminal." How far freedom of speech can go and the justifications for what is considered speech compared to the justifications for free speech are part of this thesis.

The topics Greenawalt presents are interesting and have much relevance in today's times. The problem with this book on speech is that it is too verbose. Greenawalt's style of writing makes reading this book very difficult. One needs to review passages, words, and paragraphs several times before what the author is saying is understood. Greenawalt tells the reader at the outset that he will repeat himself, which he does—but to excess.

His subject is a scholarly one. Freedom of speech is an important topic, and, certainly, trying to determine what constitutes free speech, what truly is free and to be protected, is a topic worthy of a book. But Greenawalt overdoes it. This work took about a decade, and the author appears to have put in every minute detail he could think of. The ideas are good and refreshing; however, the writing is complicated. One needs time and patience to understand and digest this work.

ROSLYN MURASKIN

Long Island University
Brookville
New York

HANRIEDER, WOLFRAM F. *Germany, America, Europe: Forty Years of German Foreign Policy.* Pp. xviii, 509. New Haven, CT: Yale University Press, 1989. $29.95.

As German reunification looms, the Federal Republic of Germany (FRG) nears achievement of the most cherished objective of its tortuous and triumphant forty-year recovery from World War II. Much attention is paid to Japan's postwar successes; we can now appreciate the equally remarkable foreign policy achievements of the Bonn government.

There is no better guide to its relationships within the West's grand coalition than this stimulating book.

Hanrieder's years of patient observation and reflection, lodged firmly within a realist perspective, have culminated in a thorough, elegantly written volume, a model of organization and analysis. It contains penetrating assessments of the political, military, and economic aspects of the FRG's relations with its Western partners, rich commentaries on American and French policies, and rewarding observations on contemporary international politics, the economic life of the North Atlantic region, and the process of European integration.

He emphasizes politics, treating the recurring debates on Western military doctrines and deployments, the struggles over European integration, and U.S.-European economic frictions as—at bottom—the constant conduct of politics by other means. The key here is the shifting distribution of power, particularly the decline of American hegemony. However, he highlights the multilevel nature of postwar international relations, the interplay of territorial-geostrategic, economic interdependence, and security realms of interaction, with which states must grapple simultaneously. His analysis turns on the tensions between interdependence and nationalism, military security and economic health, the domestic roots of foreign policy and the eternal constrains under which it operates.

Several major themes emerge. One concerns the early and close association of Bonn with American hegemony, containment, and deterrence, and then the mounting frictions as each fundamental feature of American policy eroded or became less compatible with German interest and objectives. Another is Germany's search for a suitably independent stature while remaining within, and working through, its intimate North Atlantic and Western European associations. Much is therefore said about the German problem—how the American embrace of the FRG and the latter's membership in the European Community were always intended to contain German power and autonomy and thus were not readily reconciled with German aspirations to restore a single national community.

Stunning developments have put reunification within reach, necessarily pushing the German problem to center stage once again. Even without having anticipated these events, Hanrieder concludes with wise counsel on the necessity to focus American policy on the creation of an all-European security compact to replace the once stable but no longer suitable division of the continent. Decay of the old order has outrun his expectations but has made all the more urgent his proposed response.

PATRICK M. MORGAN

Washington State University
Pullman

AFRICA, ASIA, AND
LATIN AMERICA

AZIMI, FAKHREDDIN. *Iran, the Crisis of Democracy, 1941-1953*. Pp. ix, 433. New York: St. Martin's Press, 1989. No price.

This book, although limited to Iran's political development in a period rather removed from the 1970s and 1980s, is useful in providing background for the revolution and its aftermath. Azimi analyzes both the composition of and the interrelationship between the main pillars of Iranian political power between 1941 and 1953: namely, the court, the *majlis* (parliament), the cabinet, foreign embassies, and the Iranian people. As this narrative shows, power and influence continually shifted between these

various elements with ephemeral alliances constructed between them.

The heyday of the foreign embassies occurred during World War II. The British manipulated key pro-Western politicians, while the Soviets played an important role through their brief occupation of Azerbaijan and their use of the Tudeh (Communist) Party. The Americans exercised little influence in this period, but their later role was already foreshadowed. American interest in containing Soviet influence and in encouraging U.S. economic ties resulted in the first wave of U.S. military and economic experts.

As the book demonstrates, the shah who was put into power by the Allies in 1941 was less aggressive politically than the ruler that emerged after the fall of Mohammad Mossadeq in 1953. Throughout the period, the shah steadily increased his power at the expense of the *majlis* and cabinets by amending the constitution and developing supporters among Iran's political personalities. Above all, he cultivated key army officers until his grip on that institution was unchallenged. Thus a small window of opportunity for democracy was closed.

During the war the importance of the *majlis* had increased as a forum for the exchange of political opinions. Under the Allies, press censorship was relatively relaxed and greater public freedom led to the emergence of political groups mainly centered on well-known figures. Unfortunately, the cabinets were weak—there were at least twenty cabinets during the 12 years covered by the book—and they did not represent any clear political views rooted in public support. Nor were political groups able to organize into political parties that could capture the *majlis* as a result of free elections. Most important, however, was the shah's fight against any increase in the power and influence of prime ministers or their cabinets. The only exception to this rule was Mossadeq, who was able to build up an alliance with the Iranian people capable of overruling the shah, but his rule was cut short by foreign influence.

This book is well written and has an extensive bibliography for those interested in reading more. It can be recommended to anyone interested in modern Iranian politics.

LOUAY BAHRY

Washington, D.C.

HARRISON, SELIG S. and K. SUBRAHMANYAM, eds. *Superpower Rivalry in the Indian Ocean: Indian and American Perspectives.* Pp. ix, 309. New York: Oxford University Press, 1989. $36.00.

This book is a collection of analytical essays by three American and three Indian authors that originated as working papers for the Indo-American Task Force on the Indian Ocean. The task force met in late 1984 in New Delhi under the sponsorship of the Carnegie Endowment for International Peace and the Institute of Defense Studies and Analyses (IDSA), New Delhi, with support from the Ford Foundation. The essays, however, have subsequently been revised and updated by the authors and brought together as a coherent volume through superb editorial efforts by Selig S. Harrison of the Carnegie Endowment and K. Subrahmanyam of IDSA.

As expected from its title, the book examines the implications of military deployment by the United States and the Soviet Union in the Indian Ocean and recommends measures of arms control in the region. To the delight of its readers, it delivers more than might have been expected from other such books on the superpower rivalry. To begin with, the rivalry is defined not simply as a naval competition in the blue-water Indian Ocean. It is cast broadly in terms of direct as well as indirect competition to safeguard military, political, and economic stakes in this "vast region embracing the Indian Ocean, the Persian Gulf, and 42 littoral states." The analyses thus take full account of the diversity of the region and the complexity of interactions involving U.S., Soviet, and other extraregional military forces as well as such emerging regional powers as India.

Following the introduction by the editors, who provide useful summaries of the essays by the chapter authors, the book begins with analyses of "emerging security issues in the Indian Ocean." Walter K. Andersen, on leave from his position as the State Department's political analyst for India, Sri Lanka, and the Indian Ocean in the Bureau of Intelligence and Research, presents "an American perspective" and Vice Admiral M. P. Awati, who retired in 1983 as flag officer and commander in chief, Western Command of Indian Navy, presents "an Indian perspective."

Rejecting the conventional discussion on "superpower rivalry" in the Indian Ocean, which tends to assume a simple action-reaction process between the two superpowers, Andersen develops a more sophisticated view of indirect interactions involving third parties and complex motives. While the U.S. decision in 1979 to establish a powerful and permanent naval presence in the northwest quadrant of the Indian Ocean was obviously motivated by fear of the loss of access to Persian Gulf oil, the continuous Soviet naval presence in the region is attributed by Andersen to the Soviet hopes for enhancing political influence with the littoral states. Admiral Awati, on the other hand, believes that the Indian Ocean is a potential, if not an actual, theater of superpower strategic confrontation. This is so because the Indian Ocean is an attractive deployment area for U.S. submarine-launched ballistic missiles, which would greatly complicate Soviet antisubmarine-warfare problems. After examining U.S. power-projection efforts centered around the Rapid Deployment Force/U.S. Central Command and a more modest "essentially defense-oriented" Soviet effort, he sees qualitative equivalence between the U.S. "image of a Soviet Union moving nearer the Gulf and spreading its military net in an ever widening circle, against a background of instability in Iran and in the Arab Gulf states" and the Soviet image of increased rapprochement between China and the Western allies. Awati, however, blames the United States for having set the pace of the cold war in the region and therefore obliges it to initiate any move toward détente.

The two chapters that follow the security analyses deal with the "emerging economic issues in the Indian Ocean," with Joel Larus, professor of politics at New York University, presenting an American view and C. Raja Mohan, a research associate at the IDSA, an Indian one. Noting the unparalleled economic diversity of the region, Larus provides a comprehensive and balanced analysis of the key economic issues of exploration and exploitation of both the mineral and the living marine resources in the 200-mile exclusive economic zones, the deep seabed, and Antarctica. Steering a midcourse between the Reagan administration's rejection of the Enterprise, an operational arm of the pending International Seabed Authority, and the vociferous demands by the Third World nations for its full realization, Larus proposes a pragmatic application of the concept of common heritage to the future deep-sea mining of polymetallic nodules and Antarctic development. Raja Mohan's essay is highly critical of U.S. Indian Ocean policy and rejects common assumptions about the dependence of the United

States and the West on the petroleum and strategic materials of the region and the threat to the security of the sea lanes there posed by the hostile forces.

In Chapter 5, "Arms Limitation in the Indian Ocean: Retrospect and Prospect," Subrahmanyam examines past arms control efforts, including the Indian Ocean Zone of Peace proposal, and finds fault with the U.S. policy of naval supremacy and unilateral interventionist force projection in the region. Denying the view that "the Kremlin is out to exploit anarchy in the world," he sees India and the United States, and in fact the whole world, as having common interests "in ensuring the freedom of the seas, access to the oil resources of West Asia, and safeguarding the sea lanes." Matters of common interest such as these, Subrahmanyam asserts, can be solved through a collective approach.

The final chapter, "India, the United States, and Superpower Rivalry in the Indian Ocean," by Harrison, is an excellent analytical synthesis that contains hopes for superpower cooperation, especially in light of the Soviet withdrawal from Afghanistan and the end of the Iran-Iraq war, to establish effective arms control measures centered around mutual-restraint agreements in Iran and Pakistan. Especially noteworthy in Harrison's recommendations is the pivotal role expected of India in the regional peace and security. Noting the nonalignment stance of Indian Ocean states with significant Indian population and the growing interventionary capability of India in the region, with particular sensitivity toward Pakistan, Harrison recommends U.S. policy in harmony with the legitimate interests of India. This means, in particular, a U.S. military-aid policy for Pakistan selectively chosen to enhance the latter's ability to resist Soviet advances in the region without undermining India's security.

The book concludes with an appendix containing the "conclusion and recommendations" of the task force. These call for, among other things, negotiations between the interested parties to reduce tensions in the region, clarification and redefinition of U.S. commitment to Pakistan, and Indian confidence-building initiatives to help remove U.S. suspicion about India's military-aid relationship with the Soviet Union.

What is so remarkable about the work of the task force and about this book, then, is that the policy experts from the two countries separated by two oceans seem to have more to agree than disagree on with respect to appropriate measures of international security in the region of the Indian Ocean. Several propositions emerge as areas of consensus between the six authors: the United States and the Soviet Union have not been on a direct collision course in the blue-water naval competition; nor is a steadily expanding role of the Indian navy a threat to the United States, because the two countries share an interest in keeping sea lanes and access to Gulf oil open to all nations. Arms control in the region is thus not only desirable but also possible. The only catch is the requirement of U.S. initiative.

When the task force met, it was against a background of continuing tension between the superpowers in the Indian Ocean and Persian Gulf region. There was then a sense of urgency for arms control, but its prospect was dim precisely because of the tension and unwillingness on the part of the United States to give up its go-it-alone policy under the worst-case fear of Soviet intervention at the Gulf's choke points. The tension has now subsided but so, obviously, have the sense of urgency and the risk that U.S. force projection in the region would provoke superpower confrontation. What, then, will persuade the United States to move toward a more collective Indian Ocean policy against the forces of institutional inertia, bureaucratic politics, and a unilateralist attitude in Washington? It is the fundamental shortcoming of the book that such vital questions of the politics of policy remain unanswered. For a book of prescriptive policy, however, it is praiseworthy not only for the sensibleness of the alternative policy that it recommends but also for the comprehensive analyses of the military and economic environment of this critical region.

SUNG HO KIM

Ohio University
Athens

JAGCHID, SECHIN and VAN JAY SYMONS. *Peace, War, and Trade along the Great Wall: Nomadic-Chinese Interaction through Two Millennia.* Pp. ix, 266. Bloomington: Indiana University Press, 1989. $29.95.

Sechin Jagchid and Van Jay Symons present a straightforward thesis: trade was the main element in determining whether or not there would be peace along the shifting borders between the northern nomads and the Central Kingdom of China. Jagchid and Symons make a strong case that economic considerations weighed heavily in the deliberations of both the Chinese and the nomads over whether to go to war against the other side at any given moment.

The time frame of their study is enormous, stretching all the way from the second century B.C.E. to the middle of the seventeenth century C.E. They are able to focus their analysis, however, by concentrating primarily on three institutions that were already in place before the beginning of our era: a system of frontier markets, the exchange of nomadic "tribute" for Chinese "bestowals," and intermarriage between the ruling groups.

There can be little doubt that the nomadic people of the north were less likely to extract forcibly from the central plains such items as grain, cloth, tea, and metal products when the Chinese were willing to exchange them for the horses, furs, wool, precious stones, and other goods they had to offer. Additional elements, however, also entered into the policy calculations governing movements across the network of defensive walls thrown up by the Chinese. Among these were the rise of charismatic leaders, the forging of confederations, internal strife, demographic shifts, and climatic changes.

The present volume is actually a revised and condensed translation of Jagchid's book written in Chinese on the same subject that was published in 1972. Symons has added much new material from modern Western scholarship, but there is only a little from Mongolian sources and none whatsoever from sources in Persian, Arabic, Turkic, Korean, or other relevant languages. The vast majority of references are to Chinese texts. Although Jagchid, the son of a Mongolian statesman, and Symons, an economic historian, commendably strive to correct a traditional pattern of "Chinese ethnocentrism and arrogance," they are often entrapped by the Sinitic terminology of their sources. For example, they define *yüeh* (Han-period pronunciation *gʸwat*) as a "general term for non-Chinese from the South, pejorative" when really it is the same ethnonym as the first syllable of "Vietnam." When the Chinese were temporarily well disposed toward the Hsiung-nu (Han-period pronunciation *Hʸung-nâ*, or Huns), they changed the characters used to transcribe their name from "Malevolent Slaves" to "Respectful Slaves" and wrote the title of the Hsiung-nu ruler with characters that Jagchid and Symons say mean "good man." Actually, they

mean nothing of the sort and are merely one alternative Chinese transcription of what may have been a Palaeo-Siberian word. Such are the perils of trying to reconstruct a truthful account of inner Asian history based largely on Chinese sources.

VICTOR H. MAIR

University of Pennsylvania
Philadelphia

LANGER, ERICK D. *Economic Change and Rural Resistance in Southern Bolivia, 1880-1930*. Pp. ix, 269. Stanford, CA: Stanford University Press, 1989. $42.50.

Erick Langer's work represents an analysis of two very different types of rural resistance within the context of the southern Bolivian economy's decay of the nineteenth and early twentieth centuries. The economic backdrop throughout the half century covered by Langer can only be characterized as fragile or in decline. The silver economy collapsed. Replacing it was tin mining, with its production enclaves located elsewhere. Tin would come to dominate the economy, while its bosses succeeded in dominating national politics. Resistance to changes in the late nineteenth and early twentieth centuries thus came from both the Indian peasantry and the elites, each calculating mechanisms for recovering lost power and eroding privileges. Both regional groups, commoners and oligarchs, experienced the historical conflicts presented by new and more powerful forces, including strong elites from the national capital of La Paz, foreign capital and new investments in more profitable mining in distant regions, and curtailed access to land and credit. Thus, while the Indians had had to deal with whites since the times of Spanish conquerors in the sixteenth century, the elites were now dealing with the fluctuations of a world economy and Europe's needs for primary materials.

Langer states early on that his interests are focused on the "non-elites" of the Andean world. In truth, however, this work provides a much broader framework, while concentrating on the southern region of Bolivia during the era of most significant transitions in the mining industry and capital penetration. The regions chosen for the study comprise the department of Chuquisaca, which included the provinces of Cinti, Tomina, Azero, and Yamparaez. Each of these provinces receives separate treatment in self-contained chapters. Four other chapters provide the introduction, an analysis of the regional mining economy, a depiction of the regional oligarchy, and the conclusions.

Langer uses a flexible concept of resistance that enables him to see resistance from the perspectives of organized and ad hoc reactions to economic and social changes, from regional levels to community levels, from ideologically driven considerations to less abstract calculations. Whatever the perspective, he demonstrates the variegated nature of actions, from passive resistance in the form of calculated absenteeism to organized strikes.

As the fortunes of silver mining declined, regional oligarchs turned increasingly to land as a refuge for their finances. In the event, they tried to squeeze more output and greater obligations from Indians. Their practices included the political and extralegal forms of coercion. The consequences were dire for the Indians' communal traditions, and the observance of reciprocal obligations became less reliable. One example of political coercion was the *revisita*, the process by which the plots of each community Indian household were measured and parceled out, in effect signaling the alienation of land that for centuries had been considered

part of the community (the *ayllu*). Similarly, it augured a significant change away from the tradition of tribute collection to the more onerous taxing system. Indians resisted both by resorting to the courts and by individual acts of defiance. The *revisita* process also led to one of the few occasions of cross-*ayllu* cooperation. As *haciendas* became the sole source of income for Sucre's oligarchy, the oligarchs began to crack down on Indian tenants who refused to pay or to leave the property. *Hacienda* owners resorted to forced evictions and, on occasion, abduction to collect outstanding debts.

The story of Chuquisaca's oligarchy, centered in the department's capital of Sucre, is one of stagnation and decay. It evokes images of Thomas Mann's *Bildungsroman*—stories of family empires crumbling and the atrophy of personal mores, the result of changes in the regional economy and in the world demands for Bolivian goods. The political ascendancy of La Paz sealed the fate of Chuquisaca's aristocracy. La Paz, the de facto hub of Bolivian trade and production in the late nineteenth century and the formal seat of the national government by 1898, posed a formidable threat to Sucre's leaders, who owed their historical prominence to centuries of colonial privileges, silver mining, and effective dominance of Indian labor and lands on the basis of longstanding codes of reciprocity.

From the regional oligarchy's perspective, the reality of secular decadence did not often lead to altered behaviors. Indeed, economic rationalism was not one of the characteristics of Chuquisaca's elites. Any attempt at using structural-functionalist paradigms here would simply fail. In the face of evanescing fortunes, turn-of-the-century oligarchs built formidable homes in the latest Parisian styles, organized social clubs that reinforced their endogamous relations, and provided venues for conspicuous consumption. As Langer points out, "ostentation, in the form of extravagant parties and the wholesale renovation of houses in [Sucre's] core on a Parisian model, [was] indicative of the backward-looking nature of the elites during this period."

MARK D. SZUCHMAN

Florida International
  University
Miami

SHAIKH, FARZANA. *Community and Consensus in Islam: Muslim Representation in Colonial India, 1860-1947.* Pp. xiv, 257. New York: Cambridge University Press, 1989. No price.

Farzana Shaikh raises a strong voice against those who give primacy to colonial sociology and its subsequent organizational and ideological structures as the source of Muslim solidarity and political separatism in British India. Shaikh divides scholars into those who, as she puts it, see Muslims in India as "more Indian than Muslim" in contrast to those who emphasize, quoting William Roff, an "'Islamically supplied'" political discourse. Shaikh's goal in this book is to review the political theories and actions of leading Muslim spokesmen in India to show that that discourse, rooted partly in Mogul culture and primarily in persistent themes in Islamic political models, must be taken seriously in understanding political processes. She makes an intelligent and carefully reasoned contribution to this argument, critiquing many other scholars, from Peter Hardy to Ayesha Jalal, along the way.

The structure of the chapters suggests the nature of her argument. Chapter 1 reviews "the model of Muslim political action" as one that from classical times on has insisted on a divide between Muslim and non-Muslim as the fundamental sociological, political, and moral fact, a divide meant to find expression in the context of Muslim rule. The second chapter looks at late nineteenth-century British views of Indian society that posited relentless heterogeneity as the dominant characteristic of India and conceived of Indian participation in political life as a highly limited representation of that heterogeneity. One suggestive aspect of Shaikh's analysis is to identify different meanings of "representation" that come into play in both Muslim and British positions. Central to the argument here is that colonial theories are significant because they overlap substantially with indigenous understandings. That interaction is then presented in the remaining four chapters, chronologically organized.

Shaikh's method raises questions. The method neglects competing strands within Muslim tradition. It imputes a causal connection to Islamic models that may not exist and looks for an Islamic consciousness even when Muslim symbols are not adduced. It stresses the continuity of symbols like *ijma* and *qaum* whereas more striking is the new use made of these terms (as *ijma* moves away from reference to the *ulama* and *qaum* moves toward a census or statistical definition, rather than reference to the well-born). Nonetheless, Dr. Shaikh is persuasive in her insistence that Indian political actors did not merely respond passively to British categories. Her bold approach, moreover, clearly stimulates a return to central questions at the heart of modern South Asian society.

BARBARA D. METCALF

University of California
Davis

WILLIAMS, PETER and DAVID WALLACE. *Unit 731: Japan's Secret Biological Warfare in World War II.* Pp. xi, 303. New York: Free Press, 1989. $22.95.

YOUNG, MARILYN J. and MICHAEL K. LAUNER. *Flights of Fancy, Flight of Doom: KAL 007 and Soviet-American Rhetoric.* Pp. xxvi, 333. Lanham, MD: University Press of America, 1989. $29.50. Paperbound, $18.25.

Superficially, both of these books are about conspiracy, but in each the term has a radically different meaning. *Unit 731* is a grisly story of human depravity and evil. It is a graphic description of Japanese research and experimentation in biological warfare near Harbin, during World War II, under the direction of General Ishii, a medical researcher who turned his prodigious talents to morally bankrupt ends. Unit 731 was his creation and under his leadership it tested its deadly products by systematically killing, in extremely painful ways, an estimated 3000 human beings it referred to as *muratas*, or lumps of wood. Its methods included the vivisection of live subjects and ill-conceived field tests that killed Japanese troops as well as unknown numbers of Chinese.

As the story unfolds, some familiar themes of twentieth-century political history emerge. Unit members excused themselves from responsibility for their actions by pleading that they had merely obeyed orders that had to be obeyed. People at the top echelons of government, possibly even the emperor himself, knew of the unit's activities. Indeed, Tojo developed an aversion to seeing films of the unit's gruesome experiments. And there was the deceitful corruption of language that Orwell did his best to discredit. The cells charged with conducting "field tests" designed to spread death and disease were designated as "Epidemic Prevention and Water Supply Units."

Following the war, many members of Unit 731 who escaped Soviet occupation forces in Manchuria achieved prominent, influential positions and success in post-war Japan. They were not brought to trial at the Tokyo War Crimes Trials. The burden of the book is that they escaped trial because the U.S. occupation forces struck a deal that gave Unit 731 members immunity in exchange for the information they had so inhumanely accumulated. Not only that, but investigators sent from U.S. agencies were deceived by both U.S. occupation forces and members of Unit 731 they interviewed. Thus Williams and Wallace forcefully conclude that there was "clear complicity on the part of the U.S. in the crimes of Unit 731" and that MacArthur's headquarters attempted to cover up its complicity.

Unlike their fellow unit members who reached Japan, those captured by Soviet forces were put on trial at Khabarovsk. In contrast to the cover-up regarding the Tokyo trials, Williams and Wallace argue, the evidence recorded at Khabarovsk was "accurate in most details," but, regrettably, it was dismissed by the United States as cold-war propaganda.

Williams and Wallace have clearly and concisely told an important story that should attract wide interest. Even if there are faults in their argument and evidence, they have admirably succeeded in establishing a convincing case to answer.

By contrast, *Flights of Fancy, Flight of Doom* is a disappointing book that is longer than it needed to be. It is concerned with the ways in which both the U.S. and Soviet governments sought to exploit the shooting down of KAL flight 007 for their respective propaganda purposes.

Young and Launer are interested essentially in the use of language, rhetoric, and the media rather than the usual concerns of strategists and students of international relations. Part of their method is thus a detailed textual analysis of U.S. and Soviet press commentary. The problem is that this method fails to address some basic questions about the incident.

The book does not, for instance, ask whether the tragic shoot-down was the result of a local Soviet commander overstepping his authority and hence neither a decision of the Soviet government nor something it wanted—which is not to excuse the action taken.

Young and Launer argue that President Reagan seized on the incident in an attempt to show that the Soviet Union was the evil empire he claimed it to be. But in doing so, he compromised U.S. surveillance and intelligence sources by going public too quickly. Then, having seized the initiative as he did, he lost it through ineptitude.

For their part, the Soviet leadership sought to turn the shoot-down to their advantage by linking it to questions that would lend credibility to the movement in Western Europe against the Pershing cruise missiles. About the Soviet press of the time, Young and Launer offer the unsurprising and somewhat banal assessment that it acted as an arm of the state. In so doing they fail to recognize that even in the United States the press and public may, in some short-lived instances, be at the mercy of what officials choose to make known. Simply, there are times, as during the Cuban missile crisis, when any government would seek to have the press serve its purposes, which is not to say that the Soviet press has the freedom of the Western press.

In this book the term "conspiracy" is identified with what the authors argue is an implausible explanation of the incident offered by another author, whom they describe as a "conspiratist rhetor." Why an unconvincing explanation should be associated with conspiracy in this way is far from clear. Nor is their terminology in this instance an isolated example. Others include "analogizing," "authorial world," and "evidentiary value," which may be quite acceptable to American readers but are likely to be regarded by readers from other continents as the evidence of an American tendency to use unnecessary and obscuring jargon.

Finally, it is a pity that this book was not written later, when it could have included a comparative analysis of the way the shooting down, in mid-1988, of an Iranian airline by the U.S. warship *Vincennes* could have been included. But even this might not have succeeded in clarifying any important questions and addressing them succinctly.

PAUL KEAL

University of New South Wales
Sydney
Australia

EUROPE

CORVO, MAX. *The O.S.S. in Italy, 1942-1945: A Personal Memoir.* Pp. x, 324. New York: Praeger, 1989. $29.95.

It was only in 1986 that Washington declassified its last Office of Strategic Services (OSS) records on World War II Sicily and Italy. Max Corvo, operations chief of the key intelligence network in Italy, has mined these newly available materials, added accounts from his own voluminous papers, and provided us with a richly detailed "personal memoir" of how he perceived the OSS at work.

Corvo provides an all too convincing picture of the awesome bungling and maddening confusion brought about by those with competing interests in intelligence performance: State Department figures, British and American commanders, and Italian groups of all persuasions. His unit had to skate dangerously around established procedures to procure the most basic needs, such as radio sets for agents operating clandestine stations.

One intriguing feature of this book is the recollections by Italian and American agents who participated in the scores of two- and three-man sabotage and intelligence-gathering missions behind German lines. Another is Corvo's observations on key Italian personalities like Feruccio Parri, Raffaele Cadorna, Luigi Longo, and Guiseppe Romita, important actors in the tumultuous transition from wartime to peacetime Italy. Any competent Hollywood writer could carve out a dozen or more scenarios from this book.

Corvo's main objective is not to add to the record but to correct it. He shows that much of his effort had to go toward overcoming the stultifying effects of interunit rivalries and patronizing indifference bordering on contempt from both military and civilian superiors—superiors who had little grasp of the motivations of enraged Partisans, divergent elements in the Comitato della liberazione nazionale per l'alta Italia, or groups working for or against a Communist takeover of north Italian industry. Corvo feels that histories critical of the OSS underestimate its invaluable services in forging enduring links with Italians who later showed appreciation by guiding their country along a path Americans preferred: between the Scylla of monarchism—a British aim—and the Charybdis of communism. Allen Dulles comes off badly here: he claimed credit for negotiating the surrender of the last large German forces; but the OSS on its own, thanks to much earlier parleys, was already about to accept German surrender.

The OSS was ordered disbanded even before V-E Day, before its potential usefulness in guiding postwar Italy could seriously be discussed. Corvo himself was precipitously bundled out of military service. Corvo provides evidence that at least some of this lack of support for the OSS could have come from ethnic prejudices against "Italo-Americani" or, even more stupidly, against "those Sicilians."

The book comes equipped with a useful glossary, a fine index, and a first-rate bibliography, especially welcome for its many items by Italians. There are no maps, however, and a better editing job would have eliminated some stiffly written sentences and some jumbled paragraphs.

MARTIN WOLFE

University of Pennsylvania
Philadelphia

STAVRAKIS, PETER J. *Moscow and Greek Communism 1944-1949*. Pp. xvi, 243. Ithaca, NY: Cornell University Press, 1989. $28.95.

The Greek civil war of 1944-49 has attracted the attention not only of Greek scholars seeking to better understand this tragic chapter in modern Greek history but also of American scholars for whom U.S. intervention in that conflict holds the key to an understanding of the origins of the cold war and of subsequent American involvement in other countries, including Vietnam, threatened by Soviet communism. These efforts have profited in recent years from the opening of American diplomatic archives for that period.

A nagging problem, however, has remained. Since the Soviet Union played a vital role in the Greek conflict, and since postwar U.S. policy was to a large extent a response to Soviet initiatives, we cannot hope to fully understand this policy unless we also have a clear understanding of Soviet intentions and actions. The lack of documentary evidence from the Soviet side has made a study of Soviet involvement in Greece impossible.

In *Moscow and Greek Communism*, Peter J. Stavrakis claims to have overcome this obstacle at least partially. The basis for this assertion is the recent appearance in Greece of several accounts by Greek Communists who participated in the civil war and the publication in the Greek press of excerpts from the archives of the Democratic Army of Greece and of the Communist Party of Greece (KKE).

Unfortunately, Stavrakis's claims are not supported by these documents, at least not by those documents that he examined. Whatever insights these Greek Communist sources may provide are limited to the inner workings and conflicts within the leadership of the KKE. They tell us almost nothing of the activities of Soviet agents in Greece or of their contacts with and the extent of their influence over the KKE, let alone of Soviet objectives there. They are, in fact, remarkable for their silence on all these issues.

Stavrakis therefore is reduced to deducing Soviet objectives in Greece from the actions of the KKE leaders, who, however, as he himself reports, in the absence of explicit directions from Moscow, "relied on their conviction that the best way to please Moscow . . . was to pursue the goal of revolution." In fact, Stavrakis candidly admits that his work is "based largely on perceptions of Soviet conduct itself." To make matters worse, these perceptions or evidence is often of questionable authenticity and is stretched by Stavrakis beyond what is reasonable or prudent.

For example, according to Stavrakis, in August 1945 the Soviet press took on a strong anti-British character. What real evidence does he provide to support this assertion, and what sources did he consult? Lamentably, none. He deduces the anti-British bent of the Soviet press solely on the basis of a single, unattributed document in the Department of State records that reports that some otherwise unidentified Soviet Balkans specialist by the name of Belenkov delivered a lecture marked by sharp antipathy to

British policy. Sadly, this example of shabby, if not high-handed, scholarship is not isolated.

ALEX MITRAKOS

City University of New York

WHEALEY, ROBERT H. *Hitler and Spain: The Nazi Role in the Spanish Civil War, 1936-1939.* Pp. ix, 269. Lexington: University Press of Kentucky, 1989. $24.00.

In this volume, historian Robert H. Whealey of Ohio University examines the role of Adolf Hitler and Nazi Germany in the Spanish Civil War of 1936-39, an event often described as the dress rehearsal for World War II. Deceptively brief—only 142 pages of text—Whealey's study is the product of some 25 years of immersion in a stunning array of both published and archival sources and makes a solid contribution to our knowledge of a small but significant episode in the political history of interwar Europe.

According to Whealey, whose analysis simultaneously embraces all four of the "interrelated" political, military, economic, and ideological dimensions of Nazi policy toward Spain, Hitler achieved a spectacular, if "tenuous," victory in the Civil War in three fundamental respects. To begin with, the *Führer*'s military and economic assistance, which was extended jointly with his erstwhile Italian ally Benito Mussolini, was "essential" to the triumph in the war of his proto-fascist favorite, General Francisco Franco. Second, on the international scene, the occasion of the war enabled the Nazi chief so effectively to weaken the ties between Britain, France, and the Soviet Union as to forestall any "Grand Alliance" of these powers against Germany until as late as 1941. By the same token, the intense concentration of the other European powers on the Spanish situation between 1936 and 1939 also permitted the Nazi leader to pursue, more or less undisturbed, his ideologically much greater commitment to expansion in Eastern Europe. Indeed, suggests Whealey, Hitler's aggressions against Austria and Czechoslovakia in the late 1930s were keyed directly to events in Spain and were brought to a head in 1938-39 precisely because of his perception that the Spanish crisis was about to conclude. Finally, contends Whealey, Hitler's motivations and policies in Spain itself were essentially experimental, involving the extension of limited, but critical, military aid and, in particular, the dissemination of some especially telling anticommunist propaganda. In fact, according to Whealey, the latter tactic was doubly effective, exploiting, on the one hand, the conservative fears of Britain and France while, on the other, encouraging the adherence to the famous Anti-Comintern Pact of Italy, Japan, and, eventually, Spain itself.

Notwithstanding these successes, however, Whealey believes that Hitler's apparent victory in Spain was "not complete." Thus, despite the ostensibly successful outcome of the conflict, the *Führer* did not obtain General Franco's unconditional postwar support and hence failed to secure Germany's vulnerable southern flank in Europe after 1941.

For the most part, Whealey's conclusions are neither revisionist nor terribly surprising. Nor, for that matter, is his presentation especially exciting. Nevertheless, his exposition is invariably judicious and fair-minded—qualities by no means common in Spanish Civil War historiography—and is founded throughout on detailed and meticulous scholarship—the bibliographical apparatus alone is worth the volume's relatively modest cost. In short, although Whealey himself is apparently not fully satisfied

with the exhaustiveness of his research, his book constitutes as definitive an account of this significant aspect of pre-World War II politics as we are likely to have for a long time to come.

JOHN W. LONG

Rider College
Lawrenceville
New Jersey

UNITED STATES

MARKS, CAROLE. *Farewell—We're Good and Gone: The Great Black Migration.* Pp. x, 209. Bloomington: Indiana University Press, 1989. $37.50. Paperbound, $12.95.

Whether or not one accepts the neo-Marxist theories of capitalist exploitation, of "core" dominance of vulnerable migrant workers drawn from dependent "peripheries," this book is still worth reading. Unfortunately, historians continue to import their models a generation or so after they become antiquated. Remember psychohistorians who discovered Freud about the time psychology was demolishing many Freudian assumptions? And neo-Marxist historians who describe the mass exodus of labor from capitalist-exploited "colonies"—the South, Africa, Mexico, Asia—just at the moment when workers are pouring out of East Germany and massive demonstrations are dismantling Marxist states throughout Eastern Europe?

Aside from its ideological base, this book is an interesting though incomplete synthesis concerning the great black migration of 1916-30. Professor Marks's major theses are that most black migrants were urban and nonagricultural; that they left not just to raise salaries but because the newly emerging industrial South provided them neither racial justice nor economic opportunity; and that Northern businessmen provide pull incentives as powerful as the South's push factors. She deemphasizes traditional explanations for the migration—boll weevil infestation, disfranchisement and the rise of Jim Crow legislation, and the European war that terminated European migration. Migration in fact accelerated during the decade of the 1920s. She also provides valuable information on factors that sustained the migration once it began: communication by way of family, friends, service agencies, and newspapers, especially the influential *Chicago Defender*.

Marks concludes that, once in the North, black workers did not experience upward mobility. Despite the fact that the migrants were the South's most skilled and educated blacks, they encountered significant institutional barriers to success. Salaries in low-wage industries that employed them—packing houses, stockyards, steel mills—were only marginally higher than in the South. The migrants were used frequently as strike breakers, white workers resented them, and Northern employers used a mixed labor force of blacks, native whites, and immigrants to control laborers. Blacks were not assimilated because they continued to come in large numbers.

The analysis is strongest when it pertains to narrative and weakest when it speculates on economic theory. For instance, chapter 3 is an analysis of Southern economic history heavily rooted in theories of Northern colonialism and drawn largely from the works of Woodward, Ransom, Sutch, and other sources from the 1950s, 1960s, and 1970s. For a chapter devoted to explaining the economic history of the South between 1880 and 1920 to neglect references to Gavin Wright's *Old South, New South*, Gill Fite's *Cotton Fields No More*, and Pete Daniel's *Breaking the Land* represents a serious omission. Less well known economic historians argue that much of the New South's capital came from within the region, and that Northern control often resulted in better care of workers, and superior technology and entrepreneurial skills.

A less substantive problem occurs in a chapter on assimilation. Although it is certainly true that black migrants did not return to the South during the years of Marks's study, it might be interesting to consider these migrants after their retirement. During the 1970s and 1980s the South experienced a substantial net inmigration of blacks. If these reverse migrants were the out-migrants of the years 1916-30, that fact might substantiate many of Marks's hypotheses while undermining others.

On balance, this is an important synthesis worth reading.

WAYNE FLYNT

Auburn University
Alabama

PENCAK, WILLIAM. *For God and Country: The American Legion, 1919-1941.* Pp. xviii, 411. Boston: Northeastern University Press, 1989. $40.00.

One of the most controversial American voluntary associations of the twentieth century, the American Legion has been both denounced as a repressive, proto-fascist organization and praised as a patriotic defender against subversive forces at home and abroad. In this book, William Pencak, an accomplished young historian, provides a generally balanced account of America's largest veterans' organization. His extensively researched work is based on numerous manuscript collections, including the archives of the American Legion and its main critic, the American Civil Liberties Union.

Although rejecting charges that the Legion was proto-fascist, Pencak confirms that the organization was decidedly nationalistic and conservative, and often repressive. Included is direct evidence that many Legionnaires did use illegal action, including outright vigilantism, against people they viewed as subversives—not only communists, but also socialists, pacifists, and radical labor organizers.

There is much new material here, particularly on the organization's role in the Red Scare, its opposition to Prohibition, and its attempts to thwart the organizing drives of the Congress of Industrial Organizations in the 1930s. Also fully detailed are the Legion's effective lobbying efforts, from those on behalf of veterans' benefits and increased national defense to those in support of antiradicalism by the House Committee on Un-American Activities and by the Federal Bureau of Investigation.

Pencak also tries to understand the organization on its own terms. Although the Legion saw its role as a defender of "Americanism," its own explanations of that never went beyond platitudinous statements. Pencak interprets the group's views and actions as based on a communitarian notion of liberty. Indeed, he argues that philosophically, the "Legion's defense of an Americanism based on the populace's acceptance of its duty to a historically rooted community finds powerful support in Edmund Burke."

Linking the American Legion with Burkean thought may be problematic, but Pencak is on firm ground when he connects the Legionnaires' sometimes violent suppression of dissent with a conservative vigilante tradition in America, from attacks on abolitionists by "gentlemen of property and standing" to assaults on civil rights activists by Southern segregationists. Like them, the dominant majority in the Legion generally identified the community and the nation with the status quo and refused to allow radical or even significant dissent. At the same time, it also sought to bolster a culture of patriotism in America's young people.

Using the Legion's archives, Pencak shows the complexities and contradictions within an organization that numbered more than a million members by 1939. The Legion was seldom totally united, but the compromises achieved by the national leadership often meant acquiescence in the actions of predominantly conservative positions, such as the extreme antilabor activity within the California organization and the exclusion of blacks from membership in the South. Although Pencak usually seeks to understand the Legion's position, he does not excuse actions such as these.

This thorough and well-written history is the fullest account yet of the early years of the American Legion and supersedes all previous studies.

JOHN WHITECLAY CHAMBERS II

Rutgers University
New Brunswick
New Jersey

WARD, DAVID. *Poverty, Ethnicity, and the American City, 1840-1925: Changing Conceptions of the Slum and the Ghetto.* Pp. xvii, 263. New York: Cambridge University Press, 1989. No price.

Focusing on urban America between roughly 1840 and 1925, historical geographer David Ward analyzes changing interpretations of the slum and the ghetto. He frames the study around contemporary debates over the relationship between poverty, ethnicity, and environmental conditions in the inner city. More specifically, in explaining urban poverty Ward convincingly argues that recent disputes over the role of internal cultural factors versus external environmental forces have significant antecedents in conceptualizations of poverty in the mid-nineteenth century, when the first large wave of Irish and German immigrants entered northeastern cities. It was then that the "essentially geographic formulation of poverty" emerged; it emphasized the relationship between the unhealthy physical environment of the inner city and the presumed immoral, criminal, or "pathological social conditions among its impoverished residents."

Although the book pinpoints the persistence of "geographic considerations of culture and environment and of people and place" in explanations of urban poverty, immigration, and residential patterns, it also shows the dynamics of historical change. Drawing on a variety of contemporary public and private policy records of both "hostile and sympathetic outsiders," Ward carefully documents the emerging use in the mid-nineteenth century of the term "slum," "defined as those parts of the city where the removal of the affluent had left behind a concentration of impoverished people"; the consolidation of slum as a concept by 1900; the complicated transition from slum to ghetto—emphasizing the growing number of immigrants from southern, central, and eastern Europe as well as blacks from the American South—during the first two decades of the twentieth century; and two distinct periods of reexamination from the mid-1920s through the 1970s and early 1980s. Ward not only pinpoints the important historical shifts but analyzes them in substantial detail.

In recent reformulations of the immigrant experience, Ward notes that the new migrants to American cities, particularly blacks, emerge as the most ghetto-ized, victimized, and weakest of all migrant groups. According to recent portraits, blacks exhibit few of the cultural resources that allowed immigrants to use the ghetto as a "decompression chamber" for their eventual rise into the suburban middle class. Yet Ward convincingly demonstrates that such current reinterpretations of the relationship between poverty, ethnicity, and urban space tend to downplay the impact of structural forces connected with the transition from commercial to industrial capitalism. More important, contemporary inner-city poverty is often viewed as a new departure; this view camouflages the historic connection between conceptions of poverty, mass population movements, slums, and ghettos over more than a century and a half.

By relying almost exclusively on external sources, however, Ward offers few insights into the changing perceptions held by the urban working class and poor themselves. Moreover, despite his emphasis on the structural impact of changes in the capitalist system, the study offers little discussion of the shifting economic composition of particular cities, along with the significance of intraethnic class formation. Finally, while western cities receive minor attention, southern cities receive none. Yet *Poverty, Ethnicity, and the American City* is a solid contribution to historical geography. It links geography, history, and contemporary public policy issues and warrants our close attention.

JOE W. TROTTER

Carnegie Mellon University
Pittsburgh
Pennsylvania

SOCIOLOGY

BURT, MARTHA R. and BARBARA E. COHEN. *America's Homeless: Numbers, and Programs That Serve Them.* Pp. xi, 176. Washington, DC: Urban

Institute Press, 1989. $25.75. Paperbound, $9.75.

WRIGHT, JAMES D. *Address Unknown: The Homeless in America*. Pp. xix, 170. New York: Aldine de Gruyter, 1989. $36.95. Paperbound, $14.95.

Both of these books try to estimate the number of homeless, to describe their characteristics and attempts to aid them, and to recommend solutions for the homeless problem. Burt and Cohen's descriptions are based on data from the Urban Institute's 1987 national survey of homeless who used soup kitchens and/or shelters, surveys of the homeless who do not use these facilities, and a review of studies. Wright uses data from the National Health Care for Homeless Program and other studies, particularly Rossi's census of the homeless in Chicago. Although these descriptions are based on different data, the results are similar. Both estimate the homeless population on any given day to be in the neighborhood of 0.5 million people. Eighty percent are male, 55 percent are nonwhite or Hispanic, a little more than half are high school graduates, and about 16 percent are children, with or without a parent. Both note problems among the homeless and estimate rates of poor physical and mental health, low economic status, and alcohol and chemical abuse, although the estimates are not strictly comparable.

The Urban Institute survey reports some of the physical and mental health conditions associated with homelessness: 50 percent of the sample scored in the mentally stressed range of a scale measuring depression, 19 percent had been patients in mental hospitals, 56 percent had at least one health problem, and about two-thirds had been in prison, jail, or a mental hospital or had been an inpatient for detoxification treatment.

Wright's analysis of data seems to be guided by his effort to show that the homeless are not really bad, not the "drunk, the addicted, and the just plain shiftless" described in the "My Turn" column in *Newsweek* by Stuart Bykofsky, but rather those who are unable to work and are not homeless by choice. I preferred the Burt and Cohen presentation, but Wright's impassioned rhetoric and his presentation of the "human face" of homelessness may be necessary to give the public a more proper perspective on the situation.

Burt and Cohen's descriptions of aid are based on the Urban Institute's study of shelters and soup kitchens and on a study of state and federal assistance in six states. Wright reviews current programs, and he outlines some of the barriers that individuals face in trying to participate in them.

Policy recommendations made by Burt and Cohen are included at the ends of descriptions and in a final chapter. Wright, as an advocate, shows homelessness as a part of the larger picture of poverty. He argues that the vast majority of the homeless are the deserving poor, that they are inadvertent victims of social changes, and, further, that we must intervene on their behalf. Both books are recommended reading for those interested in the homeless and their problems and should be assigned reading for those charged with finding solutions.

JERRY L. L. MILLER

University of Arizona
Tucson

MEYER, WILLIAM H. *Transnational Media and Third World Development: The Structure and Impact of Imperialism*. Pp. xiv, 132. Westport, CT: Greenwood, 1988. $37.95.

STARKER, STEVEN. *Evil Influences: Crusades Against the Mass Media*. Pp. vi, 212. New Brunswick, NJ: Transaction Books, 1989. $24.95.

In an era when critics pounce on every transgression, real or assumed, it is a novelty, even refreshing, for the media to pick up not one but two books that turn out to be defenders. One author, it is true, does not go out of his way to defend Western journalism. In his academic way, however, William H. Meyer presents a mass of statistical evidence to suggest that the New World Information Order is something less than the panacea for journalistic imbalances that Third World supporters and some Western social scientists have made it out to be since it was introduced at the United Nations Educational, Scientific, and Cultural Organization in the middle 1970s.

Meyer seeks to chart statistically the flow of information between developed and developing worlds to determine whether the dominant position of the Western world automatically creates "cultural imperialism," information inequities, westernization or endemic violence in the Third World. He concludes that there is no discernible pattern that supports the thesis.

This point of view is certainly calculated to arouse a vigorous rebuttal from the so-called structural social scientists. They have consistently been the noisiest and most loyal supporters of the New World Information Order. They have stubbornly argued that such an order should arbitrarily reduce the influence of the West and grant more power over information to local government in the Third World. Recent developments in Eastern Europe and the Soviet Union are sure to cause consternation in this camp.

Steven Starker's book may also be controversial but in quite a different way. The most vociferous critics of television, for example, are not going to sing the praises of a critic who points out that they are only following a tradition that originated before the invention of the printing press. Every new process for disseminating information or entertainment, start-

ing at least as far back as the balladeer, has been subjected to the barbs of critics until a new medium comes along to divert attention. It happened with newspapers, the cinema, radio, and television in successive waves. The question now is, What's next? Starker's book makes for good reading. The information is not new, nor is it the product of deep research. The charm lies in the careful selection of interesting historical data, all of which support the central thesis. The book may irritate the habitual critics, but even they may enjoy reading it. It furnishes them some perspective without ever arguing that their targets are faultless.

SIG MICKELSON

San Diego State University
California

POWELL, MICHAEL J. *From Patrician to Professional Elite: The Transformation of the New York Bar Association.* Pp. xxvi, 269. New York: Russell Sage Foundation, 1988. $27.50.

Founded in 1870, the Association of the Bar of the City of New York (ABCNY) was, until relatively recently, a predominantly white, Anglo-Saxon, Protestant association of big-firm lawyers. Although much of its old ethnic, religious, and gender exclusiveness has ostensibly been breached, the ABCNY retains an aura of clubby exclusiveness and a character quite unlike any other lawyers' association. The book under review is an account of the ABCNY that concentrates on the postwar years. Powell's research is impressively thorough, informed by the concepts of organizational sociologists of the Chicago school, and is set out in the language of political science.

Powell's principal concerns raise questions that go beyond the case study in hand. Powell is interested in how an upper-class institution survives, an institution whose membership, style, and activities repeatedly thrust it into contentious arenas of public debate and whose prestige—or pretensions, as critics argue—render it a constant, productive, and satisfying target. By choosing to concentrate on the years when so many excluded groups prized entry into the anterooms and pathways of power, Powell takes himself into deep and irresolvable debates about the nature of democracy, the costs of community, and the public good. And, of course, the ABCNY has not merely survived: it prospers, in both membership and influence. How has this happened, in times that have seemed so inhospitable to elite notions and groups?

Powell provides some intriguing answers. Essentially, the ABCNY has made a successful transition from membership based substantially on social connection to entry by professional standing. Even in mass society a meritocracy is unassailable to all but the most leveling of populists. The association also draws strength from its commendable history of legal reform. In the face of the ABCNY's efforts to oppose corruption in the courts and to improve legal services, it was the small-time lawyers and their political allies who deservedly were stigmatized as reactionary, self-seeking conservative protectionists.

On a larger political stage, Whig disdain for popular moods and local politics, and being above the need to pander to sects, constituencies, and interest groups, enabled the association to take and stand by positions that were morally correct, sometimes courageous, and that ultimately enhanced its standing. Two examples suffice. The ABCNY was preeminent among bar associations in reaching out to and supporting the granting of rights to minorities. And in times that were short on heroes, the association's restraint and caution in the face of McCarthyite panic and bigotry confirmed its

integrity and acquired the approving stamp of time.

This is an interesting and important topic, which is treated with the care and skill it deserves. It could have made a livelier read without departing at all from the standards of scholarship of which Powell is clearly conscious. Indeed, Powell's wide-ranging and imaginative handling of his material deserves a less plodding style. But despite such occasional irritations, Powell makes thoughtful and persuasive contributions to a number of important discussions. Certainly he seems to answer the questions he sets himself —which is more than many of us can do—and he is skillful in blending his own work with the findings and results of others. This is a book for lawyers—armchair and workbench—as well as social and political scientists.

SEAN McCONVILLE

University of Illinois
Chicago

ECONOMICS

ADAMS, WILLIAM JAMES. *Restructuring the French Economy: Government and the Rise of Market Competition since World War II.* Pp. xv, 400. Washington, DC: Brookings Books, 1989. $36.95.

A great deal of scholarly attention has been given to the performance of the French economy since World War II. Long regarded as incurably backward, hampered by so-called premodern attitudes and by a preference for protection and low risk, France under the Third Republic appeared to be a land of small-scale producers, content with limited markets and growth. Added to this was a lack of confidence in an ability to compete with more dynamic national economies, such as Great Britain, Germany, or the United

States. The role of the state, even during years of an apparent laissez-faire liberalism, was never absent, and the state often engaged in a politically popular defense of established businesses, small-scale enterprise, and provision of a cushion against the harsh realities of competition. After the war, the French economy experienced a remarkable period of growth, second only to that of Japan since the 1950s. Within the European context, the French economic miracle has often been overshadowed by Germany's impressive postwar recovery; yet the French enjoy a standard of living comparable to that of Germany. At the end of the war, French living standards were half of those of Great Britain, but now the French standard is higher.

Crucial to an understanding of the French recovery is the role of government policy, planning, and intervention in the economy. After the war Jean Monnet elaborated a plan that was designed to make maximum use of limited French resources with the objective of promoting economic growth and innovation. At the same time, there was a strong element of what Richard Kuisel calls "neoliberalism" that aimed at freeing up certain sectors of the economy from artificial restraints. Historians and economists who have looked at the recent history of France have pointed to a model of industrial planning. Indeed, what has been called the plan has caught the attention of those who advocate an industrial policy as a way of assuring economic growth and competitiveness. Beginning with the work of John and Anne-Marie Hackett in 1963, an abundant literature has developed around the French model for economic development.

William James Adams's book is an important and welcome addition to this literature. In his study, Adams looks at the role of the government and central planning in France to determine the degree to which government policy bears responsibility for the French economic miracle. The conclusion is that good planning depends on good planners. France had individuals who were strongly committed to opening markets to international competition, achieved through active participation in European economic cooperation. In addition, decolonization, in terms of its economic impact, proved to be a boon by liberating France from a closed market structure and further compelling greater activity in international trade competition. Adams argues that these competitive forces proved decisive and were stronger than any distortions that government intervention may have produced. The structural changes in the French economy came about in part by government action and in part by changes in entrepreneurial behavior and attitudes that accepted exposure to outside competition.

Among the many virtues of this study is a clarity of style that makes even some of the more technical analyses accessible to the nonspecialist.

KIM MUNHOLLAND

University of Minnesota
Minneapolis

MILLER, JAMES C., III. *The Economist as Reformer: Revamping the FTC, 1981-1985*. Pp. x, 110. Washington, DC: American Enterprise Institute for Public Policy Research, 1989. $14.75.

STONE, ALAN. *Wrong Number: The Breakup of AT&T*. Pp. xi, 381. New York: Basic Books, 1989. $21.95.

These books provide information that may be useful to the general public and to commentators seeking to influence that public but perhaps without changing many minds. If there is indeed something of a cyclical nature or pendulum-like swing in American reliance on regulatory actions, then reformers have good grounds for declaring that deregulation has gone too far and that the public again and predictably is being preyed upon. Banking, including the saving and loan subset, and airlines—especially with respect to safety—serve as proofs. On the other hand, as the two-armed economist always asserts to protect himself or herself, market forces are crucially important to efficiency and fair play. Deregulation, as James Miller insists in his book, must never be violated.

Miller has an ax to grind but does a fairly careful job of concealing the ideology behind his thinking, that the market mechanism is somehow an intrinsic part of nature itself and can hardly be construed as doing harm. The creeping welfare state had to be assaulted and annihilated. "I am proud of the truly remarkable results: record peacetime expansion; more than 17 million new jobs created after 1980; and dramatic reductions in inflation, unemployment, and interest rates," writes Miller. How desirable are these hamburger-frying jobs, which pay about half the wages of the former industrial jobs? Real interest—nominal minus inflation—is now some two and one-half times the rate of real growth, contrary to Miller's view and distressingly different from our national trend of near equality of these two key variables. High real interest rates, plus free trade deregulations and whatever else, have brought the high dollar and trade deficits that persist and are unsustainable. As an industrial power, our nation definitely is in decline relative to Japan and Germany. Deregulation cannot be meaningfully evaluated aside from the consequences of massive tax reductions and the upward shift of income distribution.

Alan Stone's task is much more modest and straightforward, and he succeeds in it to a large degree. He seeks to demonstrate that AT&T was technically pro-

gressive, moderately responsive to public needs, and not grossly predatory. As the expression puts it, "If it ain't broke, don't fix it."

Thus we end where we started: either you believe it or you do not. Both books are easy to read, being almost devoid of technical data or arguments.

FLOYD B. McFARLAND

Oregon State University
Corvallis

VEDLITZ, ARNOLD. *Conservative Mythology and Public Policy in America.* Pp. xi, 173. New York: Praeger, 1988. $35.95.

WEIDENBAUM, MURRAY. *Rendezvous with Reality: The American Economy after Reagan.* Pp. x, 313. New York: Basic Books, 1988. $19.95.

These two books are well matched: what Weidenbaum presents as "reality" illustrates just what Vedlitz means by "mythology." Vedlitz's interpretation wins the book-to-book contest, but the victory is rather hollow. Vedlitz's criticisms are not particularly incisive, and in the end, he fails to prove the case for his liberal recommendations. Weidenbaum's distortions of his own evidence, however, are a positive embarrassment.

Weidenbaum's avowed intent is to provide a realistic and objective analysis of the strengths and the weaknesses of Ronald Reagan's economic policies. Contrary to his disclaimer that "the results of Reaganomics constitute a mixed bag," however, it soon becomes apparent that Weidenbaum, the chairman of President Reagan's first Council of Economic Advisers, really believes that the successes far outweigh the failures. Whereas his prose suggests a seemingly balanced view—low inflation; tamed labor unions; less pork barrel; more local initiative versus no cuts in overall government spending; unceasing growth of entitlements; and too much defense money spent on weapons systems and obsolete bases—he soon presents a summary table in which the successes unexpectedly overwhelm the failures by a ratio of 7:2 (Table 1-1, p. 15). Not only does he expand the successes and compress the failures; he obfuscates the evidence. A $1.2 trillion increase in the national debt from 1980 to 1986 does not appear in the table, and a growth of over 250 percent in the budget deficit is presented merely as an increase from 2 percent to 5 percent of the gross national product.

In the same spirit, Weidenbaum later contends that as a result of the 1986 tax reforms, "the largest increases in the capital gains tax rates occur at the middle- and lower-income brackets." This contention derives from Table 5-1 (p. 92), which shows that families of four with taxable incomes of less than $12,840 annually suffered a capital gains tax increase of 9.4 to 15.0 percent—those with under $3670 got the 15.0 percent increase —while families of four with taxable incomes over $192,320 experienced an increase of only 8.0 percent. Are we seriously to believe that these lower-income families will feel "the impact of higher taxes on capital gains" when they sell all their stock certificates, real estate, and manufacturing plants? Will capital gains taxes really discourage them from investing their multitudinous savings in the American dream?

When Vedlitz presents his undocumented list of "six basic conservative beliefs, or myths," which he claims to have gleaned from a "careful review" of conservatives' writings and public statements, it seems that these must be caricatures. Do conservatives really believe that "failure and success [are] explained [by] possession of proper or improper values"? Do they really believe that government social and economic programs "have at best been ineffective and at worst have been harmful"? Does anyone seriously argue that "government program[s] or assistance" has almost always hurt American economic growth or that the "free market," unfettered by regulation, is "the most efficient and equitable mechanism for allocating goods and services"?

Weidenbaum, though never cited by Vedlitz, presents a sufficient number of simplifications to lend credibility to Vedlitz's otherwise dubious list: "Recent research suggests that much poverty is caused by the social and personal characteristics of the people classified as poor"; Weidenbaum cites no studies, however. "In spite of ever more ambitious, and expensive, attempts to eliminate poverty, the problem remains as intractable as ever. . . . The experience of the past half century seems to underscore the eternal verity of the biblical saying 'For ye have the poor with you always.'"

Few nations use as extensive an array of assistance to private enterprise as does the United States. . . . Many existing government policies adversely affect industry in important ways. . . . The business system would be much better off if all those government subsidies to private producers were eliminated, and so would the entire economy (pp. 175, 177, and 179). In a market oriented economy, individual entrepreneurs and companies that are efficient in meeting consumer needs are profitable. Those that fail to meet those needs . . . sustain losses. . . . The political process is neither fair nor effective in determining which enterprises shall prosper and which shall not. . . . The positive approach puts the onus on labor and management in each company to deal with the competitive problems that face them, which is where the responsibility belongs. (Pp. 184, 187, and 188)

Where Vedlitz devotes the meat of his book to critical analyses of the arguments of conservative writers, such as Edward Banfield, Milton Friedman, George Gilder, Charles Murray, and Thomas Sowell, Weidenbaum never even bothers to mention liberal economists or social scientists, such as John K. Galbraith, Chalmers Johnson, Charles Lindblom, or John Schwarz. And in keeping with his selective use data, he quotes Paul Samuelson and Lester Thurow only in support of deregulation.

Unfortunately, when Vedlitz comes to his concluding chapter, he fails to subject his own remedies to the same critical analyses he has applied to the conservatives'. "One of the real impacts of the Reagan administration," he declares without much evidence, "has been to limit the debate and control the agenda on policy in the United States." What is to be done? "Government at all levels can develop policies that reduce discrimination and facilitate the development of human and fiscal capital among impoverished groups. This means greater national, state and local assistance to public elementary, secondary, and higher education." In short, give more money to academics at public institutions, and they will help to eliminate the "negative social, economic, and political environments, leading to lack of skills, lack of opportunity, and lack of inheritance of human and fiscal capital resources."

One final note on the production values of these books. *Rendezvous with Reality* comes in a neatly designed dust jacket with tributes from Paul Volckner, Paul McCracken, and Henry Kaufman; its tables are nicely formated; its 300-plus pages have few typos; and it retails for under $20.00. In contrast, *Conservative Mythology and Public Policy in America* has no dust jacket; its tables look like photo offsets from a near-letter-quality dot-matrix printer; its 173 pages contain a noticeable number of typos, and the publisher reports that it retails for $35.95. As of December 1989, it was not even listed in *Books in Print. Rendezvous with Reality* says little of importance in support of conservative economic policies, but it looks nice and is moderately priced. *Conservative Mythology* presents a reasonable, though unspectacular, liberal critique of conservative policies. It looks lousy and is exorbitantly expensive. Neither book is worth the price.

MICHAEL MARGOLIS

University of Cincinnati
Ohio

OTHER BOOKS

ALEXANDER, JEFFREY C. *Action and Its Environments.* Pp. xii, 342. New York: Columbia University Press, 1988. $35.00.

ALMOND, GABRIEL A. *A Discipline Divided: Schools and Sects in Political Science.* Pp. 352. Newbury Park, CA: Sage, 1989. $39.95. Paperbound, $18.95.

ANDERSON, MARGO J. *The American Census: A Social History.* Pp. xiii, 257. New Haven, CT: Yale University Press, 1990. Paperbound, $11.95.

ARNOT, BOB. *Controlling Soviet Labour: Experimental Change from Brezhnev to Gorbachev.* Pp. xv, 305. Armonk, NY: M. E. Sharpe, 1988. $37.50.

BAKER, ROSS. *The New Fat Cats: Members of Congress as Political Benefactors.* Pp. ix, 92. Winchester, MA: Unwin Hyman, 1989. $18.95. Paperbound, $9.95.

BARAK, AHARON. *Judicial Discretion.* Pp. xiv, 270. New Haven, CT: Yale University Press, 1989. $27.50.

BEITZ, CHARLES R. *Political Equality.* Pp. xviii, 253. Princeton, NJ: Princeton University Press, 1989. Paperbound, $12.95.

BETHEL, DAYLE M., ed. *Education for Creative Living: Ideas and Proposals of Tsunesaburo Makiguchi.* Translated by Alfred Birnbaum. Pp. xvii, 227. Ames: Iowa State University Press, 1989. No price.

BOIA, LUCIAN, ed. in chief. *Great Historians from Antiquity to 1800: An International Dictionary.* Pp. 440. Westport, CT: Greenwood Press, 1989. $65.00.

BOOTH, JOHN A. and THOMAS W. WALKER. *Understanding Central America.* Pp. 130. Boulder, CO: Westview Press, 1989. $32.50. Paperbound, $13.95.

BRAND, DONALD R. *Corporatism and the Rule of Law: A Study of the National Recovery Administration.* Pp. 340. Ithaca, NY: Cornell University Press, 1988. $39.95.

CHAPMAN, TOBIAS. *In Defense of Mystical Ideas: Support for Mystical Beliefs from a Purely Theoretical Viewpoint.* Pp. 115. Lewiston, NY: Edwin Mellen Press, 1989. $39.95.

COHEN, WILLIAM S. and GEORGE J. MITCHELL. *Men of Zeal: A Candid Story of the Iran-Contra Hearings.* Pp. xxxi, 384. New York: Penguin Books, 1989. Paperbound, $9.95.

COLEMAN, WILLIAM D. and HENRY J. JACEK, eds. *Regionalism, Business Interests and Public Policy.* Pp. 236. Newbury Park, CA: Sage, 1989. $49.95. Paperbound, $19.95.

CORDASCO, FRANCESCO and MICHAEL VAUGHN CORDASCO. *The Italian Emigration to the United States, 1880-1930: A Bibliographical Register of Italian Views.* Pp. xiv, 187. Fairview, NJ: Junius-Vaughn Press, 1990. $32.00.

CORNIA, GIOVANNI ANDREA, RICHARD JOLLY, and FRANCES STEWART, eds. *Adjustment with a Human Face.* Vol. 2, *Country Case Studies.* New York: Oxford University Press, 1988. $55.00.

DAVIES, CHARLOTTE AULL. *Welsh Nationalism in the Twentieth Century.* Pp. 139. New York: Praeger, 1989. $39.95.

DILLON, G. M. *The Falklands, Politics and War.* Pp. xii, 284. New York: St. Martin's Press, 1989. No price.

DOCKRILL, MICHAEL. *British Defence since 1945.* Pp. vii, 171. New York: Basil Blackwell, 1989. No price.

DREIJMANIS, JOHN, ed. *Karl Jaspers on Max Weber.* Pp. xxiv, 216. New York: Paragon House, 1989. $18.95.

DUNCAN, PETER J. S. *The Soviet Union and India.* Pp. viii, 150. New York:

Council on Foreign Relations Press, 1989. Paperbound, $14.95.

EDEN, ROBERT, ed. *The New Deal and Its Legacy: Critique and Reappraisal.* Pp. xi, 263. Westport, CT: Greenwood Press, 1989. $47.95.

EIBL-EIBESFELDT, IRENAUS. *Human Ethology.* Pp. xvi, 848. Hawthorne, NY: Walter de Gruyter, 1989. $69.95.

EICHENGREEN, BARRY and PETER H. LINDERT, eds. *The International Debt Crisis in Historical Perspective.* Pp. 282. Cambridge: MIT Press, 1990. $25.00.

EIDELBERG, PAUL. *Beyond the Secular Mind: A Judaic Response to the Problems of Modernity.* Pp. xvii, 177. Westport, CT: Greenwood Press, 1989. $39.95.

EL-NAGGAR, SAID, ed. *Privatization and Structural Adjustment in the Arab Countries.* Pp. xii, 269. Washington, DC: International Monetary Fund, 1989. Paperbound, $18.50.

FERGUSON, JAMES. *Papa Doc, Baby Doc: Haiti and the Duvaliers.* Pp. 216. New York: Basil Blackwell, 1989. Paperbound, $9.95.

FEUER, LEWIS. *Imperialism and the Anti-Imperialist Mind.* Pp. vi, 265. New Brunswick, NJ: Transaction Books, 1989. Paperbound, $17.95.

FOX, STEPHEN C. *The Group Bases of Ohio Political Behavior, 1803-1848.* Pp. xix, 349. New York: Garland, 1989. $50.00.

FRANKS, C.E.S. *Dissent and the State.* Pp. vii, 288. New York: Oxford University Press, 1989. Paperbound, $14.95.

GABRIEL, JÜRG MARTIN. *The American Conception of Neutrality after 1941.* Pp. x, 289. New York: St. Martin's Press, 1989. $45.00.

GARTHOFF, RAYMOND L. *Reflections on the Cuban Missile Crisis.* Pp. viii, 236. Washington, DC: Brookings Institution, 1989. No price.

GARVER, JOHN W. *Chinese-Soviet Relations, 1937-1945: The Diplomacy of Chinese Nationalism.* Pp. xi, 301. New York: Oxford University Press, 1988. $34.50.

GELLER, L. D. *The American Field Service Archives of World War I, 1914-1917.* Pp. 144. Westport, CT: Greenwood Press, 1989. $49.95.

GIAMMANCO, ROSANNA MULAZZI. *The Catholic-Communist Dialogue in Italy: 1944 to the Present.* Pp. xiii, 171. New York: Praeger, 1989. $37.95.

GOLDSCHEIDER, FRANCES K. and CALVIN GOLDSCHEIDER, eds. *Ethnicity and the New Family Economy: Living Arrangements and Intergenerational Financial Flows.* Pp. xvii, 197. Boulder, CO: Westview Press, 1989. Paperbound, $21.95.

GORDON, WENDELL and JOHN ADAMS. *Economics as Social Science: An Evolutionary Approach.* Pp. ix, 254. Riverdale, MD: Riverdale, 1989. $33.00.

GOTTFRIED, FRANCES. *The Merit System and Municipal Civil Service.* Pp. 200. Westport, CT: Greenwood Press, 1988. $37.95.

GRAUBARD, STEPHEN R., ed. *In Search of Canada.* Pp. x, 396. New Brunswick, NJ: Transaction Books, 1989. Paperbound, $19.95.

GREEN, LESLIE. *The Authority of the State.* Pp. viii, 273. New York: Oxford University Press, 1988. $49.95.

GURR, TED ROBERT, ed. *Violence in America.* Vol. 1, *The History of Crime.* Pp. 279. Newbury Park, CA: Sage, 1989. $17.95.

GURR, TED ROBERT, ed. *Violence in America.* Vol. 2, *Protest, Rebellion, Reform.* Pp. 371. Newbury Park, CA: Sage, 1989. $19.95.

HABERMAS, JÜRGEN. *The New Conservatism: Cultural Criticism and the Historians' Debate.* Edited and translated by Shierry Weber Nicholsen. Pp. xxxv, 270. Cambridge: MIT Press, 1990. $22.50.

HAKOVIRTA, HARTO. *East-West Conflict and European Neutrality.* Pp. xv,

291. New York: Oxford University Press, 1988. $59.00.

HALE, SANDRA J. and MARY M. WILLIAMS, eds. *Managing Change: A Guide to Producing Innovation from Within.* Pp. xi, 181. Lanham, MD: Urban Institute Press, 1989. Paperbound, $14.95.

HOFFMAN, JOHN. *State, Power and Democracy.* Pp. xi, 219. New York: St. Martin's Press, 1988. No price.

HOROWITZ, IRVING LOUIS. *Persuasions and Prejudices: An Informal Compendium of Modern Social Science, 1953-1988.* Pp. xix, 642. New Brunswick, NJ: Transaction Books, 1988. $39.95.

HUBER, ROBERT T. *Soviet Perceptions of the U.S. Congress: The Impact on Superpower Relations.* Pp. viii, 197. Boulder, CO: Westview Press, 1989. $36.50.

HUDSON, GEORGE E., ed. *Soviet National Security Policy under Perestroika.* Pp. xv, 343. Winchester, MA: Unwin Hyman, 1989. $49.95. Paperbound, $19.95.

JACKSON, JOHN H. and EDWIN A. VERMULST, eds. *Antidumping Law and Practice: A Comparative Study.* Pp. xi, 520. Ann Arbor: University of Michigan Press, 1989. No price.

KIRKENDALL, RICHARD S., ed. *The Harry S. Truman Encyclopedia.* Pp. 368. Boston: Hall, 1990. $60.00.

KOENKER, DIANE P., WILLIAM G. ROSENBERG, and RONALD GRIGOR SUNY, eds. *Party, State, and Society in the Russian Civil War: Explorations in Social History.* Pp. xiv, 450. Bloomington: Indiana University Press, 1989. $39.95. Paperbound, $12.50.

KONCZAL, MICHAEL A. and GERALD V. FLANNERY. *Defamation Law in Louisiana, 1800-1988.* Pp. 160. Lanham, MD: University Press of America, 1989. $32.50.

LAING, ELLEN JOHNSTON. *The Winking Owl: Art in the People's Republic of China.* Pp. 204. Berkeley, CA: University of California Press, 1989. $45.00.

LAMBORN, ALAN C. and STEPHEN P. MUMME. *Statecraft, Domestic Politics, and Foreign Policy Making: The El Chamizal Dispute.* Pp. ix, 211. Boulder, CO: Westview Press, 1988. $29.50.

LIU, WILLIAM T., ed. *China Statistical Abstract 1989.* Compiled by the State Statistical Bureau of the People's Republic of China. Pp. xvii, 105. New York: Praeger, 1989. $55.00.

LOPEZ, GEORGE A. and MICHAEL STOHL, eds. *Dependence, Development, and State Repression.* Pp. xv, 271. Westport, CT: Greenwood Press, 1989. $47.95.

MAIER, MARK H. *City Unions: Managing Discontent in New York City.* Pp. xii, 221. New Brunswick, NJ: Rutgers University Press, 1987. $26.00.

MALINOWSKI, BRONISLAW. *A Diary in the Strict Sense of the Term.* Pp. xxxiv, 315. Stanford, CA: Stanford University Press, 1989. $42.50.

MANDELBAUM, MICHAEL, ed. *The Other Side of the Table: The Soviet Approach to Arms Control.* Pp. 215. New York: Council on Foreign Relations Press, 1990. Paperbound, $16.95.

MATTHEWS, MERVYN, ed. *Party, State, and Citizen in the Soviet Union: A Collection of Documents.* Pp. xxxix, 385. Armonk, NY: M. E. Sharpe, 1989. No price.

MAULITZ, RUSSELL C., ed. *Unnatural Causes: The Three Leading Killer Diseases in America.* Pp. 212. New Brunswick, NJ: Rutgers University Press, 1989. $37.00. Paperbound, $15.95.

MAZMANIAN, DANIEL A. and PAUL A. SABATIER. *Implementation and Public Policy.* Pp. 348. Lanham, MD: University Press of America, 1989. Paperbound, $16.75.

McCREA, FRANCES B. and GERALD E. MARKLE. *Minutes to Midnight: Nuclear Weapons Protest in America*. Pp. 200. Newbury Park, CA: Sage, 1989. $27.95. Paperbound, $14.95.

MEDDING, PETER Y., ed. *Studies in Contemporary Jewry*. Vol. 5, *Israel: State and Society, 1948-1988*. Pp. xvi, 430. New York: Oxford University Press, 1989. $29.95.

MEDHURST, KENNETH N. and GEORGE H. MOYSER. *Church and Politics in a Secular Age*. Pp. xvi, 392. New York: Oxford University Press, 1988. $69.00.

MEINERS, ROGER E. and BRUCE YANDLE, eds. *Regulation and the Reagan Era: Politics, Bureaucracy and the Public Interest*. Pp. xiv, 304. New York: Holmes & Meier, 1989. $49.50. Paperbound, $19.95.

MELANSON, PHILIP H. *The Murkin Conspiracy: An Investigation into the Assassination of Dr. Martin Luther King, Jr.* Pp. 224. New York: Praeger, 1989. $21.95.

MELENDEZ, EDGARDO. *Puerto Rico's Statehood Movement*. Pp. viii, 194. Westport, CT: Greenwood Press, 1988. No price.

MESA-LAGO, CARMELO, ed. *Cuban Studies*. Vol. 19. Pp. x, 339. Pittsburgh, PA: University of Pittsburgh Press, 1990. $32.95.

MOMMSEN, WOLFGANG J. *The Political and Social Theory of Max Weber*. Pp. xiv, 226. Chicago: University of Chicago Press, 1989. $39.95.

MORGAN, JANE. *Conflict and Order: The Police and Labour Disputes in England and Wales, 1900-1939*. Pp. xii, 306. New York: Oxford University Press, 1988. $59.00.

MORO, RUBÉN O. *The History of the South Atlantic Conflict: The War for the Malvinas*. Pp. xvi, 360. New York: Praeger, 1989. $49.95.

MORRIS, TERENCE. *Crime and Criminal Justice since 1945*. Pp. x, 198. New York: Basil Blackwell, 1989. $34.95.

MURPHY, JOHN F. *State Support of International Terrorism: Legal, Political, and Economic Dimensions*. Pp. vii, 128. Boulder, CO: Westview Press, 1989. $39.95.

NEE, VICTOR and DAVID STARK. *Remaking the Economic Institution of Socialism: China and Eastern Europe*. Pp. xi, 405. Stanford, CA: Stanford University Press, 1989. $48.50.

NORTON, ANNE. *Reflections on Political Identity*. Pp. viii, 209. Baltimore, MD: Johns Hopkins University Press, 1988. $24.50.

PERRY, MICHAEL J. *Morality, Politics and Law: A Bicentennial Essay*. Pp. ix, 323. New York: Oxford University Press, 1988. $29.95.

PINKUS, BENJAMIN. *The Jews of the Soviet Union: The History of a National Minority*. Pp. xviii, 397. New York: Cambridge University Press, 1988. No price.

PRYBYLA, JAN S. *Market and Plan Under Socialism: The Bird in the Cage*. Pp. xv, 348. Stanford, CA: Hoover Institution, 1987. Paperbound, $18.95.

RAAB, ALEXANDRE. *The Manifesto of Entrepreneurial Democracies*. Pp. 128. Montreal: Sagesse Editions, 1989. $15.95.

RACHLIN, ALLAN. *News as Hegemonic Reality: American Political Culture and the Framing of News Accounts*. Pp. 151. New York: Praeger, 1988. $37.95.

RAFAEL, VICENTE L. *Contracting Colonialism: Translation and Christian Conversion in Tagalog Society under Early Spanish Rule*. Pp. xiii, 230. Ithaca, NY: Cornell University Press, 1988. $28.95.

RALEIGH, DONALD J., ed. *Soviet Historians and Perestroika: The First Phase*. Pp. xvi, 291. Armonk, NY: M. E. Sharpe, 1989. No price.

RESEARCH AND POLICY COMMITTEE OF THE COMMITTEE FOR ECONOMIC DEVELOPMENT. *Finance and Third World Economic Growth*. Pp. xvii, 195. Boulder, CO: Westview Press, 1988. Paperbound, no price.

RICH, P. J. *Elixir of Empire: The English Public Schools, Ritualism, Freemasonry, and Imperialism.* Pp. 156. London: Regency Press, 1989. £9.95.

RUSSETT, BRUCE, HARVEY STARR, and RICHARD J. STOLL. *Choices in World Politics: Sovereignty and Interdependence.* Pp. vi, 325. San Francisco: Freeman, 1989. No price.

RYWKIN, MICHAEL. *Soviet Society Today.* Pp. xii, 243. Armonk, NY: M. E. Sharpe, 1989. $12.50.

SCHLUCHTER, WOLFGANG. *Rationalism, Religion, and Domination: A Weberian Perspective.* Translated by Neil Solomon. Pp. xxiii, 595. Berkeley: University of California Press, 1990. $75.00.

SCHOLLIERS, PETER, ed. *Real Wages in 19th and 20th Century Europe: Historical and Comparative Perspectives.* Pp. xii, 255. New York: St. Martin's Press, 1990. $39.95.

SCHRAG, PHILIP G. *Listening for the Bomb: A Study in Nuclear Arms Control Verification Policy.* Pp. xi, 139. Boulder, CO: Westview Press, 1989. $28.50.

SEED, PATRICIA. *To Love, Honor, and Obey in Colonial Mexico: Conflicts over Marriage Choice, 1574-1821.* Pp. viii, 322. Stanford, CA: Stanford University Press, 1988. $39.50.

SPRINGBORG, ROBERT. *Mubarak's Egypt: Fragmentation of the Political Order.* Pp. xi, 307. Boulder, CO: Westview Press, 1989. $39.95.

STOKEY, NANCY L. and ROBERT E. LUCAS with EDWARD C. PRESCOTT. *Recursive Methods in Economic Dynamics.* Pp. xviii, 588. Cambridge, MA: Harvard University Press, 1989. No price.

SUNDELIUS, BENGT, ed. *The Committed Neutral: Sweden's Foreign Policy.* Pp. vii, 214. Boulder, CO: Westview Press, 1989. Paperbound, $28.95.

THAMBIPILLAI, PUSHPA and DANIEL C. MATUSZEWSKI. *The Soviet Union and the Asian Pacific Region: Views from the Region.* Pp. ix, 219. New York: Praeger, 1989. $42.95.

THIO, ALEX. *Deviant Behavior.* 3d ed. Pp. xvii, 540. New York: Harper & Row, 1988. $30.75.

THOMPSON, TERRY L. *Ideology and Policy: The Political Uses of Doctrine in the Soviet Union.* Pp. viii, 220. Boulder, CO: Westview Press, 1989. Paperbound, $28.95.

THORSEN, NIELS AAGE. *The Political Thought of Woodrow Wilson, 1875-1910.* Pp. xiv, 272. Princeton, NJ: Princeton University Press, 1988. $34.50.

TROYER, RONALD J., JOHN P. CLARK, and DEAN G. ROJEK, eds. *Social Control in the People's Republic of China.* Pp. viii, 224. New York: Praeger, 1989. $37.95.

USLANER, ERIC M. *Shale Barrel Politics: Energy and Legislative Leadership.* Pp. xi, 241. Stanford, CA: Stanford University Press, 1989. $32.50.

WALICKI, ANDRZEJ. *Stanislaw Brozowski and the Polish Beginnings of 'Western Marxism.'* Pp. viii, 349. New York: Oxford University Press, 1989. $66.00.

WALSH, EDWARD J. *Democracy in the Shadows: Citizen Mobilization in the Wake of the Accident at Three Mile Island.* Pp. xiv, 227. Westport, CT: Greenwood Press, 1988. No price.

WARE, ALAN. *Between Profit and State: Intermediate Organizations in Britain and the United States.* Pp. xi, 308. Princeton, NJ: Princeton University Press, 1989. $42.00.

WEINER, MYRON. *The Indian Paradox: Essays in Indian Politics.* Pp. 336. Newbury Park, CA: Sage, 1990. $28.00. Paperbound, $14.00.

WILLIAMSON, PETER J. *Corporatism in Perspective: An Introductory Guide to Corporatist Theory.* Pp. 250. Newbury Park, CA: Sage, 1989. Paperbound, $17.95.

WOOLF, D. R. , ed. *Studies in History and Politics*. Vol. 6, *Intellectual History: New Perspectives*. Pp. 204. Lewiston, NY: Edwin Mellen Press, 1989. No price.

WYMAN, HASTINGS, Jr. *The 1989 Guide to Southern Politics*. Pp. 117. Lanham, MD: University Press of America, 1989. Paperbound, $19.75.

INDEX

In Memoriam

George D. McCune
1924-1990

It is with regret that all at Sage Publications mark the passing on May 19, 1990, of George David McCune—publisher, colleague, and friend.

George McCune's career spanned four decades of publishing. Beginning in 1952 at Macmillan, Inc., he served initially as a college division traveler (field representative). In his 13 years with Macmillan, he subsequently served as Assistant Director of the College Division, Vice President and Director of Sales, Director of The Free Press, and founding President of Macmillan's Junior College Publishing Division, Glencoe Press (in Beverly Hills). In 1966, he joined a fledgling publishing company, Sage Publications, Inc., founded in New York in 1965 by Sara Miller, his future wife. Together the McCunes built Sage (relocated in southern California) into an international professional publishing enterprise with affiliates in London and New Delhi.

In September 1989, in order to pursue further visions, Mr. McCune passed the presidency of Sage Publications to his son and colleague, David F. McCune. At the time of his death, George McCune was actively engaged in planning activities and programs for the McCune Foundation, incorporated in March 1990 to benefit higher education. He is succeeded as President of the McCune Foundation by his wife, Sara Miller McCune (Publisher and Chairman of Sage Publications, Inc.).

George McCune's vision, integrity, perseverance, and capabilities are evident in every facet of his many publishing accomplishments. It is more difficult to pay tribute to his personal qualities: breadth of intellect, unflagging loyalty to family and friends, and a keen ability to ask the most thought-provoking questions.

The name *Sage* combines the names of Sara and George. In that way he will always be a part of Sage Publications. But his legacy is more than that—as we continue to grow, his memory inspires us all.

New from Sage!

ARMS RACES
Technological and Political Dynamics

edited by NILS PETTER GLEDITSCH
International Peace Research Institute, Oslo
& OLAV NJOLSTAD, University of Oslo
with RAIMO VAYRYNEN, University of Helsinki, Finland
& DIETER SENGHAAS, University of Bremen

What factors drive arms races? What role does military technology play in arms build-ups? How have arms build-ups differed under various political systems?

Arms Races combines deep theoretical analysis with extensive empirical studies to provide readers with an in-depth understanding of the issues involved in the arms race. The contributors consider the driving forces of the arms races, a major area of research and debate within peace studies, strategic studies and international relations. They focus both on internal factors to the dynamics of the arms races—such as bureaucratic politics, inter-service rivalry, and the military-industrial complex— and on external factors, such as long term economic trends and interactive arms dynamics between the two superpowers. Existing case studies of the development of strategic weapons systems and the many quantitative studies of the causes and consequences of the arms race are extensively reviewed.

Peace Research Institute, Oslo
1989 (Autumn) / 400 pages / $45.00 (c) / $18.95 (p)

SAGE PUBLICATIONS, INC.
2455 Teller Road
Newbury Park, CA 91320

SAGE PUBLICATIONS LTD
6 Bonhill Street
London EC2A 4PU, England

SAGE PUBLICATIONS INDIA PVT LTD
M-32 Market, Greater Kailash I
New Delhi 110 048 India